The Politics of Environmental Concern

The Politics of Environmental Concern

Second Edition

Walter A. Rosenbaum
University of Florida

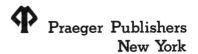 Praeger Publishers
New York

For Jean

Published in the United States of America in 1977
by Praeger Publishers,
200 Park Avenue, New York, N.Y. 10017

Library of Congress Cataloging in Publication Data

Rosenbaum, Walter A
    The politics of environmental concern.

    Bibliography: p. 299
    Includes index.
    1.   Environmental policy—United States.
2.   Environmental protection—United States.
3.   Industry and state—United States. I. Title.
HC110.E5R67   1977   301.31'0973   76–41964
ISBN 0–275–24150–5
ISBN 0–275–64820–6 pbk.

Printed in the United States of America

789 090 987654321

Contents

1. The New Environmental Politics

The patron saint of Birmingham, Alabama, is not Robert E. Lee, as one might suppose, but Vulcan. Atop Red Mountain overlooking the city, the community has erected a 55-foot-high cast iron statue of the Roman god in a smithy's apron, a lofty reminder that for more than a century, since Birmingham fashioned the Confederacy's weapons, steel has been the sinew of the local economy. At night, according to a tourist guide, the steel industry illuminates the city: "Birmingham at night is a startlingly beautiful sight, a city punctuated by the rise and fall of flames from the many steel furnaces." Though tourist literature may rhapsodize about the nocturnal delights of the city's furnaces, they are often invisible by day, for a thick blanket of smog frequently envelops the area, the residue of 25,000 tons of waste poured into the atmosphere yearly by the city's mills. Still, over the years few complained, because Vulcan was benevolent; the incessant furnaces fired a vigorous economy, and air pollution was the price of economic security.

Then something happened.[1] Early in the week of November 14, 1971, the U.S. Weather Bureau warned that a huge mass of stagnant air had settled over many eastern states, reaching from Massachusetts southwestward through New York, Pennsylvania, West Virginia, and Tennessee, then cutting sharply southward into parts of Georgia and Alabama. The air hung like a dead weight over such industrial centers as Pittsburgh, New York, Charleston, and Birmingham. No longer ambient, without strong winds to carry the waste away, it was heavily fouled, increasing in pollutants and potential toxicity. On Monday,

November 15, the National Weather Service in Birmingham issued its first air stagnation alert. The air pollution index, a measure of the suspended particulate matter in the city's atmosphere, was approaching 700 micrograms per cubic meter of air (ug/m^3)—the federal government considered 260 the maximum safe level. Only the extremely high level of suspended particulates was a novelty; air pollution had been common for decades. Although federal experts believe that particulate concentration in cities should not exceed 260 ug/m^3 more than once a year, the *average* mean daily pollution count in Birmingham had been 275 during the previous year. In heavily industrialized North Birmingham, the air was technically "unsafe" almost every day; throughout the metropolitan area the airborne particulates had exceeded safe margins during sixty-seven days in 1970.

But the situation on Monday, November 15, was ominous. As the day progressed, the particulate count climbed above 700, and the effect might be lethal if the rise continued; as the level approached 1,000, warned a federal environmental official, "you might start finding bodies on the street." The next day the count climbed to 771, close to the level considered a disaster by federal officials. On Wednesday, November 18, the count still hovered at a threatening 758. The air was now stinging, inert, and hazardous; public officials acted. Thus began the Battle of Birmingham. It started with crises and confrontation—a battle between Washington and U.S. Steel which serves to mark the advent of the Environmental Era in the United States.

THE BATTLE OF BIRMINGHAM

It fell to the Jefferson County Health Department to trigger the battle. On Wednesday, November 18, 1971, with the city's air dangerously fouled, the department's director sent an urgent telegram to twenty-three major industries in the city urging them to curtail 60 per cent of their production in the hope that smoke emissions would be drastically abated. Five of the major polluters, including giant U.S. Steel, took no significant action. "No action was required, none was volunteered," commented a company official. Now convinced that an environmental disaster might be impending and angered by the intransigence of U.S. Steel, the director of the County Health Department appealed directly to Washington. Would the Environmental Protection Agency obtain an immediate court injunction halting further production in twenty-three major Birmingham industries—including U.S. Steel—until the emergency had passed? The Environmental Protection Agency acted immediately. Armed with new emergency powers from the recently enacted Clean Air Amendments of 1970, the agency aroused U.S. District Court Judge Sam C. Pointer from his sleep in Birmingham early Thursday morning and obtained a temporary injunction halting further production in the twenty-three Birmingham firms, the first injunction obtained under the new law. The spur to this unusually vigorous demonstration of federal muscle had clearly been U.S. Steel. "U.S. Steel did nothing," declared one federal official, "although they have the major plants involved and contribute 35 per cent of the particulate emissions."

For most of Birmingham's residents, November 17 must have been remarkable. For the first time within memory, the stacks of the city's mammoth steel complex belched no smoke skyward. U.S. Steel had banked its open hearth furnaces to only 35 per cent operating capacity, barely enough to prevent their shutdown. More than five thousand workers at U.S. Steel had been temporarily "furloughed" without pay and thousands more were idled elsewhere; if the injunction continued, many more would be home. But in the afternoon, the particulate count was down to 410, still above the 375 level customary for a pollution alert, yet apparently decreasing.

Then the crisis disappeared. On Friday, November 18, a brisk west wind accompanied by a cold drizzle rapidly blew the stagnant air from the city. The particulate count dropped to only 41, convincing federal officials that the emergency had passed; federal attorneys now confronted Judge Pointer with a request, quickly granted, to lift the injunction and permit the companies to resume operation. By evening, Birmingham's furnaces were again incandescent for the pleasure of tourists and the profit of the community.

The confrontation between steel and the federal government left bitterness, recrimination, and newly awakened hope. U.S. Steel spokesmen charged that public officials had been irresponsible in seeking the injunction and protested that the company had been made unfairly the villain in the incident. But local environmentalists thought it had been an overdue lesson to Birmingham's industrial giants. "There was a time, until recently, that industry could do as it pleased in Birmingham," noted one ecologist. "But now the message is going out that if industry wants to come to Alabama, we want them to be responsible citizens who can't pollute at will."

U.S. Steel apparently did not hear the message. The company had promised to invest $12 million in new facilities that, it asserted, would enable it to shut down its five open hearths—the key to clean air in Birmingham—by May, 1974. But early in 1974 no hearths had closed; the company requested that Washington extend the deadline because technical problems prevented compliance with the original agreement and thousands of employees would have to be dismissed if the existing hearths were banked. The U.S. Environmental Protection Agency (EPA), now responsible for enforcing the agreement, concurred; a new deadline was set for November, 1975, and EPA assured irate environmentalists that the new understandings were "nonnegotiable."

By April, 1975, Birmingham's air, though cleaner, was still so contaminated that the EPA required Alabama officials to create a special pollution abatement procedure for the city. On April 30—a day before U.S. Steel's new abatement deadline would take effect—the EPA, yielding to the company's argument that it confronted insurmountable technical problems in closing its hearths, granted the company an additional thirteen months to phase out the five facilities. Noting that the hearths were each pouring 7,500 pounds of iron dust daily into the city's air, the state's attorney general was outraged: "U.S. Steel has this intolerable, bully-boy attitude that the law does not apply to them," he complained. Still, a new agreement existed: the company would close two hearths by June, 1975, the rest by June, 1976.

Late in 1975, the company paid a $35,000 fine for operating two hearths beyond the agreed shutdown date.

In June, 1976, the company asked the EPA to permit it to continue operating two hearths through 1977.

EPA officials, their patience finally exhausted, refused another extension. "We do not understand EPA's opposition," complained the company's Birmingham plant manager. Observing that the company had spent $60 million in Alabama for new pollution control devices, he asserted that continual operation of the open hearths until new facilities could be constructed "would permit an orderly transition with a maximum contribution to both employment and steel production and minimal effect on air quality." In language uncommonly acid for federal officials, EPA's deputy administrator responded by denouncing U.S. Steel for "compiling a record of environmental recalcitrance which is second to none." Retorted the chairman of U.S. Steel: "A vicious attack. . . . Our record in this field is admirable."

It had taken five years, the combined efforts of the EPA, the federal courts, and Alabama's attorney general, hundreds of administrative man-hours, and several hundred thousand dollars in public expenditures to close three of U.S. Steel's five hearths. The victory was incomplete; Birmingham's air was still polluted, two hearths burned on, and environmentalists counted the battle two-fifths lost. Nonetheless, the Battle of Birmingham was a remarkable episode in the nation's environmental history. Its beginning inaugurated an era of vigorous ecological politics unprecedented in the United States. Its continuation was evidence that the environmental movement could no longer be considered a transient political novelty but had produced, instead, a major realignment of public authority behind ecological preservation.

THE EVOLVING POLITICS OF ECOLOGY

The first confrontation between Washington and U.S. Steel that November day in 1971 was remarkable not because U.S. Steel was chastened by Washington's action but because such a direct public confrontation had occurred at all. Never before had Washington exercised emergency powers to order a total, immediate cessation of production within a major industrial complex in the name of pollution abatement. When Richard Nixon assumed office, Washington possessed neither this power nor an Environmental Protection Agency to enforce it. Air pollution emergencies had occurred for decades prior to Birmingham's; the Donora, Pennsylvania, disaster of 1948 claimed forty lives, and residents of Los Angeles, Pittsburgh, and New York know smog alerts as a way of life.[2] Still, the public had seemed largely indifferent to the problem, and public officials were unwilling to do much about it. In short, air pollution was not a major issue. Birmingham announced, publicly and emphatically, that air pollution, like other ecological issues, had now become a major item on the public agenda.

The echoes of the first great Earth Day had barely subsided when Washington first confronted U.S. Steel in Birmingham. Congress had just written the Clean Air Amendments (1970) with their tough, new air pollution contraints; other radically new environmental legislation would follow. The environmental movement, buoyed by public interest and tangible political victories, enjoyed a brief euphoric moment. It was "Year One on the ecological calendar," exclaimed one jubilant senatorial foe of the Supersonic Transport (SST) when Congress refused to continue funding the program in 1971. A few weeks earlier, President Nixon, in an unprecedented move, had halted construction of the Cross Florida Barge Canal, in which the federal government had invested $50 million. Environmentalists had arrested the projected trans-Alaskan pipeline with litigation growing from the new National Environmental Policy Act.[3] The years between 1968 and 1972, it now appears, were the high renaissance of ecological politics in the United States. During that period, there coalesced a potent combination of organized group activity, awakening public consciousness of environmental ills and growing environmental deterioration that produced an unprecedented period of environmental activism and achievement. That period, which inaugurated what President Nixon had called the Environmental Decade, is well past. Significant transformations have occurred; changing circumstances have produced a new political context in which environmental politics now proceeds.

The Public and Ecology

In the early 1970's, environmentalists mobilized for political action in a uniquely congenial climate of opinion; perhaps at no time in this century was the American public more receptive to the environmental gospel. The public's willingness to echo ecological sentiments—at least so long as the sentiments stayed comfortably vague—amplified the ecologist's message in Washington, state capitols, and city halls. Public officials are quite often instruments of public opinion; they tend, especially, to become acutely responsive to public sensitivities when they perceive that something approaching a consensus has developed on some policy matter. So it was with ecology. "The environment" had leaped to public attention, suddenly and surprisingly, and officials could not ignore it. "Not since the Japanese attack on Pearl Harbor," noted one normally cautious observer, "has any public issue received such massive support in all the news media, local as well as national."[4]

An indication of the sudden emergence of public environmental concern is evident in Table 1, which compares public responses to a question dealing with the domestic matters that ought to concern the government as the public rated those issues in 1965 and 1970. This surge of public interest had numerous political benefits for ecologists.[5] Beyond convincing public officials that a large and articulate constituency for ecological protection had unexpectedly emerged, it contributed to generating a "crisis" atmosphere that seemed to demand a swift and incisive governmental response. It is almost axiomatic in American politics that groups seeking to force new items on the public agenda have to create this crisis climate before public institutions will respond. Moreover, the swift upsurge of public environmental con-

TABLE 1. "Which three of these problems would you like to see government devote most of its attention to in the next two years?"

	Percentage of Public Mentioning Item		Five-Year Change
	1970	1965	
Reducing amount of crime	56	41	15%
Reducing pollution of air and water	53	17	36
Improving public education	31	45	-14
Helping people in poor areas	30	32	-2
Conquering "killer" diseases	29	37	-8
Improving housing, clearing slums	27	21	6
Reducing racial discrimination	25	29	-4
Reducing unemployment	25	35	-10
Improving highway safety	13	18	-5
Beautifying America	5	3	2

SOURCE: Gallup Poll *Index,* June, 1970, p. 8.

cern caught the American business community by surprise and threw it on the defensive, thereby putting a traditionally formidable sector of opposition to many environmental regulations at a disadvantage that, momentarily, disarmed it politically.

This environmental consciousness had been cultivated, in some respects, by environmentalists. The environmental coalition had been steadily broadening its social base and size by vigorous recruitment in the late 1960's; the Sierra Club and Audubon Society, for example, had doubled their membership in this period. It was a diverse coalition: traditional conservation interests like the National Wildlife Federation, newer militant groups like Friends of the Earth, college students (many scarcely graduated from the war protest movement), the League of Women Voters, other good-government associations, and groups broadly committed to public interest policies. Part of its success turned on imaginative strategies for capturing public interest. In a sense, the Battle of Birmingham actually began in the late 1960's when environmentalists fashioned a broad national alliance called the Breather's Lobby to enlist support for more stringent federal air quality standards. Undoubtedly, the public agitation for environmental protection peaked on April 22, 1970, when the first Earth Day was celebrated. The televised teach-in that day reached more than a million viewers; thousands of other citizens participated through pollution demonstrations, workshops, and public lectures conducted in hundreds of local communities.

In the wake of all this, public and private institutions sought to demonstrate a newly acquired environmental consciousness and the nation endured a period of environmental chic. The Boy Scouts, anxious to be relevant as well as prepared, initiated Project SOAR (Save Our American Resources). Business, quick to propel the ship of its fortunes on a strong breeze of opinion, rapidly acquired an environmental voice; eight of the nation's largest corporations produced an expensive twenty-three-page insert in the country's largest circulation periodical to answer the title-page question: "What Are We Doing About Our Environment?" The Forest Service's famous Smokey the Bear yielded equal billing to Woodsey the Owl, who advised: "Give a Hoot—Don't Pollute!"

This heightened public environmental interest has largely dissipated, and, as a result, the political setting of environmental action has altered. The changing public mood was predictable. "Public attention," as Anthony Downs has observed, "rarely remains sharply focused upon any one domestic issue for very long—even if it involves a continuing problem of crucial importance."[6] Thus, opinion polls routinely revealed by the mid-1970's that ecological issues had been replaced in public concern by matters such as high unemployment, the rising cost of living, crime, foreign affairs, and—in the aftermath of Watergate—apprehension over official ethics. A typical finding, interesting because it focused on the same individuals over a five-year period, demonstrated that in one western state support for increased taxes for pollution control had declined among a panel of representative citizens from 70 per cent in 1970 to 22 per cent in 1974.[7] Then, too, the American public had been diverted to other social ills by the pervasive "energy crises" in 1973 and the sagging economy of 1974–76. Although this apparently had not turned the public against environmental protection (some opponents of ecological measures had attempted to convince the public that unemployment and the energy crisis would be intensified by the new ecological measures), it had divested the movement of its consensus image and ready public emotion.

Indeed, the surge of pollution concern during 1969–71 projected even then a deceptive image of massive public preoccupation with and commitment to environmental protection. Citizen interest was not necessarily durable or deep. Polls indicated that the public concern for environment was confined largely to pollution and did not commonly embrace numerous other significant issues such as solid waste management, noise control, better land management, and preservation of open space and resources (note the low importance attached to beautifying America in Table 1). Pollution was far from being the most important social issue to most Americans even in the early 1970's. The best showing made by an environmental issue on a spontaneous list of concerns voiced by citizens during this period was a ninth place in 1970 when pollution was mentioned by a scant 4 per cent of the sample.[8]

Public approval especially diminishes when the tangible costs of environmental protection become evident. The polls in the early 1970's indicated that a majority of Americans believed the government was spending insufficient funds on pollution abatement and other environmental programs, but the public seemed disinclined to allot even small amounts for environmental protection themselves. In 1969, for instance, almost two-thirds of a sample public told the Opinion Research Corporation that they would not spend $100 a year in taxes to control water and air pollution; the Gallup organization that year finally found a majority in favor of increased pollution taxes —if the increase did not exceed $10 annually. Even in 1971, when environmentalism was popular, almost 40 per cent of one national poll indicated they were willing to spend "nothing" to banish air pollution. Estimates indicate that the American consumer will have to pay directly $67.7 billion in the cumulative costs of pollution control between 1974 and 1983. Part of this cost will include $200 to $800 for emission controls on new automobiles, a higher rate for electric power consumption to offset industry pollution equipment, and higher costs for food, chemical products, and other commodities whose manufacture involves new pollution abatement expenses.[9] The costs of environmental restoration may seem particularly objectionable to many citizens because they are "buying" an intangible product for future delivery at a real current cost; one pays several hundred dollars for auto emission controls in return for cleaner air in five years.

This alteration of the opinion climate in which environmentalists must now politically operate has had several repercussions. The burden of the political battle is now increasingly borne by the active organized minorities representing the major ecological interests; without the psychological leverage of strong public interest, they are increasingly thrown upon their own resources in the political struggle. It also means that the air of crisis is largely gone and, in its place, a more deliberative and reflective attitude toward ecological matters has emerged in governmental circles. Voices of opposition and dissent to new environmental policies are likely to receive more careful and interested hearing. Moreover, as public concern shifts to other matters, so does media attention; it becomes harder to arouse and interest the public in the fate of environmental measures; public officials feel greater freedom of action to follow their own logic in deciding how to implement policy.

The diminishing public salience of environmentalism is important, not least of all, because it accompanies a shift in the area of primary political action for those involved in environmental politics. In the early 1970's, mobilization and agitation were primary strategies as conservationists sought to arouse public officials to place ecological matters on the institutional agenda of government. That has been largely achieved; the political struggle has shifted in good part to the legislative hall, bureaucratic chambers, and the judicial cloister. Compared with the noisy, acrimonious, and widely observed mobilization period, the politics of policy formulation and implementation—the business of governmental institutions—is quiet and often invisible to the public. It is a different political arena with different institutions, strategies, and participants but no less important than the earlier phase.

Governmental Involvement

The federal government has assumed the leadership in formulating and implementing environmental policy; the critical struggles over environmental management now occur in Washington. The years between 1969 and 1973 produced a remarkable outpouring of innovative Congressional legislation on environmental affairs—the bullhorn yielded to the briefcase as ecologists, working through the legislative process, encouraged perhaps the most singular period of environmental legislation in national history. Among other achievements, Congress rewrote national water and air quality programs through the Clean Air Amendments (1970) and the Federal Water Pollution Control Act Amendments (1972), created the National Environmental Policy Act (NEPA) with its unprecedented requirement for federal "environmental impact statements," and mandated the first comprehensive federal assistance program to the states in conserving the country's valuable coastal lands. The magnitude of federal involvement in these new programs can be gauged from the fact that thirty-three agencies, departments, and boards now routinely create, comment on, and review impact statements; eleven departments are involved in water quality control, seven in air quality maintenance, eight in solid waste and coastal zone management. Today, the federal grant program to assist local government in constructing waste treatment facilities, an $18 billion authorization, is second only to the federal highway program as Washington's largest public works enterprise.

A useful measure of Washington's policy priorities is the federal budget. In 1955, all environmental programs represented a minuscule 3 per cent of the federal budget, including virtually nothing for pollution abatement. By fiscal year 1976, Washington authorized $6.9 billion for environmental management—ten times the dollar amount authorized in 1969 but still a very modest 2 per cent of the total budget. In contrast, the United States was spending 25 per cent of the 1976 budget on defense, 5 per cent on commerce and transportation, and another 5 per cent on veterans' benefits.[10] Thus, environmental programs are much more generously funded yet far from a high national priority.

In any event, Washington's environmental sensitivity has been rather sudden; like their state and local counterparts, federal officials were slow to recognize most environmental problems and approached the few they did notice at a glacial pace. As early as 1912, for instance, the International Joint Commission had warned Washington that pollution in the Great Lakes was "generally chaotic, everywhere perilous and in some cases disgraceful."[11] Since then, Lake Erie has deteriorated almost to the stage of a "dead" lake ecologically, and a joint federal-state effort is only now underway to save endangered Lake Michigan from a similar fate. The Donora air pollution disaster occurred in 1948, but it was 1955 before Congress passed the first, modest air pollution legislation; at the time there were no viable state programs at all. The first temporary water pollution control legislation was enacted by Congress in 1948; permanent measures came about in 1956. As late as 1964, the Democratic Party's platform gave slight attention to the environment and then spoke primarily of conserving natural resources and expanding recreational facilities; the Republican platform was silent about the environment.[12]

An interest in land and resource use came only slightly earlier and very unevenly to federal officials. Before 1900, the U.S. government asserted little effective control over public lands and their resources; on the contrary, it handed over huge portions of the public domain with all its richly varied resources to a variety of private interests, usually through the principle of "preemption," which was written into a variety of federal statutes.[13] During the latter part of the nineteenth century, in addition, Congress bequeathed great swaths of public land to the railroads to encourage their expansion. During

Lincoln's administration alone, more than 75 million acres of public land were disposed in this manner; before the giveaway ended, 180 million acres—an area larger than France, England, Scotland, and Wales—were devoured by railroad interests.[14] Despite a vigorous reform effort under Theodore Roosevelt (who coined and popularized the term "conservation"), the federal government continued to permit oil, timber, cattle, and minimg interests to use federal reserves with little supervision, and, although outright resource giveaways were sharply abated, major private resource users still found that they could do business with Washington—legally and occasionally illicitly. (The Teapot Dome Scandal that fouled Warren Harding's reputation involved the selling of oil leases on federal reserves in return for bribes to major administration officials.) While the two Roosevelts were successful in getting more than 150 million acres of national land set aside for national parks and forests, Congress was a fitful and balky partner in the enterprise. "Uncle Joe" Cannon, the legendary Speaker of the House, had fought Theodore Roosevelt and William Howard Taft on every major Presidential effort to set aside public land for national parks with the battle cry "Not one cent for scenery"; this indifference to governmental stewardship of resources, coupled with an indulgence of their private use, was the dominant Congressional mood until recently.

Although the federal interest in environmental protection developed tardily and conservatively, it seems somewhat enlightened when compared to the record of the states. Generally, the states have followed, rather than anticipated, federal environmental programs; environmental protection at the state level, consequently, was until recently very meager. Virtually no significant air or water pollution legislation existed in the states prior to 1960—in most, none at all. Between 1951 and 1962, only eleven states had any law relating to air pollution on their statute books; since then, thirty-six have added some form of air pollution control. Prior to 1966, only thirteen states had made any serious effort to regulate the emission of air pollutants within their boundaries, and, even more significantly, only a handful had begun to tackle the most essential problems, such as the regulation of sulfur oxide emissions and the establishment of ambient air standards. With the exception of some state regulation and support of municipal sewage treatment facilities, the situation in water pollution control until the late 1960's was equally void of incisive state action.

State stewardship of land and resources was somewhat better than pollution control, but land and resource management has only recently become a major preoccupation in most statehouses. More than 6 million acres of land had been set aside by the states for parks and recreational facilities by 1960, but millions of acres of public lands had been, or were being, surrended to private interests. The states had been enthusiastic participants in the land giveaways throughout the nineteenth century. Maine and Pennsylvania sold enormous tracts for 12 cents an acre to the railroads and other commercial enterprises, while North Carolina auctioned hardwood stands to timbermen for 10 cents an acre. Such unbridled generosity gradually diminished, but the states, until very recently, did relatively little to prevent the transformation of open land, public and private, into commercial use. In recent years, rural land has been converted into urban developments, highways, airports, and other projects at a rate approaching 1 million acres a year. Wetlands—beaches, estuaries, tidal flats, lagoons, and the like—have been under equally intense pressure. Through dredging, filling, and other practices, the total wetlands once available in the United States, about 127 million acres, have been diminished to about 70 million acres—a 60 per cent decrease. Of the 3,700 miles of shoreline on the Atlantic and Gulf coasts, only 105 miles (or about 3 per cent) were available for public use in 1965. As will be noted later, a major effort among the states began only in the late 1960's to protect public lands and to regulate the use of natural resources in the interest of the environment.

As government at all levels assumes greater authority in environmental management, the terms of ecological politics alter. Increasingly, environmentalists and their opposition must concentrate upon gaining and exploiting access to Congress, state legislatures, and the administrative labyrinth that attends all government. Achieving environmental goals becomes difficult because business and other traditional opponents to most measures advocated by ecologists enjoy secure access to and powerful influence in the legislative and administrative process. Moreover, policy becomes more controversial and divisive even among those who marched behind the same ecology banner in the mobilization struggle; disagreements among erstwhile

ecological allies is inevitable when choices must be realistically assessed. Thus, lamented one environmental lobbyist watching an alliance of business and unions in support of pesticide management
dissolve into squabbling factions, "Industry is worried about next
year's profits and the union is worried about the immediate loss of jobs
so that the threat from pesticides twenty years from now is easy to
bargain away."[15] The pace of policy-making also slows, and bargaining, with the compromise it customarily extracts, must be accepted
as a political reality.

Finally, an unforeseen consequence of governmental involvement is
that Congress, in an uncustomary leap of imagination, mandated
regulatory programs for air and water pollution that far exceeded
existing technical capacities to achieve within the time period ordained for them. This, as we shall observe in Chapter 5, has meant
that a whole new scientific research and technology foundation has
had to be created concurrently with the effort to control pollution.[16]
It has produced intense and prolonged conflicts between ecologists,
administrators, scientists, and the business community over virtually
every major technical aspect of the new pollution and abatement
programs. Implementation has been slowed considerably, and re-
trenchment in goals and compliance deadlines have occurred. Generally, this has worked to the disadvantage of environmentalists by
opening up countless points in the administrative process where opposition to programs can be mounted and where compromise and bargaining must occur.

The struggle over ecological policy within governmental institutions also throws into sharp relief the major role that the American
business community plays in ecological politics. This involvement of
the private sector in pollution abatement procedures is as significant
as any other development in environmental politics because American
enterprise exerts a powerful direct and indirect political voice in ecological matters.

Business Involvement

American business is understandably concerned with environmental policy, especially with its regulatory aspects. The private sector
must bear a major burden of the anticipated expense for future pollu-

tion control. The Council on Environmental Quality estimates that between 1974 and 1983 American corporations must make a minimum capital investment of $47.7 billion for water pollution control technology and an additional $137.7 billion for air pollution abatement (this amounts to more than 95 per cent of the nation's total outlay for air pollution control).[17] Before the late 1960's, American business allocated little time or resources to pollution abatement. Beginning in 1970, American business began to divert increasing capital toward research in pollution control techniques. The manufacturing industry increased its pollution control research expenditures by 12 per cent between 1970 and 1972, the nonmanufacturing companies by a healthy 127 per cent. Such industries as iron and steel, chemicals, and textiles were initially slow to respond to the need for pollution control research, but most major sectors of the economy are increasing investments now. Arguments continue over the capital that industry should invest in environmental protection, with critics alleging that most major industries are slow and niggardly in their allocations. However, many companies are reporting a sizable investment in actual equipment. According to reliable estimates, some of the heaviest industrial polluters were spending a significant amount of their 1974 total capital outlay on effluent controls: iron and steel, 10 per cent of capital expenses; nonferrous metals, 25 per cent; pulp and paper, 18 per cent. Overall, American business was collectively spending a moderate 5 to 6 per cent of its total capital on pollution control —an economically acceptable figure, according to most experts.

Since the beginning of the Environmental Decade, the business community has maintained an ambivalent attitude toward environmental policies emanating from Washington. In 1970, *Fortune*'s survey of 500 top business leaders found more than 80 per cent professing a willingness to restrain the introduction of new products, to forgo increased production, or to reduce profits if this would contribute to environmental protection.[18] During this period, corporations spent lavishly to advertise that business had an ecological conscience. Unfortunately, in many instances this demonstrated only bad faith when numerous enterprises congratulated themselves for accomplishments quite unsupported by deeds. Corporate spokesmen often predicted that ecology measures would lead to economic disaster; the U.S. Chamber of Commerce dourly anticipated that "all existing firms will be adversely affected" by new pollution regulations. Corporate spokesmen sometimes lashed out at environmentalists indiscriminately; in the words of the chief counsel of an eastern utility, they were all "birdwatchers, nature fakers and militant enemies of progress."[19] Environmentalists frequently acquired a lasting conviction that the corporate executive was the environmental devil incarnate. Indeed, environmentalists often assume that the only way to keep the feet of errant business on the path of ecological virtue is to cudgel corporations with heavy fines and other harsh enforcement procedures.

However, effective environmental protection requires voluntary cooperation and a minimal goodwill from business; it is prohibitively expensive, time-consuming, and counterproductive to rely upon judicial force or punitive fines to get such cooperation, which, in any event, can never be wholly coerced. Thus, American business enjoys an inescapable political asset in environmental politics: it must be included in the formulation of regulatory programs to ensure their success, and its collaboration must be secured by making meaningful concessions to its viewpoint as the price of compliance.[20]

THE POLITICAL ANATOMY OF ENVIRONMENTAL ISSUES

Changes in the environmental movement since its first flourishing in the early 1970's have not altered its general direction. "Ecology" has risen from virtual political invisibility to continuing political salience. As a nation, we will be involved in the complex and critical business of establishing through our political institutions a national public policy on the environment through the next several decades. To public officials has fallen the difficult but essential task of translating this environmental concern into authoritative policy. How public officials make environmental policy is, from the viewpoint of this book, the essence of environmental politics; we are concerned largely with the institutions, actors, and influences that now mold environmental policy and with the policy's substance. This is not the whole story by any means, but it is the portion we shall emphasize. Let us briefly examine, in more specific terms, what shall concern us.

The bundle of issues bound together by the word "ecology" may have introduced new items on the governmental policy agenda, but the study of public policy-making itself is a venerable enterprise.

Political analysts have created a multitude of schemes, many of great sensitivity and sophistication, in an effort to explain how and why public policies develop. Since our purpose is to create a relatively simple and serviceable model for identifying the important components in the policy process, we can borrow from the literature on public policy several widely recognized concepts useful in explaining the development of environmental policy.[21]

Issue Development

To explain how public officials respond to specific issues before them, it is profitable to examine several aspects of the issue's rise to governmental concern.

To begin, it makes a difference *whether one is dealing with a relatively new or old policy problem.* Generally, when public officials confront a major issue that has not previously absorbed much governmental attention, the breadth of the political battle may be quite wide, the possible solutions quite numerous, and the situation generally fluid. In a new policy area, for instance, there is likely to be keen competition among the various groups concerned with the policy to establish their influence and access to governmental decision-makers in order to set the course of future policy and strongly influence it subsequently. Legislators, bureaucrats, and executive leaders, often lacking a heavy investment in an established policy formula, may be more open to evaluating and enacting a broad range of policies than they will be after a policy line has developed. Various sections of the public may be strongly mobilized and intensely involved in the policy issue, adding another element that may be manipulated by the various participants in the policy struggle. Conversely, when policy-makers deal with an issue upon which government has already acted, different conditions are likely to prevail. Lines of group access to officials are likely to be established, working relationships among the groups stabilized, and understandings reached. Moreover, an established policy often amounts to an agreement on, or settlement of, political conflict among competing interests concerned with that policy; these interests tend to resist a major revision of policy with the new blood-letting likely to follow. Public interest may be considerably diminished as well. Established policies, in addition, are enforced through bureaucratic agencies with often great commitments to the policy *status quo,* and legislators may, as well, have strong preferences for the established policy formula. Thus, policy changes in "old" policy areas are likely to be relatively modest and difficult to bring about, for there are strongly resistant, conservative pressures at work. In short, the political problems of *creating* a major policy are different from those *changing* the direction of such a policy. This explains why it is useful to take time to examine the political history of various envrionmental policy problems.

This distinction between new and old policy areas might seem immaterial to environmental politics, for we have noted that ecology is a rather new issue. However, while the concept of ecology and the many issues it embraces are genuinely new, many other items now considered in the ambit of ecology have long concerned government. For instance, air and water pollution abatement in most respects is a new policy problem, but questions of land and water use, resource allocation, and related problems have long been grist for the governmental mills. Thus, the political context in which policy is made for different environmental issues currently in the news will differ to some extent among the issues. To understand the current policy struggle surrounding a specific environmental issue, therefore, it pays to examine its age.

Issue development also involves some concern with the nature of the policy problem itself. Obvious as this seems, it still deserves emphasis because the substance of a problem has at least two critical political implications: It defines the range of groups involved in a policy area and establishes some boundaries for policy alternatives. To the nonscientist and nonecologist, at least, even a modest examination of the complexities of an environmental problem may seem to lead into a thicket of technicalities unless the political implications of such details are emphasized. For example, during 1971 and 1972, Americans were treated to numerous television commercials, sponsored by petroleum companies, asserting that "the pulse of America" beat to the flow of refined petroleum. One showed a grandmother baking her pies (with natural gas), a jolly family outing in the station wagon (gas-propelled), and a community snugly warm on a frigid winter's evening (through heating energy from petroleum). This might have seemed, upon first inspection, a rather commonplace commercial, but it would seem considerably more to one moderately acquainted with the Alaskan pipeline controversy. During the period of these commercials, the nation's major petroleum refiners were locked in a struggle with conservationists over construction of the Alaskan pipeline to the largest oil reserves yet discovered in North America, reserves upon which the companies held leases. The focus of the struggle shifted to Washington, where public officials were then deciding whether, in light of the pipeline's environmental impact, the cross-Alaskan line should be permitted. The apparently innocuous appearance of grandmother baking her pies as a paean to petroleum appeared, in fact, to be a skillfully timed presentation to build public sympathy (and pressure) for the Alaskan development. As this example suggests, studying the nature of environmental policy problems can provide clues to which interests are likely to be involved, and in what manner, in the resolution of the issue.

The nature of environmental problems also sets some limits on solutions. Air and water pollution, for example, are so intimately associated with almost all industrial processes in the United States, and industry itself is so pervasive, that public officials must depend on considerable cooperation from American business if pollution abatement is to succeed; government cannot force, or enforce, pollution control unilaterally. In a different area, public policy-makers cannot reduce the growth of strip mining in the United States, despite widespread acknowledgment of its vicious environmental consequences, unless they are prepared to alter existing policy concerning the use of fuel by the electric power industry. These policy issues are interlocked because strip mining is an increasingly important fuel source for power generators, and, hence, the problems cannot be realistically separated.

The Group Structure

To know how interest groups are involved in environmental policy-making is not to know all, or explain all; but an analysis of environmental policy devoid of attention to interest-group activities would be artless and quite unsatisfactory. The activity of groups in the policy process has been widely studied and its importance recognized. Groups are largely responsible for organizing and mobilizing demands for governmental policy, for exerting pressure on public officials to take action, and for organizing the various viewpoints on policy problems. In large part, therefore, the strength of group activity on various sides of policy questions determines how widely and effectively various policy issues will be represented to government. Indeed, it is largely through groups that issues are politicized in the first place —that is, brought within the ambit of public institutions. In order to understand which environmental issues are likely to be salient to public officials, or what conflicts are likely to develop over them within public institutions, or to predict the future importance of various environmental issues in government, some inspection of the strength, diversity, and viewpoint of interests organized in environmental policy battles is fundamental.

In addition, public policy-makers are very likely to weigh the costs and consequences of environmental policy decisions in group terms. This is not to suggest that various groups are the only components in the public officials' subjective map of the political world, but almost all studies of official decision-making emphasize that group viewpoints and the group consequences of policy choices do weigh heavily in official thinking much of the time. It is a matter of fundamental political intelligence for officials to discover, in any case, where important interests stand on policy questions, environmental or otherwise. All this underscores the fact that what groups do in the political arena —how they represent their interests, to which officials they speak— is likely to have substantial consequences in shaping public policy.

Finally, as we shall frequently emphasize, once policy decisions are formulated in general terms by legislators and executives, they are implemented, and in good part further developed, by the administrative arm of government in which organized interests play a major role. All administrative agencies have their "clientele groups"—those organized interests affected by the agency's responsibilities and working with the agency in making administrative policy. Once these clientele groups gain and stabilize their "access" to administrative officials (the variety of these groups may be great and their access patterns complex), they exert enormous influence in the creation and application of policy through the administrative branch. In short, there is no point in the policy-making process at which group activity ceases to be significant.

Such an abbreviated discussion of groups does little more than hint at their significance in the political process, but it should underscore, at least, why a separate chapter will be devoted to inspection of group involvement in the formulation of environmental policy.

The Governmental Setting

Anyone concerned with the making of environmental policy must, of course, turn to governmental institutions. As always, it is well not to be misled by the formal divisions of power in the Constitution. In theory, the federal government consists of three separate branches with differing responsibilities; in fact, however, the national government (and state governments, all of which follow the federal pattern) are actually composed of separate institutions that share many functions, and, more specifically, each has a major part in *making* policy. For example, the President assumes the initiative in much policy formulation, yet administrative agencies often promote legislation through the President or directly to Congress; thus, Congress is by no means the center of most policy formulation in government. The application of policy is primarily the business of the huge bureaucratic structure, but in the process of determining how policies—which are often written in very general terms—will apply in specific instances, the administrator often makes additional policy himself. Finally, although in theory the courts may only be declaring what the law is, in fact they often make policy in the process of interpreting the law. One must therefore look beyond the formal constitutional façade of the federal government into all branches in search of policy-making components.

It is also crucial to note that a governmental "policy"on any issue amounts to the way in which government deals with an issue through *all* branches. For instance, Congress may formulate a policy for dealing with air pollution by declaring the government's intent to limit the emission of certain pollutants from automobiles. This is merely a declaration; it will have no effect until it is administered through the executive branch and interpreted in the courts. In the administration and adjudication of the policy, in fact, will its actual impact be determined. This means, clearly, that there is often a differ-

ence—perhaps a great one—between what government declares it will
do and what it is doing in a particular policy area. Any sophisticated
analysis must approach governmental policy-making with an eye toward the cumulative impact of all branches in actually fashioning the
operative policy.

Finally, it should be emphasized that, in order to understand the
making of public policy, some attention must be given to the procedures that define *how* the decisions will be made. All decision-making
rules are "loaded" in the sense that they will favor some policy outcomes over others. To an important degree, the rules make policy in
that they preclude some decisions while encouraging others. For example, in the 1960's, the federal government declared its intention to
stop many serious cases of interstate water pollution. But virtually
nothing was done by Washington to diminish many blatant instances
of severe interstate water pollution. Part of the blame for this can be
attributed to the cumbersome and time-consuming procedures that
Congress ordained for acting against such pollution. In this case,
Washington's passiveness was in good measure the result of rules for
dealing with major interstate polluters.

The Substance of Policies

Finally, to understand how and why policies get enacted, one must
turn to the substance of policies themselves. There are several aspects
of policy that deserve particular emphasis.

It is clearly important to know *what policy alternatives are facing
public officials.* In many cases, certain alternatives are impossible or
so difficult as to be virtually impossible. Sometimes, courses of future
action depend heavily on past policy decisions or on commitments
made by policy-makers to politically influential parties in the policy
process. All these considerations, among others, mean that policy-
makers are never free to choose among all or most of the conceivable
alternatives. To understand how policy is actually fashioned, therefore, one must often attend to past decisions and to the realistic
constraints upon the decision-makers in the present. With these considerations in mind, it is easier to understand why some policy choices
are more likely than others.

Also, all policy choices of consequence involve a *distribution of costs and benefits* among a multitude of important interests; how these costs and benefits are distributed by different policies often provides an important insight into how policy-makers will view their choices. Both costs and benefits can be tangible or intangible, hidden or obvious. One obvious tangible set of costs and benefits is economic. If there is to be a governmental ban on DDT, then chemical firms manufacturing that product are likely to absorb some high, short-run costs. If the government decides to discourage further increases in the amount of timber that commercial lumbering companies may remove from federal lands, the timber industry stands to lose future income, whereas manufacturers of alternative building materials may profit. However, costs and benefits can also be reckoned in political terms. A policy may bestow political benefits by assigning the implementation of a new law to an administrative agency with which certain interests enjoy cordial relationships; in another case, representatives of an interest may be appointed to critical decision-making posts within the governmental structure as part of a policy concerning that interest. Conversely, political "costs" may be assessed against various interests by diminishing appropriations for programs of concern to them, or by reorganizing the agencies with which they have customarily dealt on various policy matters. Or, perhaps, a major piece of legislation will not include a set of interests within those granted some form of governmental favor. In any case, the variety of costs and benefits to flow from a particular policy can vary enormously. The important point is that the pattern in the distribution of such gains and losses will have a significant influence in shaping support and opposition to any policy formulated in government.

The many factors that shape public policy include numerous influences besides public officials and governmental institutions themselves. Even when one has a reasonably accurate idea of what factors enter into the making of policy, one may be uncertain of their relative influence. All this points to the complexity of environmental policy-making and underscores how rudimentary is the outline of these factors we have presented. Still, the factors we have discussed are clearly important in shaping the present and future course of environmental policy and will serve as organizing points for the subsequent discussion. We shall turn next to an examination of the environmental problem itself, the issue, as a beginning toward policy analysis.

NOTES

1. The Birmingham story is adapted from reports carried between November 18 and November 25, 1971, and between April, 1975, and August, 1976, by the *New York Times,* United Press International, the *Miami* (Florida) *Herald,* and the *St. Petersburg Times.* Additional data were supplied by the U.S. Environmental Protection Agency, *Progress in the Prevention and Control of Air Pollution,* Annual Report of the Administrator of the Environmental Protection Agency, March, 1972.
2. A useful summary of air pollution indices in the years immediately prior to 1970 may be found in Philip Nobile and John Deedy, eds., *The Complete Ecology Fact Book* (Garden City, N.Y.: Doubleday Anchor Books, 1972), pp. 195–209. A detailed examination of three such crises is contained in John C. Esposito, *Vanishing Air* (New York: Grossman Publishers, 1970), chapter 9.
3. Many of the issues involved in the SST controversy are discussed from an environmentalist's viewpoint in William A. Shurcliff, *S/S/T and Sonic Boom Handbook* (New York: Ballantine Books, 1970). The Barge Canal incident is summarized in Walter A. Rosenbaum and Paul E. Roberts, "The Year of Spoiled Pork: Comments on the Role of the Courts as Environmental Defenders," *Law and Society Review,* August, 1972, pp. 33–60.
4. Harold Sprout, "The Environmental Crisis in the Context of American Politics," in Leslie L. Roos, Jr., ed., *The Politics of Ecosuicide* (New York: Holt, Rinehart and Winston, 1971), p. 49.
5. The public interest in ecology is clearly evident in the compendium of polls found in Hazel Erskine, "The Polls: Pollution and Its Costs," *Public Opinion Quarterly,* Spring, 1972, pp. 120–35.
6. Anthony Downs, "Up and Down with Ecology," *The Public Interest,* Summer, 1972, p. 38.
7. Reiley E. Dunlap, "Decline in Public Support for Environmental Protection: Evidence from a Panel Study: 1970–1974," *Rural Sociology,* forthcoming.
8. The Gallup Poll *Index,* February, 1970, p. 5.
9. Estimates on consumer expenses may be found in Council on Environmental Quality, *Environmental Quality: The Sixth Annual Report of the Council on Environmental Quality* (Washington, D.C., 1976), pp. 527, 552.
10. Budget estimates for environmental protection are taken from *ibid.,* appendix F. Other budget estimates may be found in U.S. Office of Manpower and Budget, *The Federal Budget.*

11. Quoted in Charles R. Ross, "The Federal Government as an Inadvertent Advocate of Environmental Degradation," in Harold W. Helfrich, Jr., ed., *The Environmental Crisis* (New Haven, Conn.: Yale University Press, 1970), pp. 178–79.

12. The history of federal pollution legislation is summarized in Council on Environmental Quality, *Environmental Quality, 1970: The First Annual Report of the Council on Environmental Quality* (Washington, D.C., 1970), pp. 43–44.

13. Such legislation includes the Pre-Emption Act of 1841, the Swamp Land Act of 1850, the Mining Act of 1866, and the Desert Lands Act of 1877. For a discussion of the political implications of these acts, see the excellent summaries in Earl Finbar Murphy, *Governing Nature* (Chicago: Quadrangle Books, 1967), pp. 208 ff.; and Grant McConnell, *Private Power and American Democracy* (New York: Vintage Books, 1966), chapter 7.

14. A résumé of these "great giveaways" may be found in Stewart L. Udall, *The Quiet Crisis* (New York: Holt, Rinehart and Winston, 1963), chapter 5.

15. *New York Times,* November 9, 1975).

16. This point has been made effectively by Charles O. Jones in "Speculative Argumentation in Federal Air Pollution Policy Making," *Journal of Politics,* May, 1974, pp. 438–64. See also Charles O. Jones, *Clean Air* (Pittsburgh: University of Pittsburgh Press, 1975).

17. See Council on Environmental Quality, *Sixth Annual Report,* p. 534.

18. Robert S. Diamond, "What Business Thinks about the Environment," in Editors of *Fortune, The Environment* (New York: Harper and Row, 1970), pp. 55–65. See also *A Nationwide Survey of Environmental Protection* (New York: *Wall Street Journal,* 1972).

19. The Chamber of Commerce is quoted in *New York Times,* June 4, 1972; the "birdwatcher" quote is from *New York Times,* January 13, 1973.

20. The importance of voluntary compliance is emphasized in Clarence Davies III, *The Politics of Pollution* (New York: Pegasus, 1970), pp. 201–203.

21. While I make no pretense that this is more than a rudimentary scheme, I think it includes many concepts that policy analysts would consider important and does *start* the building of analytical policy studies on environmental issues. My own thinking has been influenced on this matter by Charles O. Jones, "From Gold to Garbage: A Bibliographical Essay on Politics and the Environment," *American Political Science Review,* June, 1972, pp. 588–95.

2. The Environmental Toll

Most Americans know now that we have an "environmental problem" although they might be vague about its details. The media in mounting volume have dramatized and disseminated information about environmental abuse, ecology is now commonly discussed from kindergarten through college, and public officials have preached protecting the environment almost to the point where not only the environment but the environmental issue surrounds us. The danger in this publicity is that Americans may become desensitized to the problem or begin to suspect that the constant emphasis exaggerates the issue. One purpose of this chapter is briefly to describe the nature of the nation's major environmental problems in order to lay at rest any doubts about their gravity. However, since the nature of the problems at hand creates many of the contours in the political struggle over policy, another purpose here is to provide some preliminary insight into environmental politics.

The current environmental movement, in its broadest view, represents a concern for the total environmental quality of the United States and the world. While various ecology activists may concentrate upon particular problems, they are also striving to move Americans toward an "environmental consciousness" in which environmental ills are viewed wholistically, as a totality of problems affecting both the quality and the feasibility of life. Most environmental experts, otherwise divided on many aspects of ecology, agree that the physical environment of the nation has seriously deteriorated and that grave, possibly calamitous consequences may follow unless effective countermeasures are immediately taken. Most Americans appear to equate environmental degradation principally with air and water pollution, but public and private leaders concerned with the environment see the problem more comprehensively. It involves not only pollution but, among other issues, poor land use, uncontrolled noise, rising waste, unrestrained use of chemical poisons, reckless population growth, and unthinking destruction of the wilderness. Most of these problems are related; in the end, they combine to make life increasingly unpleasant and may seriously threaten it.

Some critics, convinced that Americans have a perverted genius for environmental contamination, lay the blame on capitalism, the establishment, or some other American culture devil. To the contrary, environmental degradation is now worldwide. It is closely associated with Western culture (now global in its impact) and particularly with industrialization, a very "dirty" process ecologically. Both the Soviet Union and Communist China have admitted serious pollution problems. In a recent report to the United Nations Economic Commission for Europe, the Soviet Union noted that it would take more than two and a half times the present river flow in that water-rich nation to adequately dilute the existing water pollution there. Both desalinization of sea water and the use of melted polar glaciers were being considered by Russian officials as possible remedies to the pollution crisis. In Venice, the air and water are so fouled with sulfur oxides that the legendary canals have occasionally turned dark brown, silver exposed to the air tarnishes, and a third of the city's historic buildings and sculpture suffer from "marble cancer"—sulfuric acid corrosion from air contaminants. Experts have warned that the Sea of Galilee is "dying" of eutrophication (oxygen depletion), while eighteen nations along the Mediterranean have recently joined to save that body from irreversible pollution.

The global sweep of environmental damage was underscored by two international events. In the summer of 1972, the first U.N. Conference on the Human Environment was held in Stockholm in response to mounting international apprehension about environmental damage. A 200-page program endorsed by 114 nations warned the world of possibly irreversible ecological damage that might be impending unless international measures were undertaken to abate it.[1] An outgrowth of the Stockholm conference was the creation of the

U.N. Environmental Program, with a staff of 100, headquarters in Kenya, and a five-year, $100 million budget. One of its first projects was the creation of the Earthwatch Program involving global environmental monitoring and the organization of a worldwide ecological information referral system. More dramatic was a study released by the prestigious Club of Rome in 1972, in which a mathematical model and computer simulation were used by experts at the Massachusetts Institute of Technology to forecast the future global impact of present environmental trends. Based on their projections, the MIT scientists made a chilling forecast:

> If the present growth trends in world population, industrialization, pollution, food production and resource depletion continue unchanged, the limits of growth on this planet will be reached sometime within the next hundred years. The most probable result will be a rather sudden and uncontrollable decline in both population and industrial capacity.[2]

Numerous economists and environmental experts have challenged some of the assumptions leading to these pessimistic conclusions, yet the global threat of resource depletion and pervasive pollution is widely recognized, as the U.N.'s recent environmental program reveals. Thus, the 1970's became a decade of not only American, but also of global environmental concern.

THE MAJOR PROBLEMS

In the United States, it is difficult to find an environment unaffected by some sort of pollution; indeed, the federal government recently launched a program to save "samples of the full range of natural environments" in the country before they disappeared entirely. The creation of new federal, state, and local environmental restoration programs in the last few years has produced some heartening signs of partial restoration. The Detroit River, gray with pollution for a half century, is blue again as ecological health and sport fish slowly return. Lake Erie, once pronounced "dead," is alive if not quite well. Oregon's Willamette River and Florida's Miami River have been reclaimed from the ecological graveyard.[3]

Still, the nation's environmental ills are pervasive. Laws are not deeds; it will take decades, even with vigorous public and private effort, to translate legislative promises into ecological realities. The air is still seriously polluted: Acid rain and snow (reaching 1,000 times normal acidity) have now been recognized as a serious ecological threat in the eastern United States, and excessive lead, presumably originating from auto emissions, has contaminated fruits and vegetables grown in some urban plots to the extent that in some cities, such as St. Louis, eating the produce would be "a clear danger to children." The Great Lakes will take decades to restore to ecological health. In 1976, the International Joint Commission, responsible for implementing agreements to clean the Lakes, admitted it "could not have foreseen the magnitude of the problem." Despite controls on the pesticide DDT, the Louisiana brown pelican was in danger of extinction from the poison in late 1974.[4] In short, a variety of environmental indicators show that the ecological battle has only begun.

Federal and state efforts have concentrated on five related environmental problems that, while far from representing all, have seemed the most serious.

Air Pollution

Air pollution is the result of several contaminants appearing in differing concentrations and combinations in ambient air. Some, like the photochemical oxidants, react with sunlight, form smog, and become visible, while others remain invisible. These pollutants and the approximate proportion of each in emissions into the atmosphere during a recent representative year can be briefly listed:

1. *Carbon monoxide (CO)*-47 per cent: a colorless, odorless, poisonous gas produced by the incomplete burning of carbon in fuels. Most of this comes from internal combustion engines, usually gasoline-powered vehicles.

2. *Sulfur oxides (SO)*-15 per cent: a poisonous, acrid gas produced when sulfur-containing fuel is burned. Industry and electric generators produce most of this.

3. *Hydrocarbons (HC)*-15 per cent: represent unburned and wasted fuel that plays a major part in forming photochemical smog. Comes from both gasoline vehicles and industry.

4. *Particulate matter*-13 per cent: solid or liquid substances of variable size that remain in the air for long periods and travel enormous distances. Industry is the major source.
5. *Nitrogen oxides (NO)*-10 per cent: produced by fuel burned at very high temperatures. Electric power plants and transportation vehicles are the major sources.

A variety of studies suggests that short exposure to high concentrations of these pollutants singly and in combination, or prolonged exposure to lesser concentrations, can produce serious health hazards or physical impairment for many individuals; the annual property damage is also enormous. The federal Environmental Protection Agency has estimated that the total annual toll of air pollution to Americans may approach $20 billion, including more than $9 billion in health costs, almost $8 billion in residential property damage, and an additional $7.6 billion in destruction to materials and vegetation.[5]

From a political viewpoint, an important aspect of air pollution is where it originates, which means, essentially, what interests are affected by air pollution controls. In Figure 1, the estimated contribution of various sources to the total United States air pollution load by weight is presented. It is noteworthy that three sources appear to account for more than three-fourths of the pollutants by weight: gasoline-burning vehicles (transportation), electric power plants (stationary sources), and industry. This means that any efforts at air pollution abatement must involve the automobile, petroleum, rubber, electric utility, and the chemical industries among the major elements within the private economic sector, in addition to numerous other enterprises interlocked with these through product-sharing and investment structures. Equally important, to speak of such industries is to mention products that are basic to the American life style and that strongly determine the nation's rate of economic growth and activity. For example, the electric power industry, producer of a commodity indispensable to private life and industry alike, has increased its output by 7 per cent yearly since 1947 to meet rising demand; this annual consumption of electric power is expected to quadruple by the year 2000.[6] Between 1964 and 1970—to cite a small yet instructive example of our electricity-dependent life style—the annual sales for window air conditioners doubled in the United States from 2.5 million to 5 million. Next to his shelter and daily bread, the average

Figure 1
MAJOR SOURCES OF AIR POLLUTANTS, BY WEIGHT

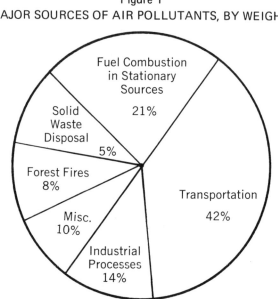

SOURCE: Council on Environmental Quality, *Environmental Quality* (Washington, D.C., 1971), p. 64.

American spends more on his car than any other item. By 1980, Detroit will be producing about 44,000 cars daily to meet this transportation demand. So, in the end, air pollution abatement directly affects not only the largest corporate interests in the nation but almost all Americans whose convenience will be affected if regulation of major air pollution sources is to be a reality.

Water Pollution

Today, one eats Mississippi River catfish at his peril. Once a staple of local cuisine, it is increasingly suspect because of contamination to it and most other fish in the great river. The Mississippi, draining 41 percent of the United States, has not proved too big to pollute; even swimming and fishing are now almost unthinkable along most of its meandering course. In one study of the river's southern end, sixty major industrial sources were found to be contaminating the water with eighty-nine organic compounds and significant quantities of cyanide, phenols, arsenic, lead, cadmium, copper, chromium, mercury, and zinc. In New York, vacationers were prevented from using the Fire Island beaches along the Atlantic Ocean at the height of the 1976 summer season when globules of gray sewage sludge washed ashore from an undetermined source. Oil spills, growing constantly, reached 13,966 separate incidents in U.S. waters during 1974, depositing an estimated 18 billion gallons of petroleum on the nation's waters.[7] Such incidents, no longer rare, constitute only the more forceful examples of the nation's growing water pollution ills.

Totally unpolluted bodies of water are almost nonexistent in the United States. Federal estimates of pollution levels among waterways in major geographic areas of the country indicate that about a third of all stream miles and almost three-fourths of the total watershed area in the nation are polluted; in some regions, such as the Northeast, serious pollution has become almost rampant. The volume and combination of water pollutants vary enormously among the nation's water-bodies but it is possible to identify the major forms of pollution. Below is a brief description of these contaminants:

1. *Industrial wastes.* These include almost every type of *organic compound* involved in industrial processes in addition to a wealth of *heavy metals* (mercury, cadmium, zinc, copper, and the like) and, in recent years, *thermal pollution* produced by infusing streams, lakes and rivers with heated water discharged by industries after its use to cool production equipment. The major source of thermal pollution is the electric power industry.

2. *Municipal wastes.* These consist primarily of human waste and detergents together with other organic compounds found in domestic effluent.

3. *Agricultural wastes.* The major components of agricultural waste are animal waste, fertilizers, and, particularly in the western United States, salt and other minerals leached from the soil during irrigation.

4. *Other sources.* Among these, *oil pollution* from oil spills in harbors and rivers is increasingly serious. *Mine drainage,* mostly in Appalachia but wherever strip mining is practiced, produces sulfuric

acid when sulfur compounds in the ground react with water; about 10,500 miles of streams in Appalachia have dropped below desirable quality levels in recent years solely because of this.

All authoritative studies predict a continuing rise in the volume of these pollutants. Within fifty years, there will probably be a fourfold increase in municipal sewage, while industrial wastes, barring a technological breakthrough, will more than double. Thermal pollution in particular seems destined to intensify. By 1980, the electric power industry, principal producer of heated water from industrial processes, is expected to require one-fifth of the total fresh water run-off in the United States to cool its generators.

The total cost of water pollution is impossible to estimate accurately because it includes both widespread tangible damages, which can be stated in terms of dollars, and aesthetic losses upon which a fair price is difficult or impossible to fix. Wherever accurate measures of water pollution damage have been determined, appreciable costs have resulted on a national scale. More than a fifth of the nation's shellfish beds have been destroyed by water pollution; the soft-shell crabfish industry has been almost totally eliminated in U.S. waters, while the annual harvest of shrimp from coastal waters has decreased from over 6.3 million pounds in 1936 to only 10,000 pounds in 1965. The losses suffered by western farmers because of increasing water salinity are expected to rise from $16 million annually in 1970 to $50 million by 2010. Taxpayers have borne and will continue to bear the major expense of purifying the nation's waters (over 80 percent of the total, at least) through tax payments to local governments for waste treatment facilities. Between 1970 and 1974, total public expenditures for waste treatment facilities financed by taxes increased, from $800 million to $3.2 billion annually.

The water pollution issue clearly embraces most significant private and public institutions in American society. The 300,000 industrial concerns contributing to water pollution are distributed among all major sectors of the economy (although paper, organic chemicals, petroleum, and steel are the principal polluters). Municipal and state governments are deeply implicated in water pollution control as formulators of public policy and as the primary financers of water treatment facilities. The federal government, now assuming the initiative in water pollution policy, appears ready to use its own taxing powers to fund research, development, and construction of water treatment facilities on an unprecedented scale at state and local levels.

Land and Water Resources

The first settlers in America encountered a virgin continent embracing, within the present United States, more than 3.6 million square miles containing some of the richest land, mineral, and water resources on earth. Until recently, Americans treated this inheritance as an inexhaustible cornucopia whose abundance should be used by the nation as private whim, economic advantage, or public expediency dictated. The culture, the law, and public officials treated nature as a "free good," an apparently limitless bounty costing nothing except the price of extracting its riches. Americans exercised little foresight in their onslaught upon this vast natural endowment. They were driven not only by hope of private reward or corporate wealth but also by a public policy inspired by the intense nationalism and the international insecurities of a new state. Not unlike the leaders of modern "developing nations"—albeit with far more promising opportunities and infinitely more resources—America's national administration pressed hard for domestic economic expansion, for the settlement and securing of the frontiers, for growth, wealth, and power of all kinds that would build the nation's international security and fortify its world economic position. In this respect, the nation's raid on resources was an environmental phase in nation-building and one which almost all the world's currently "developed" nations have experienced. The country was settled, timbered, mined, dammed, drained, dredged, filled, pitted, bored, bought, and sold with scant reflection on environmental consequences. For a century after the nation's founding, the westward frontier promised ever renewed resources over the horizon; one could abandon and thereby avoid environmental ravage by putting it to his back. "That is what the frontier has always meant to us—an escape from the consequences."[8]

For over a hundred years, prophetic voices were raised in unavailing warning against this reckless ethic. In this century, the two Roosevelts were the first leaders in American history to harness massive public concern and national energy to the task of redressing extensive damage to our natural resources. But it is becoming clear in the 1970's that the nation confronts land and resource problems requiring a far greater investment of public resources and more sweeping public policy than ever before. Environmental experts and ecology leaders have urged a rethinking of public policy concerning almost all major resources. We shall consider but a few issues currently important.

One major problem now facing the nation is the *growing scarcity of open land.* The nation is moving slowly but inexorably from an era of land abundance to an era of land scarcity, although the generous open space still visible may temporarily obscure this trend. With less undeveloped land available, however, conflicts over its use will grow more frequent and intense; there will no longer be sufficient land to satisfy all competing demands. As a result, more deliberate choices will have to be made about its use by public agencies. All this is plain enough in the statistics: About 1 million acres of rural land a year are now being converted to urban development, airports, highways, reservoirs, and flood control; suburban development alone accounts for half this annual land loss. This presents at least two significant problems. First, the disappearance of wetlands is acute. Wetlands are extremely vital areas, not only for their aesthetic and recreational value but for the continued existence of a multitude of plants and animals that could not breed or survive anywhere else. Moreover, the shellfish industry depends on the estuarine wetlands, especially as the breeding ground for its products.

Originally, the United States possessed 127 million acres of wetland, which has now shrunk by 40 percent to only 70 million acres. In California, more than two-thirds of the wetlands once available for fish and wildlife have disappeared, while Florida and numerous other states have lost at least 15 per cent of their original estuarine environments. America's loss of wetlands has been concealed from full recognition because the disappearance is insidiously slow. Dredging and filling, conversion to industrial use, and residential development proceeds across wetlands at a measured, remorseless pace that absorbs relatively small land areas at a time. Over long periods, however, the toll mounts. In the decade 1954–64, for example, New York lost almost a third of its existing estuary land, Connecticut almost 13 per cent and eight other northeastern states together about 8 per cent of all their wetlands.

Disappearing open land also means a decline in recreational opportunities and aesthetic enjoyment for many Americans. The recreation industry has, in some instances, attempted to manage open land for commercial purposes; more than three hundred American corporations are now in the business of creating recreation areas from open country. But much of this land has been lost, probably irrevocably, in its natural state, and much will never be open again. This means more than a diminished opportunity for relaxation and appreciation of natural environments; it denies many Americans, increasingly, the pleasure of living next to nothing "civilized."

Unlike concern about land use, the controversy over *water resource development* has proceeded with unabated intensity for many decades. For almost two centuries, the federal government has been the principal developer of water resource projects. The current controversy swirls mostly about the work of the Army Corps of Engineers and, to a lesser degree, of the Interior Department's Bureau of Reclamation—the principal federal agencies in this area—although a larger issue is the whole system through which Congress funds water resource projects. Water resource developments—dams, navigable waterways, reservoirs, levees, flood walls, and recreation areas—have been generously and dependably funded. Such projects have regularly absorbed several billion dollars in appropriations and, until recently, were the most heavily supported of any federal program directly concerned with the environment. These developments, like other local public works projects collectively known as pork-barrel endeavors, are esteemed in Congress because of the real or alleged economic benefits they bring to constituencies and because they promote the political fortune of the legislator who bestows them upon his constituents. The Corps of Engineers, 175 years old and a formidable political force in Washington, dominates the planning and development of these projects and thus incurs the ire of environmentalists dissatisfied with the federal water resource program.

Those sensitive to environmental problems have long criticized Congress for authorizing, with the collaboration of the Corps, too many unnecessary, uneconomical, and ecologically damaging projects in an effort to keep federal money flowing to local constituencies. In essence, environmentalists have concluded that the continuation of water resource development along its present lines will result in progressively greater environmental degradation for the sake of projects of dubious worth. Some environmental spokesmen argue that if new projects were weighed carefully for economic and environmental value, it would be discovered that the most necessary ones have already been built.

Energy Use

The 1970's marked the first stirring of energy accountability in the United States, a prodigious energy consumer whose vast resources had dulled its awareness of diminishing energy reserves. Now, for the first time, the United States has been forced to begin the difficult task of formulating a policy enabling it to bring its energy consumption in line with its actual energy supplies. Energy conservation, itself a major ecological issue, poses a host of related environmental questions in the process of its resolution.

Americans, only 6 per cent of the world's population, consume about a third of its energy production. On the eve of the "energy crisis" of 1973, per capita American energy use exceeded the rest of the globe's per capita consumption by seven times and remained twice the average of that in European nations with comparable living standards.[9] Climbing precipitously since World War II, American energy demand rose, to an extent not then appreciated, on a tide of cheap imported oil. When political motivations prompted the Arab oil exporters to cut American supplies by a modest 2 million barrels daily in late 1973, the sudden constriction of petroleum availability and its repercussions forced the public and its officials to recognize a growing gap between domestic energy use and supply.

Despite allegations to the contrary, the energy crisis is real. Until 1973, the flow of inexpensive imported crude oil disguised the nation's true energy picture. As the Committee for Economic Development explains, the 1973 embargo did not initiate the energy problem:

> Even prior to this event, the need to adjust to the growing scarcity of fossil fuels was becoming evident. The prospect of energy scarcity had been obscured during most of the postwar period because discovery of oil, in particular, exceeded consumption.... But the tide began to

change in the last few years, at least partially because of the earlier drop in prices. World energy consumption grew at an average annual rate of 5.7 percent during the period from 1967 to 1972, and oil consumption grew even faster, as cheap oil replaced coal in Europe and Japan as well as the United States. With the evaporation of spare capacity at the end of the decade, U.S. self sufficiency also ended.[10]

The essence of the domestic problem is that the United States faces the prospect of gradually diminishing supplies of virtually all its major energy sources while its energy demand remains as yet uncontrolled. An idea of the nation's present energy position can be gathered from a quick inventory of energy resources:

1. *Crude oil.*   Peak domestic production was reached in the late 1960's. Since then, the gap between demand and domestic production has steadily widened. In 1970, the gap was 4.1 million barrels per day, but by 1974 it had risen to an estimated 8.9 million barrels per day. To remedy this deficit, imported oil has risen from 1,310,000 barrels per day (bpd) in 1970 to more than 3,500,000 bpd in 1974.[11]

2. *Natural gas.*   This, the nation's dominant energy source, provides one-third of U.S. energy requirements; half our industrial energy is gas-generated. Since 1968, increased demand has exceeded new source discovery. Despite Washington's efforts to promote further gas exploration, supplies are not likely to increase beyond present levels and may decrease. Since 1970, twenty-one states have had to declare moratoria on new gas hook-ups at various times.

3. *Coal.*   Coal is America's most abundant energy reserve; the United States possesses about half the world's known coal reserves. In recent years, coal production has lagged behind demand because presently mined reserves are less productive and demands have risen. Coal now accounts for about 19 percent of the nation's energy use; it produces half the energy consumed in electric power generation. The volume of future coal supply will depend upon federal policy concerning huge western reserves that it controls. Development of these new reserves is intensely controversial because of the ecological damage anticipated.

4. *Nuclear energy.*   Once a glamour fuel, touted as the technological miracle to rescue the United States from energy scarcity, nuclear

generating plants now seem unlikely to become a major energy source in the next several decades. In 1974, nuclear power accounted for less than 2 per cent of the nation's power generation. High "start-up" costs for generating plants and technical problems have been major impediments to anticipated development.

5. *Speculative sources.* Energy has been generated from geothermal, solar, oil shale, ambient air, and residual waste sources; each presently accounts for a minuscule portion of domestic energy production. Although technically possible, generation of energy from such sources in significant quantities has yet to prove economically promising.

Given this picture, it seems evident that no short-term technological breakthrough will spare the nation a diminishing energy supply. Apparently, the United States will have to concentrate upon controlling energy demand and developing its own resources to bring supply and demand into balance. Above all, the era of cheap, abundant energy seems dead.

Environmentalists generally favor energy conservation over massive new exploration for domestic energy reserves because they believe continued exploration will accelerate the nation's energy demands and distract public attention from the reality of limited energy reserves. Thus, President Nixon's 1974 declaration of "Project Independence" and the White House's subsequent efforts to produce American energy "self-sufficiency" by the late 1980's have met with scant enthusiasm among conservationists because self-sufficiency, if possible, will mean a new raid on resources at huge environmental costs. Increased domestic crude oil production, for example, will require extensive offshore drilling on the outer continental shelf with potentially grave risks of oil spills; converting oil shale to petroleum entails large energy investments and creates air pollution problems. However, it is coal, the "energy pariah," that incites the bitterest current controversy in energy policy. Coal is the nation's most abundant energy resource, its development the key fuel in Washington's design for energy self-sufficiency, and its extraction an impending environmental disaster in the opinion of many ecologists.[12]

Coal is controversial because of its current mining technology. It was once extracted through deep-shaft mines; most future domestic coal will be strip-mined. Strip mining, or surface mining, is a technique for mining mineral seams (customarily coal) in hills and mountains by removing all soil, trees, and other "overburden," then blasting a bench into the hillside from which the mineral is easily extracted. Clearing and blasting continues down the slope until it is denuded of all original surface features. What remains is often a mound of bare, corrugated subsoil; sometimes the top of a hill is entirely removed and only the decapitated remnant is left for stripping. Harry M. Caudill, a native of Appalachia, writes about the viciousness of strip mining with the fire and eloquence of a man outraged. Though Caudill's anger is not impartial, few who have observed strip mining in action would disagree with his description of foothills after surface mining.

> The overburden is scraped off and the coal is scooped out. Inevitably such topsoil as the land affords is buried under towering heaps of subsoil. When the strippers move on, once level meadows and cornfields have been converted into jumbled heaps of hardpan, barren clay from deep in the earth. This hellish landscape is slow to support vegetation and years elapse before the yellow waste turns green.

When stripping is practiced on mountains, says Caudill, the damage is "fantastically magnified."

> Masses of shattered stone, shale, and dirt are cast pell-mell down the hillsides. The first to go are the thin remaining layer of fertile topsoil and such trees as still find sustenance in it. The uprooted trees are flung down the slopes by the first cut. Then follows the sterile subsoil, shattered stone and slate. As the cut extends deeper into the hillside the process is repeated again and again. . . . After the coal has been carried away vast quantities of the shattered mineral are left uncovered. Many seams contain substantial quantities of sulfur, which when wet produces toxic sulphuric acid. This poison bleeds into the creeks, killing minute vegetation and destroying fish, frogs and other stream dwellers.[13]

Once a minor source of coal and confined to Appalachia, strip mining has advanced to a major industry because of increasing fuel demands for electric generating plants, the need for less polluting fuels, and an expected technological breakthough that will make coal a major producer of natural gas. Stripping is, moreover, comparatively inexpensive and enables the recovery of far more coal than would otherwise be possible. At present, strip-mined land accounts for approximately half of the U.S. annual coal tonnage; to produce this, 2 million acres—an area more than half the size of New Jersey —has been stripped of soil. A major push is now underway by the coal industry to purchase mineral rights in Arizona, Colorado, Montana, New Mexico, North Dakota, and Wyoming, where strip mining would begin when the expected mineral deposits are found. Since more than 77 percent of the nation's strippable coal lies in the thirteen states west of the Mississippi, a major strip-mine industry is almost inevitable in the West. Without any restraint, this stripping will far surpass in area and coal tonnage produced anything found east of the Mississippi. Strip mining has aroused bitter opposition wherever it has appeared, even in eastern Kentucky, where coal has long been king; indeed, its proponents have frequently admitted many of its environmental ravages. As Harry Caudill's description suggests, environmentalists believe that strip mining almost totally destroys the natural ecology of entire regions, leaves ugly scars on the earth that are slow to heal, bleeds sulfuric acid from its remains to thwart soil regeneration, and contaminates nearby water until it impoverishes all about it environmentally and economically. Moreover, strip-mine operators are accused of callous negligence in failing to restore the stripped soil to better conditions. Defenders of strip mining, though acknowledging the truth in some of these accusations, argue that coal is a necessary American industry, and strip mining must eventually meet the mounting coal demand if it is to be satisfied. They also argue that environmental damage, though real, is often exaggerated and that their frequently successful efforts at environmental restoration are ignored or depreciated unfairly by their critics.

Wastes and Poisons

Solid waste is an unofficial measure of national prosperity: The more affluent the nation, the greater its volume and variety of solid wastes. Is is hardly surprising, then, that Americans are the most prolific producers of solid waste on earth—6.57 billion tons in 1972 alone. Among the wastes produced in the United States, Americans annually throw away 30 million tons of paper and paper products, 4 million tons of plastics, 100 million tires, 30 billion bottles, 60 billion cans, and millions of major appliances including cars. Americans have regarded solid waste as an annoying but inevitable problem to be managed principally by government. The volume of solid waste is now rising at such a steep rate that the customary response—bury it—will no longer suffice.

Clearly, agricultural wastes (2.28 billion tons a year) are the greatest single source, producing almost twice the volume of all other waste sources combined; following (in order of volume) are mineral wastes (1.7 billion tons), residential, commercial, and institutional wastes (250 million tons), and industrial wastes (110 million tons). The variety of products represented in each of these sources is noted in the following summary:

1. *Agricultural wastes.* 2.28 billion tons per year: manure and other animal products, slaughterhouse leavings, useless residues from crop harvesting, vineyard and orchard prunings, and greenhouse wastes.

2. *Mineral solid wastes.* 1.7 billion tons per year: primarily from mineral and fossil fuel mining and including all the debris commonly found in slag heaps, culm piles, and mill tailings. Most comes from the production of copper, iron and steel, bituminous coal, phosphate rock, lead, zinc, aluminum, and anthracite coal.

3. *Residential, commercial, and institutional wastes.* 250 million tons per year: paper and related products, plastics, tires, bottles, cans, grass and tree trimmings, food wastes, sewage sludge, and abandoned appliances.

4. *Industrial solid wastes.* 110 million tons per year: scrap metal, paper and paper products, waste plastic, bales of rags, drums of assorted surplus products, and flyash.

Although accurate data describing the total volume of national solid wastes over the years is scarce, considerable indirect evidence suggests that the volume is mounting. In general, there is an industrial and private trend away from recycling materials and toward higher materials consumption—both forecasting greater solid waste for the future. Indeed, when it comes to private consumption, the shape of the future seems to be a disposable container. By the mid-1970's, for instance, returnable bottles, the only container for soft drinks little more than a decade ago, will account for less of those sold as metal and glass throw-aways come to dominate the market. After the middle of this decade, according to predictions, seven of every ten beer containers sold in the United States will be nonreturnable as well.

As waste increases, more problems arise. The collection and disposal of the mounting waste from residential, commercial, institutional, and industrial sources—the most immediate health hazards—are becoming increasingly expensive, and the results are often unsatisfactory. The cost of manpower and machinery for waste disposal absorbs a progressively larger proportion of governmental appropriations (particularly at the local level, where most of this waste is handled), but, with the exception of the compactor truck, no significant technological innovations have appeared in waste management that might produce greater efficiency in operations. Moreover, dumps themselves are often poorly managed, unsanitary, and repulsive; open landfills—the most customary mode for disposing of solid waste—are getting scarcer and more expensive. Until now, Americans have expended little effort or imagination to develop more satisfactory methods of local waste disposal.

Recovering and reusing some portion of solid waste—customarily called recycling—is a desirable solution and may be essential. Recycling is partially a strategy for reducing the sheer volume of waste, but it may also slow the depletion of many natural resources, such as metals, timber, and minerals, through reconverting their end products to further use. Not least important, recycling may be a palliative for the junk and debris that clutters the American landscape in ugly profusion. Paper products, beverage containers, and automobiles, three major contributors to solid waste problems, illustrate the possibility for recycling. Americans deplete a large portion of their standing timber to consume more than 59 million tons of paper products yearly; eventually, much of this becomes the debris that amounts to half the roadside litter of the country. A large portion of this paper waste is technically reusable, yet the nation recycles less than a fifth of its paper production. In contrast, several other nations, including Japan, recycle almost half of theirs.

American industry manufactures about 45 billion disposable beverage containers annually and expects to avalanche the market with 100 billion a year by 1980. Between 1 and 2 billion of these are tossed away annually to decorate our highways. At the moment, only about 5 percent of all nonreturnable containers are recycled, although it is technologically feasible to process almost all. Currently, somewhere between 2.5 million and 4 million abandoned automobiles embellish the American countryside while slowly rusting to powder; after motors and accessories have been stripped, the frames are often left to the elements because they are economically unprofitable for further recycling. Appalachia alone has the dubious distinction of being "Detroit's boneyard," where about three million junked cars (almost a fifth of all junked cars in the nation) now reside. As with other waste products, the technical capacity for recycling a used car exists, but not the economic incentives. Almost an entire automobile, including the oft-abandoned frame, can be and has been reused in some way when it proved profitable. What is now needed for massive waste recycling is an economic stimulus, together with additional research, to ensure greater economy and efficiency. Government could provide such a stimulus, not only for recycling but for the elimination of many waste products, through tax incentives and research subsidization.

In 1962, Rachel Carson's informed, eloquent condemnation of indiscriminate pesticide use in *Silent Spring* opened the public debate over chemical poisons in the United States. The controversy involves a wide variety of chemical poisons—insecticides, herbicides, and biocides—widely used throughout the world and collectively called pesticides. Environmentalists and scientists have expressed acute apprehension about such lethal poisons as sodium arsenate and parathion, such "persistent" chemicals as DDT (chlorinated hydrocarbons), aldrin, dieldren, endrin, heptaclor, toxaphene, and the herbicide 2,4,5-T.[14] Like agriculturists around the world, American farmers depend heavily on chemical poisons to control plant and animal pests. In the United States, more than 900 active pesticidal chemicals have been formulated into about 60,000 preparations; more than 1 billion pounds of these pesticides are used annually here. There have been several reasons expressed for apprehension about chemical poisons. To begin, several persistent poisons such as DDT have proved lethal to animal life. DDT has been responsible for larger kills of shellfish, fish, birds, aquatic mammals, and land mammals; such toxicity may, the critics charge, ultimately destroy or seriously endanger entire ecosystems and eliminate several animal species entirely. The critics assert that persistent poisons are particularly deadly to the predators living at the top of "food chains." These "chains" begin with microscopic organisms forming the food base for more highly developed life which, in turn, supplies the food for still more developed organisms until, at the top of such a complex chain, there exist the large predators such as eagles, hawks, cats, and other carnivores with few enemies except man. The minute quantities of persistent poisons absorbed by organisms at the bottom of a "food chain" are concentrated in the bodies of their predators and this concentration continues until the animals at the top of this life pyramid may ingest massive doses of the poison into their system by eating their natural prey. Thus, persistent poisons may virtually extinguish predators at the top of a food chain if not controlled. DDT has been demonstrated to be a major cause in the death of hawks, eagles, pelicans, ducks, falcons, and the ospreys among major predators. Equally important, critics of chemical poisons state that many pesticides may also be serious hazards to human life and that substantial enough evidence exists to suggest that a major study should be undertaken to determine the effect of pesticides on humans. Finally, those concerned with chemical poisons often assert that the federal government, though empowered to exercise some control over pesticides, has been lax in investigating the effect of chemical poisons and slow to assert tight control over their use.

The pesticide controversy involves not only a multitude of issues—about which we shall say much later—but numerous interests in both the public and the private sectors of society. Within the public sector, the U.S. Department of Agriculture, the Food and Drug Administration, and the Department of Health, Education and Welfare, together with their counterpart agencies at the state government level, have been active participants from the beginning. Environmental groups, as well as scientific spokesmen, farming interests, commodity associations, manufacturers of chemical poisons, and many other private interests, are drawn into the debate. Moreover, it is a global issue. Recently, a variety of specialized United Nations agencies and representatives of most foreign governments entered the arena because any modification in the supply or use of chemical poisons, now almost universally the primary defense against agricultural damage, could have potentially profound effects on agricultural production in most nations.

Pollutants Unlimited: "Technological Displacement"

The pesticide problem illustrates the tendency of modern technology to create substances with intense environmental impacts to replace those more readily absorbed into the ecosystem. Virtually every pollution problem we have observed can be traced, in differing ways, to the creation of these environmentally damaging substances in replacement of more innocuous materials. This tendency, which Barry Commoner calls "technological displacement," appears to lie at the source of most environmental ills:

> The chief reason for the environmental crisis . . . is the sweeping transformation of productive technology since World War II . . . productive technologies with intense impacts on the environment have displaced less destructive ones. The environmental crisis is the inevitable result of this counterecological trend.[15]

One particularly important aspect of this "counterecological trend" is its capacity to generate a profusion of highly sophisticated, synthetic chemical poisons more rapidly than environmental consequences or controls can be ascertained for them. Since modern technology constantly generates new potential environmental pollutants, one cannot speak meaningfully of environmental pollutants being controlled today, or even adequately understood. "Industry's capacity to develop new chemical substances," notes the Council on Environmental Quality, "far exceeds the ability of medical and scientific investigators to determine the carcinogenic potential for the chemical."[16]

In the past ten years, the manufacture of synthetic organic chemicals has increased by 255 percent; few have been studied for their potential as agents for cancer or other human ills. Within the last few years, a great variety of familiar chemicals have been suspected to be hazardous to humans; these include benzidine (a million pounds of which is yearly used for dyes in the United States), the fluorocarbons in aerosol containers, taconite (a low-grade iron ore) tailings, and polychlorinated biphenyls (PCBs). Many of these synthetic chemicals often appear in drinking water because public waste treatment facilities cannot eliminate them from water supplies. Taconite tailings have been discovered in drinking water in Duluth, Minnesota, and PCBs in tap water in Winnebago, Illinois.

The continuing generation of hazardous substances, tomorrow's likely pollutants, will not abate within the next several decades. This constant invigoration of Commoner's "counterecological trend" means that some public authority must regulate the availability of synthetic chemicals and the conditions for using them. It emphasizes, together with other problems we have noted, why government must inevitably become the major institution in environmental management.

THE GOVERNMENTAL IMPERATIVE

It has been only a few years since public officials, citizens, and scientists, awakening to the gravity of environmental ills, began to consider their implications. Discussion has already reached the point where no informed analyst could suggest that the crisis can be resolved or even materially diminished without massive governmental participation. If a time ever existed when private—that is, nongovernmental—remedies were sufficient to check environmental deterioration, it is past. We have reached a point in history where only a nexus between government and ecology promises a chance for environmental restoration. Many of the reasons for this governmental imperative may be discerned by brief reflection on the problems we have analyzed.

The Exhaustion of Private Remedies

There are several reasons why a reliance on private means as the major cure for environmental ills is inadequate. One explanation lies in the technical nature of the problem: Almost all kinds of ecological ills are systemic and interdependent. Shrinking open space, mounting solid waste, resource depletion, and chemical poisons are not geographically bounded. Like other environmental problems, they are systemic in the sense of being spatially distributed throughout the whole national (and international) ecosystem and arise, in turn, from such cosmopolitan sources as population growth, technology, science, industry, and economic forces. Such problems exceed the capacity of private institutions to rectify, even the largest ones when acting in concert. Indeed, while corporate leaders may regard the federal government's intervention in environmental protection with ambivalence, they seem to recognize the necessity and inevitability of public institutions bearing the major initiative in this area. As one political analyst familiar with ecology has concluded, "Technologically related problems know no territorial bound, and they defy locally based efforts to deal with them."[17]

Reliance on private remedies is further negated by the interdependence of the problems. The first law of ecology, observes biologist Barry Commoner, "is that everything is connected to everything else." With a little reflection, one can trace out a multitude of cause-and-effect relationships among environmental ills. A brief illustration and a specific example can illuminate this interdependency. Let us trace a few of the factors in the United States, using the diagram in Figure 2.

Clearly, one cannot reduce air pollution without treating its immediate sources: power generation, industrial production, and automobiles. All of these are interrelated: Industrial demand affects the growth of the power industry, but industrial growth is also affected by the market for automobiles in the United States. Further, the availability of electric power for domestic use is a determinant of suburban growth, and suburban sprawl increases the demand for transportation. Behind these primary causes of air pollution are a

Figure 2
SOME MAJOR FACTORS ASSOCIATED WITH AIR POLLUTION

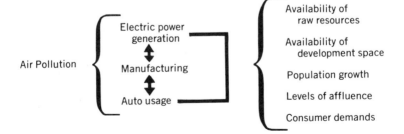

welter of secondary ones of which we have suggested but a few. A glance at these on the far right-hand column of Figure 2 indicates a number of other environmental problems ultimately related to air pollution: demands for natural resources, pressures on open space, population growth, and consumption patterns in the United States.

An Environmental Protection Agency (EPA) report on environmental problems in Helena, Montana, illustrates this interconnectedness more tangibly. The EPA discovered that two metal processing plants near the community had contaminated both air and water with sulfur oxides and heavy metals including arsenic, cadmium, and lead; these passed into the soil and vegetation, there to be absorbed into the bodies of farm animals. Eventually, these pollutants appeared in the bodies of Helena's adults and children. Metal refining, in brief, had triggered a complex chain of events leading from air and water pollution through agricultural contamination to potentially dangerous human poisoning. As these examples suggest, the interdependence of environmental problems means that the whole ecosystem is ultimately affected. As Commoner concludes, "The environment is a complex, subtly balanced system, and it is this integrated whole which receives the impact of all the separate insults inflicted by pollutants."[18] Since one cannot attack a single environmental problem without simultaneously dealing with many others, it appears that environmental protection on a national scale requires a level of manpower, money, expertise, authority, and co-ordination vastly exceeding that of private institutions. In the words of the United Nations' first world environmental conference, "The very nature of environmental problems—that is to say, their intricate interdependence—is such as to require political choices."[19]

Even is the resources did exist for private remedies, the will to use them effectively while bearing the cost probably does not; it seems unlikely that private resources would ever be marshaled for environmental protection until ecological damage became so acute as to be irremediable. The environmental problem is, in the largest sense, a cultural problem. It arises from our economy, technology, science, attitude toward nature, and life style. So great is the force of culture on behavior that it is difficult to imagine a massive, spontaneous surge of feeling for environmental protection permeating American society to such a degree that it could effectively throw off its own traditions without being forced by the weight of governmental authority. For these reasons among others, governmental leadership seems to be the only likely path.

The Primacy of Government

If governmental activity is now so crucial to environmental protection, several major consequences follow.

To begin with, a failure to find the governmental means for environmental restoration is likely to produce an ecological disaster. This is not a foregone conclusion, but it seems obvious when one considers the magnitude of our environmental ills and the limitation on private means for their solution. In effect, the nation is entering a critical period when it can solve its ecological crisis only by developing two concurrent technologies—scientific and governmental. Only when the scientific skills and resources are combined with the proper authority, organization, and action by government does a long-range restoration of environmental quality seem possible. There is no assurance that governmental efforts at environmental protection will prove ultimately effective, but without government the effort is likely to fail.

As it asserts increasing responsibility for environmental management, government must declare what environmental degradation is and what environmental quality will be. As Clarence Davies notes in his study of pollution control, governmental bodies are defining, in effect, what the nation will consider "pollution:"

> Not only is control of pollution a political problem: the very definition of pollution hinges on politics. . . . While we may be able to scientifically define what level of environmental quality is necessary for particular uses, the definition of what constitutes pollution is dependent on the public's decision as to what use it wants to make of its environment. It becomes a political decision, a voicing of the community of its concept of the public interest.[20]

In the name of the public, governmental bodies will also decide how much poison in air, water, and soil constitutes an environmental danger, what rate of resource use is compatible with good ecology, how much solid waste we can continue to produce, and other determinations that define what the nation will consider environmental degradation and restoration. Essentially, this amounts to government's defining, in most important respects, what kind of ecological quality the nation will accept.

Government must also determine the priority of ecological issues in the agenda for public action. However urgent the nation's environmental problems may seem to ecologists, environmental issues must compete among themselves and with other social problems for a position on the governmental agenda. Public officials must make numerous hard choices in determining the priority for environmental issues. In what order should environmental problems be tackled? How important is environmental protection in comparison with foreign aid, defense, or welfare? What level of funding, manpower, and organization should be achieved if various environmental programs are to be successful? While environmental issues may seem of great urgency when considered by themselves, public officials are constantly confronted with spokesmen for various interests who feel other matters are equally urgent. Government must therefore determine how much of the national resources and effort will be allocated to ecology when it must compete for support on the political marketplace against other major issues.

Critical and frequently contentious governmental decisions must also be made about the distribution of costs for environmental restoration. As we shall observe often, there are at least two aspects to this problem. First, the federal government must decide how costs will be apportioned between the public and private sectors of society for environmental protection. In pollution abatement, for example, how much of the cost for research, development, and operation of facilities should be borne by industry and how much by government? Second, an equitable method must be formulated for assigning the cost of environmental restoration to a specific polluter. This is by no means a simple problem, especially in cases where it is difficult to determine how much of a pollution problem is attributable to a particular source (as in air pollution) or where it is difficult to assess environmental damage in financial terms (as in open land loss).

Finally, government may ultimately have to decide what "trade-offs" we must make as a nation for environmental protection. Ecologists generally assert that Americans cannot have a healthy environment and continue to live as they have in the past; there must be some trade-off for environmental protection. Demand for electric power and automobiles, for example, cannot continue indefinitely, nor can the consumer's appetite for absolutely unblemished fruit be satisfied much longer if air pollution or chemical poisons are to be abated. If we continue to demand natural wood in increasing supply, we cannot hope to protect the nation's forest lands from depletion.

Thus, there is no socially costless ecology. As these examples show, to achieve real advancement in environmental protection or restoration almost assumes that the nation can in some manner successfully reduce its demands for various goods and services or abandon some cherished values. To the extent it is possible to engineer such trade-offs on a national scale, one looks toward government as the most logical agent. It can encourage, if not force, environmentally advantageous trade-offs through many methods: by taxing goods and services to enhance or diminish their desirability, by regulating resource use, by subsidies to various industries, and by its enormous capacity to stimulate research on new, environmentally advantageous technologies. Environmentalists are currently pressing federal officials to force a trade-off between the public's demand for private transportation and the need for air purification by channeling much of the money now subsidizing highway development (a major incentive for car usage) into the development of mass rapid transportation. State and local governments are taking the first tentative steps toward another trade-off: between consumer convenience and solid waste management. Several state and numerous local governments are considering, or have already enacted, laws that outlaw the use of nonreturnable beverage containers. In any event, the important point is the great potential government has, and, it is hoped, will exercise, to force national trade-offs for environmental protection.

No Ecology without Government

A few years ago, "ecology" and "environmental protection" did not exist in American public discourse; they were non-issues to most citizens and public officials. Now we are in the midst of a new "environmental decade" whose meaning and broad implications we have briefly sketched. More importantly, the nation has moved in a relatively few years from a general governmental indifference about environmental protection toward a new governmental involvement. The remainder of this book is concerned with the politics of ecology, with the actors, issues, and processes involved in governmental efforts at environmental protection. Clearly, the politics of ecology is a crucial component in any successful solution to the nation's environmental dilemmas; indeed, governmental action looms so large in determining the outcome of the struggle that to speak of ecology makes little sense unless one deals with its politics. Thus, we now turn to the events and processes through which we will either win or lose the environmental battle.

NOTES

1. See the "Declaration on the Human Environment," summarized in *New York Times,* June 17, 1972.
2. Donella H. Meadows, *et al., The Limits of Growth* (New York: Universe Books, 1972), p. 143.
3. The story of the Willamette River's recovery, the first major river restoration since the Federal Water Pollution Control Act Amendments (1972) were written, is fully told in President's Council on Environmental Quality, *Environmental Quality: Fourth Annual Report* (Washington, D.C. 1973), pp. 32–72.
4. Current environmental trends are summarized from stories in *New York Times,* May 5, 1975; July 7, 1975; February 22, 1976; and March 12, 1976.
5. U.S. Environmental Protection Agency, *The Economics of Clean Air: Annual Report of the Administrator of the Environmental Protection Agency* (Washington, D.C., 1972), pp. 1–11. This is an extremely conservative estimate because it states the annual costs in terms of figures for 1977, when the EPA assumes a significant air pollution abatement program will exist. For other estimates, see Council on Environmental Quality, *Environmental Quality: Fifth Annual Report* (Washington, D.C., 1975), pp. 494–515.
6. This may be a conservative estimate. See comments by the chairman of the board of New York's Consolidated Edison Co. in Charles F. Luce, "Energy: Economics of the Environment," in Harold W. Helfrich, Jr., ed., *Agenda for Survival* (New Haven, Conn.: Yale University Press, 1970), pp. 107–118.

7. Council on Environmental Quality, *Sixth Annual Report,* p. 447.

8. Robert Rienow and Leona Train Rienow, *Moment in the Sun* (New York: Ballantine Books, 1967), p. 245. This "raid on resources" is summarized in Stewart L. Udall, *The Quiet Crisis* (New York: Holt, Rinehart and Winston, 1963), and in an excellent collection of essays in Vernon Carstensen, ed., *The Public Lands: Studies in the History of the Public Domain* (Madison: University of Wisconsin Press, 1968).

9. A wealth of useful energy data is usefully summarized in Congressional Quarterly Service, *Energy Crisis in America* (Washington, D.C.: Congressional Quarterly Service, 1973), and *Continuing Energy Crisis in America* (Washington, D.C.: Washington Quarterly, 1975).

10. Committee for Economic Development, *Achieving Energy Independence* (New York: Committee for Economic Development, 1974), p. 19.

11. Import figures quoted from Congressional Quarterly Service, *Continuing Energy Crisis in America.* The gap in production is estimated from figures quoted in the *New York Times.*

12. The future implications of coal development in the western states is explored in Walter A. Rosenbaum, "The Dirtiest Declaration of Independence: Ecology and the American Energy Crisis," in Donald R. Kelley, ed., *The Energy Crisis in Comparative Perspective* (New York: Praeger Publishers, forthcoming).

13. Harry M. Caudill, *Night Comes to the Cumberlands* (Boston: Little, Brown and Co., 1963), pp. 311–312.

14. For ecologists, the bible in the pesticide battle remains Rachel Carson, *Silent Spring* (Boston: Houghton Mifflin Co., 1962). A useful update, in a similar vein, is Frank Graham, Jr., *Since Silent Spring* (Boston: Houghton Mifflin Co., 1970), especially chapters 7–12. A brief but illuminating introduction to chemical poisons as pollution problems is found in Charles ReVelle and Penelope ReVelle, *Sourcebook on the Environment: The Scientific Perspective* (Boston: Houghton Mifflin Co. ,1974).

15. Barry Commoner, *The Closing Circle: Nature, Man and Technology* (New York: Bantam Books, 1974), pp. 175–76.

16. Council on Environmental Quality, *Sixth Annual Report,* p. 23.

17. Harvey Wheeler, "The Politics of Ecology," *Saturday Review,* March 7, 1970, p. 63.

18. Barry Commoner, *Science and Survival* (New York: Viking Press, 1966), p. 122.

19. *New York Times,* March 17, 1972.

20. J. Clarence Davies III, *The Politics of Pollution* (New York: Pegasus Press, 1970), p. 18.

3. Beyond Birdwatching: A Political Profile of the Environmental Movement

The environmental movement caught most social prophets looking the other way. A decade ago, no social analyst could have predicted ecology's rise to major national attention. As late as 1968, the gathering of experts associated with the prestigious Brookings Institution did not list ecology among the most pressing issues that ought to be tackled immediately by the Nixon administration. In part, this lack of foresight appears to be a failure to perceive major changes that might occur in the American social climate that would make ecology more attractive to the public than previously. But there has also been a fundamental transformation in the character of group support for environmental protection, a transformation that could not have been easily discerned until recently. In this chapter, we are concerned with understanding both the social climate and group structure that buoy up the environmental movement, as well as their future implications.

WHY HERE? WHY NOW?

The United States might now seem like a logical place for an environmental movement. Americans consume more than half the world's important resources and might be expected, if only from self-interest, to be acutely sensitive to any depletion of the materials upon which the nation's prosperity depends. Moreover, since severe pollution is closely associated with industrialization and technology, the United States—the world's leader in both respects—might seem ripe for a grave pollution crisis that would awaken public sensibility to environmental abuse. Also, the nation's large scientific community might appear to be a special public capable of articulating an ecological concern of particular persuasiveness to others.

Yet, environmental protection is a bitter potion. Many of the movement's objectives are incompatible with current cultural norms; indeed, the movement's success might seem to ask for some form of cultural suicide. Effective environmental protection, as former Secretary of the Interior Stewart Udall has remarked, requires a value revolution in American society. A moderate by the standards of the current environmental movement, Udall nevertheless speaks along with numerous other environmentalists, of the need for a radical recasting of American values: "The times demand nothing less than a sustained, life-centered effort to reshape the attitudes, laws and institutions that have produced the mess that is man-made America."[1] Numerous Americans probably greet such pronouncements with skepticism, but almost all environmental experts agree that the roots of the environmental crisis lie deep in our culture. The President's Council on Environmental Quality cites among the principal causes the nation's dedication to unlimited industrial production and economic growth, an affluence that stimulates an apparently insatiable appetite for consumer goods, a burgeoning population, and technology. Other analysts add to the list our belief that nature is property to be used at its owner's discretion, our faith that science can solve any social problem before it becomes catastrophic, and our fierce dedication to private rights over public ones. A major alteration in the American life style seems to be the price of environmental clean-up, and Americans have a powerful incentive to resist paying it.

Environmental protection would also demand changes in the nation's economic structure. Major corporations would probably be required to submit to governmental controls on their use of resources, would have to invest billions of dollars in pollution controls, and might have to restrict the volume and variety of their production. No longer could unlimited production and constant growth be economic gospel; transformation in the profit structures of major industry, of course, would necessarily follow any change in this growth ethic. Most business leaders do not welcome such changes and may, in various ways, seek to delay or blunt their impact. Not least important, the basic political institutions and norms of society would be affected by any major effort at environmental protection. Governmental planning and controls over the economy would have to be extended, the ascendancy of corporate interests in governmental chambers would be challenged, and public officials would have to make hard, controversial choices between ecological values and such previously sacrosanct goals as full employment and production, continual growth of the gross national product, expanding highways, new housing starts, and a multitude of other policies no longer consistent with good ecology. Still, we are now witnessing a major environmental movement. Why has it arisen here and now? Let us examine several suggested explanations.

Environmental Degradation

The increasingly tangible evidence of environmental ills and, more particularly, the crises that finally erupt from this degradation have played a part in the mounting environmental concern. In American politics, it often takes a crisis to prompt public officials to act on social problems. Thus, a bill to control oil pollution languished in the 90th Congress until the disastrous Santa Barbara oil platform blowout of January 28, 1969, released 235,000 gallons of crude oil into Santa Barbara harbor, blackened thirty miles of white beach, and enraged normally apathetic local residents. Pressure on public officials quickly convinced Congress to pass the measure that now controls oil spills, provides new safety standards for platform drilling, and levies heavy fines on corporate violaters of its provisions.[2]

In the Pacific Northwest, environmentalists had vainly fought for decades against many of the forty dams erected across the Columbia River and its tributaries. Despite their warnings that great stretches of scenic wild river and irreplaceable animal habitat would be sacrificed to the dam builders and that major ecological damage would be inflicted upon the affected states, most public officials in the states involved remained unresponsive to such pleas. But when the Federal Power Commission in 1971 licensed two dams in Hell's Canyon that would have flooded the last remaining wild stretch of the Snake River, destroying most of its sixty-six rapids, the governors of Oregon, Washington, and Idaho were finally convinced that dam building had progressed too far at the expense of their states' natural resources. Joining with conservationists, they protested to Washington and promised to fight the projects until their abandonment. Such instances of environmental degradation triggering governmental action are not uncommon over the last decade.

Nonetheless, the gravity of environmental problems alone cannot explain the current environmental movement. Many environmental problems now on the agenda of public agencies—such as disappearing open space, the depletion of resources, pesticide use, and waste management—have not become so pervasive or visibly ominous to reach the stage that customarily arouses immediate public alarm. Moreover, Americans have lived with many serious environmental ills in the past without demonstrating much apprehension. Air pollution may have been more lethal in many communities a few decades ago, but little public concern was evident; the people of Appalachia watched the daily rape of their once lovely land for generations without much significant protest. And, as we have noted, the public's current concern over environmental matters should not be overrated. We have observed that many Americans do not seem greatly alarmed by environmental deterioration, if one judges them by their willingness to make a personal sacrifice for ecology. Perhaps many regard environmental protection, like the state of their souls, as an important issue that nonetheless fails to concern them very often.

The End of Industrialization

Some commentators believe that ecology is important because the United States, now past its great industrializing push, has room for it on the social agenda. In the view of these, ecology is most likely to be a major national issue in postindustrial societies. Not only is environmental blight likely to be serious, but such nations have attained many desired national goals: economic productivity, a measure of international political and military influence, rising education, scientific competence, and reasonable affluence. In this case, political and economic leaders need no longer concentrate on industrialization, with all the political and economic sacrifices it entails, at the expense of conflicting national policies. For, having arrived at a high plateau of economic development, the leaders are free to ponder the environmental effects of industrialization and the economic controls necessitated by environmental protection without surrendering the benefits of industrialization itself.

International affairs lends some support to this thinking. The industrialized ("developed") nations are currently far more preoccupied with global environmental ravage and its control than less industrialized ("developing") nations, which also suffer environmental blight. The developing areas apparently fear that international environmental controls might restrict or entirely arrest their own economic growth. Some of these nations assert that the industrialized nations' concern with ecology is a selfish luxury that would permit affluent countries to maintain a superior domestic and international economic status while ensuring that other nations remain economically inferior; in the end, as Anthony Lewis has remarked, ecology would then become a "fortress of the privileged" against new nations wanting wealth.[3] In effect, the industrialized nations are sometimes viewed as ecologists with a tainted conscience: Having cut the wood to timber their own mansions, they now propose to protect the forests at the expense of neighbors whose dwellings are hardly more than blueprints.

The Changing Power Structure

Another explanation for environmental politics suggests that there has been a derangement—perhaps only temporary—in the traditional power structure of the nation that had previously inhibited the emergence of ecology as a salient issue. This argument asserts that power at most governmental levels has customarily resided in different constellations of private interests, primarily major corporations and trade associations, which could force "nondecisions" upon government. They usually kept objectionable issues from engaging major governmental attention, which, in turn, prevented the issues from acquiring public importance. This "off stage power to enforce political inaction" usually prevented the passage of governmental policies that would adversely affect their reputation, economic structures, or political status.[4] These interests allegedly preferred that governmental agendas favor "private" policies that conferred benefits on a specific, limited set of economic interests, rather than "collective" policies with benefits for a diffuse, collective group such as an entire community or most of a nation. Under such conditions, this argument contends, ecological issues were seldom given much governmental attention because they were "collective" in the sense that they bestowed diffuse benefits on a large, amorphous public (in the form of a healthier environment) while imposing heavy costs on a number of specific economic interests (the expense of pollution control devices, for example). After recently studying two communities where air pollution regulations were gradually, and grudgingly, enacted, Matthew Crenson concluded that private "veto" groups were the major obstacle to pollution control in both communities long after air contamination became serious. Crenson suggests that his findings, though limited to two communities, may depict a relatively common situation at most American governmental levels.

Some commentators believe that these veto groups have suffered a gradual power deflation over the last decade severe enough to impair their previous ability to inhibit the development of collective issues they found objectionable. This power deflation, suggest the analysts, has resulted from the Vietnam War, race crises, the Watergate affair, economic problems, and other recent issues that mobilized many Americans against the real or suspected influence of private interests on public policy. Once these interests were thrown on the defensive, room was made for the emergence of such collective issues as the needs of the poor and minorities, consumer affairs, educational problems, and ecology. Commentators also note that when a few collective issues gain widespread attention, others soon follow. Once public awareness of collective problems is stimulated, a public mood is apparently created; public consciousness of yet other collective problems occurs while groups expand the scope of governmental agendas.

The environmental movement clearly draws part of its inspiration from a larger movement that might be called public interest politics, which represents a militant concern for a multitude of public needs. This movement is personified today by Ralph Nader, whom many would consider the foremost national spokesman and organizer of public interest movements in the political arena. It is revealing that Nader speaks about ecology in the larger context of public needs versus private interests, as if to underscore the fact that ecological concerns stem from a broad concern with public needs in general.

"Our institutions, public and private, are not really performing their regulatory functions," he noted in a full-page *New York Times* advertisement. "They tend not to control power democratically, but to concentrate it, and to serve special interest groups at the expense of the voiceless citizen."[5] What the public must do, he advises, is demonstrate an awakened concern not only about pollution but about urban decay, deceptive advertising, shoddy consumer goods, unequal employment opportunity, and a host of other collective American grievances. As this advertisement suggests, one ought to project the environmental movement against the larger background of public rights politics in the late 1960's and early 1970's to fully appreciate the source of the issue's impetus. Perhaps, also, the ecology movement reflects or intensifies a renewed public interest in domestic affairs that has been largely subordinated to international considerations since World War II. The bitterly controversial prolonged Vietnam War together with other international fiascoes may have soured the public on global politics and rekindled an interest in domestic problems. Americans are turning inward, so some suggest, and reversing their domestic and foreign priorities. In such an era, environmental affairs will assume a saliency previously lacking. The environmental problem, growing more ominous for years, can now be "discovered" because public officials are no longer distracted by global preoccupations.

Finally, education and, particularly, educated youth may have contributed to the mobilization of ecological concern. Some commentators link environmentalism to increasing public education. Public opinion studies reveal that a sensitivity to environmental problems is closely associated with education. This relationship was demonstrated, for example, in one of the first careful studies of public opinion and pollution, done in St. Louis in 1963.[6] The investigators found that the respondents with a post-high school education showed a greater frequency of concern with air pollution than any other social group in the study, including even those who were exposed to high concentrations of the pollution; many recent studies further verify the link between education and environmental sensibilities.[7] Reasoning from such familiar findings, some analysts conclude that the rising levels of public education in America must contribute to the vigor of the environmental movement. Others, noting the decidedly youthful cast to the movement, point to youth's distinctive contribution in mobilizing ecological concern. They note that there are currently more young Americans between eighteen and thirty-five years old than ever before in the United States and that these young people are a large, available, and politically sensitized manpower pool for the environmental forces. America's young people, the argument runs, are well educated and therefore environmentally alert. In the early 1970's, many were veterans of political protest and election struggles; moreover, with the winding down of the Southeast Asian conflict and major draft reforms, they were ready to engage their energy in other political issues. All these circumstances result in an unprecedentedly large base of youthful eco-activists with political skills to be utilized during the great mobilization drive.

Regardless of how one accounts for the new environmental movement, it is not only a reality but a very different phenomenon from earlier efforts at environmental protection. This is more apparent if we briefly examine its philosophy and political tactics.

BEYOND "CONSERVATION"

The present environmental movement is more than a newer, reinvigorated edition of the earlier "conservation" crusade. Current environmental activists often make a point of emphasizing the distinction by calling themselves ecologists, environmentalists, or eco-activists rather than conservationists. Many of the goals and much of the material strength in the older conservation movement have been absorbed into the new environmental crusade, to be sure, but the differences between the two are real and continuing.

The Environmental Ethic

The current environmental movement is unified more by a mood and shared attitudes than by a carefully wrought creed. Within the movement, one can discern a great diversity of groups espousing different, sometimes conflicting ecological priorities and philosophies of political action. Yet, amid this pluralism exists a common outlook that might be called the ethos of the movement.

A CONCERN FOR LIFE'S QUALITY. When environmental spokesmen speak of ecology today, they are apt to be concerned with the total quality of the human environment and its effect on man's survival. This truly encompassing definition of ecology, with the breadth of problems and activities it embraces, comes from expanding the original meaning of the term "ecology," which once referred to a rather exotic, obscure branch of biology concerned with the mutual relations between organisms and their environmental movement. In this respect, the focus of the environmental movement is a major qualitative leap beyond earlier conservation interests.[8] Conservationists gave paramount attention to land use. They committed much of their energy to wilderness preservation, to the wise use of natural resources such as forest and rivers, and tended to see the problems they confronted in rather fragmented terms. "Pollution" was not in the movement's vocabulary, nor was "ecology" in the sense of a comprehensive vision of man's environment and its interrelated problems. From the viewpoint of current eco-activists, the conservationists, notwithstanding their many admirable achievements, were too narrow in their vision of environmental degradation and too unsophisticated in their understanding of its causes and consequences.

Environmental spokesmen have attempted to express the scope of their current concern in various ways. "Today, we recognize that man has been engaging in activities that affect the whole life system of the planet," says one leader; "instead of focusing upon a single resource . . . we must paint on a canvas that might be a river valley, a region, a continent—or the planet itself."[9] To another spokesman, environmentalists must concentrate on "how to preserve the general ecological balances" of the planet; a third analyst speaks of ecology as "conserving resources for human use."[10] Such definitions of ecology seem to leave nothing in man's world outside the ambit of attention; some environmentalists, indeed, don't want much excluded.

The human environment is an immense complex of natural elements, man-made structures, institutions, societies and other people. . . . Environmental quality and human welfare are not two independent values. . . . It is not possible for one to remain good while the other is bad. . . .

Under this broad definition of environment all of the ills of man emerge as environmental problems—poverty, prejudice, public education, health services, militarism, inner circles and pollution all qualify as environmental crises.[11]

As a practical matter, few environmental leaders actually propose to tackle the whole catalogue of human miseries in the name of "ecology" but prefer to concentrate instead on such specific maladies as pollution, waste disposal, pesticides, and land use. Still, modern eco-activists approach individual issues with a characteristic logic. They tend to see each problem in a wholistic perspective, in relation to other environmental problems and forces. They speak of air pollution in the context of industrialization and technology, frequently link these to our culture and economy, and may, finally, view all these issues in a worldwide framework. The environmental activists may also bring to their discussion a rather sophisticated synthesis of political, economic, and scientific perspectives that allows them to move from one context to the other freely in interpreting the issues before them. With these perspectives, environmentalists increasingly talk of problem-solving in terms of broad social planning, long-term trends, and interrelated social forces. In short, their view of environmental ills tends to be total, systematic, or integrative in its definition of problems and prescriptions for their resolution.

THE TIME IS NOW.   A sense of urgency pervades the ecology movement. This apprehension ranges from cautious warnings of environmental degradation to tense predictions that the United States has reached the edge of an ecological catastrophe and will soon plummet over the precipice unless radical action is immediately initiated. The President's Council on Environmental Quality, steering a mid-course between complacency and exaggeration, represents the moderate view:

> The public has begun to realize the interrelationship of all living things —including man—with the environment. The Santa Barbara oil spill in early 1969 showed an entire nation how one accident could temporarily blight a large area. Since then each environmental issue—the jetport project near the Everglades National Park, the proposed pipeline across the Alaskan wilderness, the worsening blight of Lake Erie, the polluted beaches off New York and other cities, smog in mile-high Denver, lead

in gasoline, phosphates in detergents, and DDT—flashed the sign to Americans that the problems are everywhere and affect everyone.[12]

Still, the Council did not entirely eschew dark judgments; at one point it spoke of the "deadly, downward spiral of environmental quality." Many environmentalists, particularly scientists and other professionals associated with the movement, favor such a balanced, cautious assessment of ecological damage. While admitting the seriousness of environmental abuse, they point to the complexity of ecological relationships, the primitive state of man's ecological knowledge, and the limited environmental data available as reasons for restraint in making dire judgments about ecological ills.

Numerous other laymen and professionals in the movement, however, predict an imminent ecological crisis with few misgivings that they might be "hysterical." They forcefully assert that man is an endangered species whose existence is threatened by population pressure, technology, materialistic culture, and all the environmental ravages that follow. They would agree, at a minimum, with the judgment of the famed microbiologist and Pulitzer Prize winner René Dubos:

It would be easy, far too easy, to conclude from the present trend of events that mankind is on a course of self-destruction. I shall not discuss this real possibility but shall instead focus on the certainty that . . . all over the world, technological civilization is threatening the elements of nature that are essential to human life, and the values that make it worth living.[13]

Such pronouncements have served the movement nicely. They often capture the media's attention and stimulate popular imagination while imparting a doomsday tone to the movement's rhetoric; they also enlist manpower, particularly when the warning comes from spokesmen with considerable stature such as Dubos. And there have been many who speak similarly. One is former Secretary of the Interior Walter J. Hickel, a minor hero among ecologists for his vigorous attack on numerous environmental problems. "We are rapidly approaching a civil war of priorities in our nation: neighbor against neighbor, man against need, over the preservation or use of our resources," he has written. "Bitter voices are being raised—on the one side pleading 'Give us work, give us energy for our homes'; and on the other side shouting 'Stop the rape of our environment.' "[14] David Brower, among the movement's most militant and effective organizers, has repeatedly predicted "destruction in a decade" unless radical steps are taken to alleviate environmental ills. Among the newer militants, Stanford University biologist Paul Ehrlich, whose book *The Population Bomb* became the best-selling bible for population control advocates, has predicted a grim future:

> I *am* an alarmist, because I'm very goddamned alarmed. I believe we're facing the *brink* because of population pressures. I'm certainly not exaggerating the staggering rate of population growth; it's right there in plain, round numbers. Whatever problems I'm diverting attention from will be academic if we don't face the population-environment crisis now.[15]

Ehrlich, like other environmental militants, has often been called an alarmist, yet it is only his extreme pessimism that distinguishes him from more moderate voices in the movement. While ecology leaders and experts may disagree over the extremity and implications of environmental damage, they are seldom divided over the existence of currently serious problems.

SOCIAL RECONSTRUCTION.   Within the ecology movement, one can detect a deep disillusionment with existing American values and institutions that seem responsible for the nation's ecological problems. Radically new forms of social organization are often proposed and older ways rejected. Whether this criticism is explicit and articulate or merely implied, it betrays a social radicalism in the movement's *mystique*—even on the part of many who would not consider themselves "radical" in political terms. The movement is too heterogeneous to agree on a detailed, comprehensive formula for social reconstruction, but it does agree on the cultural causes of environmental ills. In its most extreme form, this critique of American culture represents an alienation from Western culture in virtually all respects and a yearning for an alternative culture more congenial to ecology.

Most ecologists realize that they are on a collision course with contemporary American life. They generally regard the dream of unlimited economic growth as a malignant illusion; this "growth psychology," with its emphasis on continually expanding production, demand, and resource use, is seen as the acceleration environmental degradation. Environmentalist Robert Rienow suggests that the growth myth produces a "superficial dazzle and glamor" and caters to American influence without accounting for ecological costs:

> A major evil in this national worship of the GNP is the lack of discrimination that marks its acceptance. The economist prodding the nation to growth is not disturbed by the beer-can-littered landscape or the unsightliness of the strip mining location. His concern is to stimulate the appetite, not to cultivate the taste. His is a kind of science of collective gluttony. It has been aptly remarked that "one of the weaknesses of our age is our apparent inability to distinguish between our needs and our greeds."[16]

Technology and science are viewed as serious problems because they produce environmental damage even when most other sources of environmental degradation can be controlled. "If the population declined and technology continued to breed, without any improvement in our arrangement for its prudent use," states one ecology writer, "a small fraction of the present U.S. population could complete the destruction of the physical environment."[17] The American market economy is also condemned. It does not take adequate account of environmental damage in producing and pricing goods for the market; this encourages too much demand for products that eventually create great environmental damage by failing to take account of these damages in the cost of the items. A recent national conference of environmental experts concluded:

> In the terms of familiar economic analysis, the injuries done to the environment and to the society by pollution are "external costs" or "social costs," not taken into account in the ordinary business calculations of income and expense. They have been "external costs" not for reasons inherent in the nature of things or derived from the fundamentals of economics but because the legal system has so provided.[18]

All these contributors to environmental degradation are also abetted powerfully by a government that, in the view of many environmentalists, has lacked the will, organization, and authority to deal with environmental degradation effectively. One major reason is that governmental officials, consciously or not, have usually shared the values of American business and therefore have collaborated in the economy's destruction of the environment. Complained a former member of the Federal Power Commission to an environmental conference:

> The relationships of industry . . . with government, in effect, have actually determined the inadvertency of the environmental degradation. In order to put together the complicated, long-range plans for tomorrow, an almost incestuous relationship between these unholy partners has developed and such "minor" problems as the environment have been lost in the shuffle.[19]

Many environmental leaders believe that major governmental restructuring must be accomplished if public officials are now to combat environmental deterioration. We need, suggests one ecologist, "a political economy for Spaceship Earth" in which the government undertakes this restructuring for environmental protection as a first priority. Rarely does a spokesman conclude an analysis of ecological problems without calling for a transformation in government policy, organization, or ethics in the name of environmental preservation.

Almost all environmentalists recognize the cultural components of ecological problems and admit the need for some cultural change. However, the movement's reaction to American culture, especially to prevailing economic and political institutions, was intensified, and in some cases radicalized, by a partial overlap during the early 1970's between the environmental movement and what was called the American New Left. This New Left emerged briefly as a significant political force in the United States during the late 1960's, enlisting its manpower primarily from colleges, the intellectual community, and other groups. The movement marched under many organizational banners, followed a great diversity of leaders, and often espoused inconsistent political philosophies; it was united by shared attitudes rather than by a pervasive, coherent philosophy. The New Left bitterly condemned the nation's prevailing political and economic institutions. It asserted that the country was scourged by materialism and capitalism, that its political and economic leaders were a selfish, often corrupt elite governing in their own interests, that it was an inhuman society for the disadvantaged, the nonwhite, and the young. The cure most often proposed was a radical reconstruction of all the nation's major institutions, usually along lines derived from socialist or communist principles.

Many among the New Left discovered a strong affinity between their view of the nation's social malaise and the environmental movement's diagnosis of the country's ecological problems; the ranks of environmental groups were swelled by New Left activists joining the ecology crusade, especially on college campuses. For many of these recruits the environmental struggle is simply an old battle on a new front. "Capitalism" had created Vietnam, militarism throughout the country, the repression of minorities, and other evils; it was responsible for environmental degradation, too. The same political leaders and institutions that had irresponsibly led the nation into foreign war, racial discrimination, and other immoral situations had permitted environmental degradation. Materialism and affluence had blinded the nation to its abuse of the poor at home and to the needy nations abroad; so, too, had it caused an ecological crisis. Many New Left activists quickly imposed upon ecological issues the same philosophical framework they had used to interpret other social problems, while some of the most militant environmental spokesmen borrowed liberally from New Left ideology to fashion a radical environmental rhetoric, as in the following remarks by one eco-activist:

> . . . the politics of ecology must start from the premise that present day reality is increasingly a product of a structure of economic and political power that consolidates and sustains itself through the systematic destruction of man and his physical world. The exploitation of man by man and nature by nature are merely two sides of the same coin. . . . The task of ecological radicals is to continually raise those issues which sort those who seek to patch up the status quo from those who struggle for basic transformation.[20]

Other political radicals in the environmental movement were equally militant. Says California poet Gary Snyder, "You can't be serious about the environment without being a revolutionary. You have to be willing to restructure society."[21] Another radical exhorted, "Liberate the ecosystem."

The New Left did not dominate the environmental movement numerically or philosophically; with the gradual waning of New Left strength, its contribution to environmental activism diminished. Nonetheless, the earth movement still entices enough young radicals to arouse apprehension among many New Left intellectuals. Richard Neuhaus, a radical Lutheran clergyman, has asserted that ecology can become for radicals "a seductive diversion from the political task of our time," distracting them from the task of liberating the poor from economic bondage and leading unthinking radicals into espousing policies in the name of environmentalism that are, in fact, hostile to the underprivileged. Population control, for example, is close to war on the poor. Pollution control, which requires an economic slowdown, is a selfish, middle-class wish that would deny the less advantaged an opportunity for material advancement. Indeed, argues Neuhaus, the ecology movement is largely inspired by the nation's political and economic establishment, which wants to blunt the force of radical protest by diverting its attention from economic inequalities to quests for a cleaner environment.

While environmentalists offer a variety of prescriptions for cultural change in the United States, one salient feature of the movement as a whole remains its probing, questioning, and critical stance toward the nation's basic values and institutions. Even as they disagree about remedies for our environmental ills, most environmental spokesmen sense that they are raising a profound issue: "All our problems seem to have a common root. Something is wrong with the way this nation uses its human and natural resources. And I believe that it is always healthy to reexamine, to test, the basic mechanisms we have created to run our affairs. . . . How should our society be organized to resolve the crisis of survival?"[22]

Environmental Politics

The earth movement's political strategies passed through two distinct phases in the 1970's. First came techniques inspired by the "street politics" of the war protest and civil rights movements—this during the intense activism of the early 1970's. After 1975, strategies settled into more traditional forms—litigation, lobbying, and public information campaigns—never ignored but previously obscured by the more spectacular mobilizing devices.

NEW TACTICS.   In the early 1970's, ecology groups liberally borrowed from earlier protest movements such techniques as mass demonstrations, protest rallies, and occasional civil disobedience. Some groups, such as the politically influential and effective Sierra Club, abandoned the tax shelter for the political arena by sacrificing their federal tax-exempt status in order to campaign for candidates to partisan office.

Mass demonstrations and other attention getting activities were important to the movement because they captured media attention and aroused public interest. Thus, eco-activists interrupted the inauguration of Rutgers University's seventeenth president to demonstrate against a proposed state highway to cross the campus; pots brimming with pollutants dredged from industrial outfalls were symbolically deposited at corporate offices after ecologists paraded to the doors. In frigid waters off Amchitka Island near the Alaskan coast, sixteen protesting ecologists anchored a small boat near the spot where a large underground blast was to be detonated, focusing attention on their concern for environmental damage. Such demonstrations, however, were largely an ephemera associated with the early 1970's. The strategies were largely new to the conservation movement and marked a growing political sophistication. But the public, as we have seen, soon tires of such business; moreover, these strategies had served their purpose in arousing public and official concern. The more enduring, and important, weapons for political battle remain litigation and lobbying.

LITIGATION AND LOBBYING.   Lawsuits have risen in importance through the 1970's as an effective weapon for environmentalists. Indeed, one of the most significant innovations in the movement was the development of groups specializing in litigation—particularly the Natural Resources Defense Council and the Environmental Defense Fund—to bring a high level of continuing pressure for environmental protection through judicial procedures. This litigation has grown for several reasons. Much of its customarily high cost is often absorbed by environmental lawyers donating their expertise. Customary opponents of environmental groups do not enjoy the same great advantage of influence in the courts that they customarily enjoy in legislative and administrative battles.[23] Moreover, a variety of recent laws have greatly encouraged citizen environmental lawsuits:

- Section 102(2) (C) of the National Environmental Policy Act (1970) requires opportunity for citizen review of "environmental impact statements" prepared by federal agencies and permits citizens to sue to ensure that agencies properly prepare such material.

- Section 505(a) of the Federal Water Pollution Control Act Amendments (1972) permits citizen suits against any public or private party violating provisions of its major sections.

- Section 304 of the Clean Air Act (1970) empowers citizens to seek compliance with basic regulatory features of the act when violations are discovered.

These provisions, by explicitly permitting citizen "standing to sue" in environmental litigation, also remove any doubt of citizen "standing," once a formidable obstacle to the environmental lawsuits. Additionally, twenty-one states and Puerto Rico now require state agency "impact statements" analogous to the federal ones; citizens, in these cases, customarily enjoy standing to sue for noncompliance. The courts have generally become more receptive to the ecological viewpoint. One manifestation is the recent unprecedented decision of the U.S. Court of Appeals (District of Columbia) in ordering the federal government and private oil companies developing the trans-Alaskan oil pipeline to pay half the cost of litigation borne by environmental groups that had successfully sued both the government and the companies for violations of environmental law. Reasoned the court: "Where litigation serves as a catalyst to effect change and thereby achieves a valuable public service," the plaintiffs could be considered "private attorneys general" serving the public interest and worthy of public compensation.[24] Such a ruling clearly encourages other ecology groups to press public interest litigation because, in effect, they may be partially subsidized by judicial fiat. The number of lawsuits initiated by environmentalists, though difficult to estimate, is undoubtedly large and growing; the EPA alone has approximately 500 suits pending annually, many instigated by ecologists. Lawsuits, finally, are sometimes useful for harassing the opposition and obstructing unwanted legislative or administrative proceedings. Although not a primary purpose, these disruptive tactics are occasionally utilized by environmentalists to wring concessions from the opposition as the price of freedom from judicial wrangling.

Like all other major interests, environmentalists use lobbyists and lobbying techniques at all governmental levels. More than thirty environmental groups have registered representatives in Congress.[25] The larger national associations, such as the Wilderness Society and the National Wildlife Federation, employ their own Washington lobbyists. Many environmental groups support collaborative organizations, such as Environmental Policy Center, formed in 1972 with eleven employees, to concentrate upon lobbying for a variety of strong environmental measures. Many of these collaborative programs are supported partially by private foundations. The majority of environmental groups, however, have no Washington lobbyists; many are unrepresented in state capitols. It falls, therefore, to a relative handful of the largest groups to bear most of the responsibility for political action in Congress and the states—a burden that could not be shouldered without generous volunteer help.

WHO WANTS ECOLOGY?   The ecology movement speaks in middle- and upper-class accents. Those most often counted in the ranks of ecology groups are usually white, middle- to upper-class, well-educated, relatively young Americans. Public opinion polls and surveys indicate that the ecology movement depends heavily on these groups for manpower, financial support, and political effectiveness. Conversely, ecology draws relatively meager interest among most blacks, the poor, and the least educated.

Ecology's failure to engage less advantaged groups seems ironic when projected against the environmental realities confronting the poor, blacks, and the underprivileged generally. The highest sustained rates of air pollution are often found in the core of cities where large numbers of such individuals live; the inner cities, more often than not, are grim models of "visual pollution" in the form of urban decay and suffer the most from "noise pollution." Pesticides are used there in especially heavy dosages to combat flies, roaches, and rodents. In general, whether they live in cities or not, the least advantaged Americans suffer as much or more from environmental degradation than the relatively affluent, educated citizen.[26] Nonetheless, ecology remains a peripheral concern to most disadvantaged Americans because their more urgent needs are adequate employment, decent diets, better housing and education, health care, and other essentials. It is not surprising, given these elemental needs, that improving the quality of the air might seem less compelling than getting food for one's family or protecting one's children from disease. Many spokesmen for the disadvantaged believe that the ecology crusade may divert the nation's interest and resources from the greater task of improving the lot of the disadvantaged. As black leader Whitney Young asserts:

> The war on pollution is one that should be waged after the war on poverty is won. Common sense calls for reasonable national priorities and not for inventing new causes whose main appeal seems to be in their potential for copping out and ignoring the most dangerous and most pressing of our problems.[27]

Those responsive to the needs of the disadvantaged often argue that a massive attack on environmental degradation would mean diminishing the nation's rate of economic growth, cutting back on affluence, and in general drastically reducing new forms of wealth, capital, and opportunity that the poor desperately need to improve their condition.

This division of social support has produced mixed political consequence for the ecology movement. On the positive side, the middle- to upper-class base of the movement includes the largest number of Americans and brings to it those citizens with the greatest political experience, resources, and interest, in addition to giving the movement support from those social sectors to which American government has traditionally been the most responsive. At the same time, its feeble appeal to the disadvantaged not only deprives the movement of additional manpower, political weight, and social appeal but creates a potentially dangerous cleavage that, under the right circumstances, could become a socially polarized struggle pitting the more affluent's demands for environmental protection against the less advantaged's desire for social advancement.

Environmental leaders, conscious that the movement's social roots are broad but not deep, have been trying to build alliances with labor and the disadvantaged in recent years. The most ambitious effort was the 1976 conference, sponsored by the United Auto Workers, to find a common program for ecology and labor. Although UAW's president attempted to rally the coalition behind opposition to "corporate environmental blackmail" there is little evidence of strong environmental sentiments in the labor movements.[28] In the latter 1970's, ecology remains, as it has always been, a middle-American preoccupation.

THE ORGANIZATIONAL BASE.

The long-range fortunes of the movement depend upon the skill, strength, and determination of the organized interests that promote environmental protection and represent its continuing base of stable political support. More than 3,000 organizations in the United States are concerned with some aspect of the environment; half the politically active groups did not exist before 1970. The majority of ecology organizations—about 2,500—work at local levels and seldom assume national importance. Most environmental groups are small (almost two-thirds have fewer than 500 members) and confine themselves to disseminating information, attending public meetings, and participating in hearings on environmental matters by public agencies. National environmental policy is most often affected by the 250 national and regional organizations and 400 state environmental groups with the membership, resources, and status to fight major political battles. Between 1970 and 1971, membership in the five largest environmental groups jumped by 400,000, a 33 per cent rise in one year.[29] Contrary to many predictions, membership in most environmental organizations has continued to grow, albeit more slowly than in the early 1970's.

Those groups most active in politics constitute a small but expanding segment of the ecology movement. These active groups will become familiar to anyone following current environmental policy.

The Sierra Club.   Politically militant and aggressive, the Sierra Club has a reputation as a tough, sophisticated political opponent. Founded in 1892 by the great American naturalist John Muir, the club remained relatively small and active primarily in the West until recently, when it climbed to 135,000 members in forty-one chapters throughout the nation. The club's reputation was fashioned, in good part, during the years when it was led by David Brower, its executive secretary for seventeen years before leaving the organization in 1969. Under Brower's direction, the club defeated an effort to place dams across the Colorado River that would flood segments of the Grand

Canyon and thwarted numerous other efforts to develop wilderness areas commercially. The club asserts a hard-line "preservationist" viewpoint that resolutely opposes destruction of any wilderness area for almost any purpose; this fundamentalist position has often separated the club from more moderate environmentalists who favor multiple use of wilderness areas and has caused most of its opponents to call it extremist. In recent years, the club has fought the proposed Alaskan oil pipeline, the development of California's Mineral King Mountain by commercial recreation interests, further hydoelectric dam construction, and the introduction of SST jet transportation in the United States. It remains the best-known environmental group in politics.

The Audubon Society.   Founded in 1905 and with a current membership of approximately 210,000, the society is a federation of state and local chapters, many of which (like the Massachusetts state chapter) exert considerable political influence within their own regions. The society is primarily concerned with the enjoyment, preservation, and enhancement of wildlife in all varieties. It has been especially active in fighting pesticides and other poisons that affect the food chain, in gathering funds from public and private sources to buy wilderness preserves, and in encouraging public agencies to use existing public resources to protect animal life, particularly endangered species. The society maintains a lobbying office in Washington and many state capitals; in many communities, its local chapter is often the only environmentally active organization. While usually moderate on most environmental questions, the society has often sided with more militant groups such as the Sierra Club in political combat.

The Izaak Walton League.   The league represents a mixture of straight conservationists and sportsmen. Founded in 1922, the league has 56,000 members distributed among state chapters in a loose federation that gives the local units great autonomy; in many respects, the league has been far more effective at the state level than in national politics. Since it is a confederation of sportsmen and conservationists, the state units tend to take positions according to which of the elements dominates the membership. Generally, it favors the development and enhancement of recreational facilities on public lands but not without some attention to wilderness preservation. Thus, it helps to bridge the gap that sometimes develops between sportsmen and conservationists on resource use. Operating principally through lobbying, publications, and other familiar forms of political action, the league leans toward a more traditional, "conservationist" view of environmental problems.

The National Wildlife Federation. Generally considered the only militant and effective sportsmen's group, the organization is a federation of state councils representing rod-and-gun clubs. Although the affiliated clubs represent about 3.5 million members, few are active in the organization and most of its money comes from conservationists who buy the club's attractive magazines, wildlife stamps, and other publications. The federation has very close ties with state fish and game departments, commercial recreational interests, and other groups concerned with the enhancement of recreational fishing and hunting activities. The federation maintains a Washington lobby but is more effective at state levels. Since it usually sides with those wanting to expand hunting and fishing opportunities, it often opposes strict "preservationist" organizations like the Sierra Club and sometimes incurs the criticism of conservationists for its relatively mild position on wilderness development.

Friends of the Earth. Created by David Brower after a split in the Sierra Club resulted in his dismissal as its executive secretary in 1969, FOE is hard-line preservationist and vigorously political in its approach to ecological issues. The organization, according to Brower, wants "conservation to go on the attack, to . . . reclaim shopping centers, not swamps, cities, not mountains, polluted rivers, not free-flowing streams. More space and less development, more wild animals and fewer people are the political aims of Friends of the Earth." The organization tries to provide information to environmental groups for ammunition in their battles in legislative halls and other political arenas. Current membership is less than 15,000, but it's growing. Following Brower's philosophy, FOE fights its political battles wherever major political decisions affecting the environment are made. Already active in Washington, FOE is becoming a presence in many state capitals.

The League of Conservation Voters. Originally an electoral arm of Friends of the Earth, the league became fully autonomous in 1972. A nonpartisan organization, it published appraisals of the environmental record for most members of the House of Representatives, raised and distributed $50,000 in campaign contributions for selected Congressional contenders in 1970, and published evaluations of environmental views for the major Presidential contenders in 1972 (although it endorsed none). The league is still small, its electoral impact uncertain; it has been increasingly active in state and national elections as the 1970's progressed. At the moment, the league represents the first national environmental organization committed to a wholly political program.

The Environmental Defense Fund. When he founded it in 1967, flamboyant lawyer Victor Yannacone ensured its fame among ecologists by his unofficial motto: "Sue the bastards." Though Yannacone left the group, it has grown in activity and impact and is today the most effective legal weapon in the environmental movement. The fund is a coalition of sixty lawyers, 700 scientists, and other experts who collaborate in preparing and presenting cases before the nation's courts in which they seek to protect public rights to a safe environment. Although the fund operates on a modest budget, mostly dues from its 25,000 members, it has been extremely successful in achieving its objectives. Relying on a mixture of well-presented, carefully prepared scientific testimony and imaginative, vigorous legal argument, the fund has succeeded in getting DDT banned in several states, in halting the Alaskan pipeline until careful environmental studies could be made, and in halting construction of three major federal canal-and-dam projects in an unprecedented defeat for the Army Corps of Engineers. Most significantly, the fund has apparently succeeded in establishing the right of citizens to defend a claim to a clean environment as a "public right" in the courts. In 1972, the fund had more than forty suits in the courts or under consideration.

The Natural Resources Defense Council. Founded in 1970 with Washington headquarters, the NRDC has assumed the leadership, together with the Environmental Defense Fund, in initiating major environmental lawsuits at the federal level. The NRDC is staffed mostly by lawyers and depends upon foundation and environmental group support for most of its funding. In addition to legal action, it carries out a number of citizen education campaigns (such as its 1974 Project Clean Water, which distributed materials and notices of pending federal and state action on water quality to interested citizen groups) and regularly monitors compliance of the EPA and other federal agencies with environmental law. In any recent year, the NRDC had initiated approximately fifty lawsuits on ecology issues.

Zero Population Growth.   Created by biologist Paul Ehrlich in 1970 to proselytize for population control as the only alternative to a major world catastrophe, ZPG has been particularly active on college campuses. New and relatively small, the group is zealous, forceful, and colorful in proclaiming its message. Concentrating almost exclusively on population problems, ZPG follows a philosophy of active political involvement but is too new to have yet demonstrated what political muscle, if any, it possesses.

In addition to organizational diversity, there are several important philosophical divisions among environmentalists. There is a fundamental, persisting division between preservationists who want wilderness and other resources saved from almost all man-made alterations and moderates who accept "multiple use" (for preservation, recreation, and commercial interests); this not only results in a difference in organizational philosophies—the Sierra Club's hard-line preservationism against the Audubon's less militant position, for instance— but often divides groups internally. There are also differences among priorities for environmental action: The Izaak Walton League and the National Wildlife Federation tend to be responsive to the concern of sportsmen, Zero Population Growth places population problems above all other considerations, and the Audubon Society pays particular heed to wildlife issues. Also, as we shall shortly note, the interest of governmental bureaucrats involved in ecology may diverge in significant respects from the interest of those not committed to particular governmental agencies or politics.

Besides ecology groups, a great variety of other interests are continually involved in the politics of environmental protection. American business and governmental agencies, in particular, are among the most important of these interests that also shape the political pattern of environmental struggles.

Business, Bureaucrats, and Ecology

Except for government, no other institutions in American society are more deeply implicated in the struggle to make environmental policy than are the nation's corporations. Whether considered as single firms, trade associations, or entire industrial groups, businessmen have become increasingly aware of environmental issues and alert to their political interest in ecology.

CORPORATE POLITICS. American business has reason to be deeply involved in environmental politics. First, since industry is the principal source of many pollutants, it will be heavily regulated by any governmental policy to abate pollution; industry produces about three-fourths of the most damaging air pollutants and more than half the volume of oxygen-demanding wastes discharged into municipal sewage systems. Much of the cost and initial responsibility for installing pollution control devices must also be borne by business. The consumer will eventually pay much of this cost in higher prices, but corporations are nonetheless affected. Business must absorb some of this cost, may be adversely affected in some cases by the increased cost of their products, may have to close economically marginal plants when pollution control equipment is required, and may have to "write off" some future projects as losses.

Business is also a major resource consumer, vitally concerned with any restrictions on resource availability that government might impose for ecological reasons. A number of industries, for instance, will be affected by any changes Washington may dictate in corporate access to federal lands. The lumber industry obtains more than 35 per cent of all its commercial softwood from federal forests, cattle and sheep raisers graze their herds on 273 million acres of federal reserve, and an additional 64 million acres of public domain is leased for private mineral exploitation. If tough environmental safeguards are imposed on oil companies developing new fields such as the Alaskan reserve at Prudhoe Bay, the cost and volume of petroleum production would be significantly affected. Not least important, American industry has been thrown on the defensive by the environmental movement. Numerous environmental experts have harshly assailed industry for its pollution and alleged callousness regarding environmental protection; the public commonly views business as the source of environmental ills and often as the villain in environmental politics.[30] Corporations, extremely anxious to demonstrate that they are maligned by environmentalists, want to prove they are also working for a cleaner environment.

Since 11 million corporations speaking through 3,000 trade associations constitute the American business community, it is far too pluralistic to possess a single voice on environmental issues. The largest corporations and trade associations that frequently set the policy stance for most business have, however, demonstrated some fairly consistent political strategies on environmental issues. Although many environmentalists regard any statement of corporate environmental concern as a case of the devil quoting scripture, business leaders profess a will to cooperate with governmental efforts at environmental protection and appear to accept, if not always welcome, ecology as an enduring political issue. This is apparent not only at the top stratum of business leadership, but also at middle and lower levels as well.

A fairly typical attitude was expressed by one large southern land developer: "I'm not even sure what ecology means. But whatever it means, it's here to stay and it will enter into all future development projects." Business seldom welcomes federal intervention in the economy, but in the case of pollution control, major corporations generally prefer the federal presence because it prevents the confusion of fifty different state regulatory systems while ensuring that no major corporation will escape regulation and thereby enjoy a market advantage. For these reasons, the auto industry did not initially oppose federal emission standards for new cars, and industrial users of fossil fuels prefer that Washington take the initiative in establishing air quality standards. Large corporations have occasionally been models of environmental responsibility, as when the Ford Motor Company voluntarily acknowledged in 1973 that some of its engineers had tampered with engines used on new cars to "certify" their compliance with federal emission controls or when Monsanto Chemical Company, the nation's only manufacturer of PCBs, ceased further distribution when tentative evidence suggested the chemical might be an extreme hazard.

Still, although American business may profess its commitment in principle to environmental protection, it is most often unenthusiastic about the practical details. The public record ordinarily reveals considerable corporate resistance to and dissatisfaction with initial governmental efforts to protect the environment; conflict, not concord, most often marks the relationship between business and its regulators. Business tends to adopt a common stance toward most regulatory measures. It frequently argues (1) that an ecological problem is exaggerated by experts, (2) that regulatory policies will be excessively harsh, dangerously retarding national economic growth and imposing unjustifiably heavy costs on firms, and (3) that evidence supporting a pollutant's regulation is unreliable. Recent variations on these themes include the following:

1. Industrial spokesmen at a national conference called for a moratorium on the "imposition of any new environmental standards" because new standards will "use up money that business could invest to increase output and thus hold down inflation."

2. The leading car manufacturers requested Congress to declare a "five-year moratorium on any new safety and emission standards."

3. The president of the International Paper Company declared that the goals of federal water pollution legislation "will drastically change the competitive posture of many of the major basic industries of the United States, like steel, aluminum, chemicals, petroleum and pulp and paper."

4. In response to federal warnings that the fluorocarbons in propellants used in spray cans may damage the earth's ozone layer, the Aerosol Education Bureau responded: "Without experimental evidence, it would be an injustice if a few claims—which even critics agree are hypotheses—were to be the basis of regulatory or consumer reactions."[31]

When Oregon's legislature required a deposit on beer and soft-drink containers and established strict new air and water pollution controls, the Western Environmental Trade Association, an Oregon business and labor group pledged to fighting "environmental hysteria," unloosed the following broadside:

> There have been a great many ill-conceived and unsound environmental programs which seriously endanger the public welfare. . . . As a result of over-zealous, erroneous governmental regulations and actions, that segment which produces jobs and profits has been rendered a serious economic blow.[32]

To which most corporation leaders are likely to respond (at least privately), "Amen."

In fact, these gloomy predictions seldom seem justified. The Council on Environmental Quality, for example, found no support for the allegation that the new environmental regulatory programs have caused significant unemployment, have forced the closing of numerous factories, or have otherwise damaged the economy.[33] Nonetheless, warnings of impending economic ills often enlist other interests into an alliance with business when it appears that they, too, will suffer from ecological regulations. Thus, among those opposing California's program to control development on the state's ecologically vulnerable coast were real estate developers, oil and gas interests, logging companies, the construction trade unions, and others who termed the plan "a nongrowth policy."[34]

It is not surprising, then, that the record of American industrial response to ecology has been a grudging resistance. The auto industry balked and delayed so long in developing auto emission control equipment that the government finally had to file suit against Detroit's four major auto makers in 1969 to force a more cooperative attitude; in subsequent efforts to achieve further controls by 1975, the industry was only slightly more cooperative.[35] The oil industry emasculated much of the 1966 Clean Waters Act by getting it written in a manner that made it almost impossible for the federal government to sue successfully an oil company responsible for a major oil spill; massive efforts by environmental interests in 1970 finally changed the bill.[36] The nation's steel firms have generally opposed existing federal air and water pollution standards; earlier efforts by local government to achieve air pollution abatement was frequently thwarted when major steel corporations expressed willingness to accept "reasonable" controls but refused to make any effort to promote them, thus denying their considerable support to pollution control and delaying it through the power of inertia. Business leaders frequently complain that they have been unfairly accused of environmental negligence, but their public record often seems to justify the indictment. It is hardly surprising, then, that one study of community leaders in fifty-one important American cities in the early 1970's revealed that almost 95 per cent of them listed industrial corporations and their executives as the opponents of air pollution control.[37]

Whatever the truth may be, business is also spending millions of dollars in advertising to convince Americans that it is a conscientious environmental guardian with impressive accomplishments. This is an important strategy. If successful, it can create public goodwill that may be tapped and directed to industry's advantage in policy struggles; it can delay or diminish efforts to achieve greater governmental control of industrial pollution by undercutting popular support. All major American industries subject to environmental legislation have paid handsomely for media space to assure the public they are on the side of the angels in environmental affairs. Here is a sampler of such advertising:

> *Standard Oil:* "Great strides are being made in the control and reduction of automotive pollution by the automobile manufacturers and the petroleum industry, assisted by Federal, State and local governments. . . . The development of F-310 is . . . an important advance. To our knowledge, F-310 is the most significant step taken to date by any oil company to provide a gasoline which helps reduce air pollution."
>
> *Republic Steel:* "We were concerned about ecology long before it became a household word. Our program began more than thirty years ago."
>
> *Private Electric industry:* "Buildings with *the electric climate* put nothing into the air around them . . . because electricity is the cleanest source of energy."
>
> *Glass Industry:* "Working toward the ULTIMATE recycling system. Which means a system that will channel the components of trash into a new useful life."
>
> *Can Industry:* "Cans are good guys. We've already set up recycling centers for used cans. . . . More are coming. This costs us money but doesn't cost you anything."

Industry has also utilized advertising to influence public opinion on specific environmental issues. To arouse public support for the massive development of western coal reserves—a move widely opposed by ecologists—American utility companies seized upon the Arab boycott of American oil in 1973 and spent millions on a campaign in all major American magazines and newspapers to remind that "America has more coal than the Middle East has oil . . . let's dig it!" When U.S. Steel was threatened by a federal court contempt citation for failing to negotiate with the EPA on control of air pollution from its Clairton Coke Works, the company spent $60,000 to inform Pittsburgh residents in two daily newspapers: "Clairton is one of the cleanest coke-making operations in the nation" and to warn: "U.S. Steel can't make steel in Pittsburgh without coke from Clairton. Period."[38] In an effort to counteract public criticism of corporate pollution, many of the nation's major businesses formed Keep America Beautiful, Inc. (KAB), "to urge more individual anti-pollution action and less criticism of business and government." Predicting it would obtain more than $450 million in free media time and space for its programs, the KAB's chairman announced the group's theme would be "People start pollution. People can stop it."

Many corporations have made themselves vulnerable to charges of misleading or blatantly false advertising (like the large western utility that depicted a lobster, apparently content in power plant wastes, that in fact came from "nowhere near the plant"). Corporate leaders admit that such deception is regrettable but argue that it represents only a small portion of all corporate environmental advertising. They point out that the public often blames industry for environmental problems that the public itself helps to create, and too often believes the worst allegations of environmentalists rather than considering the commendable environmental achievements of industry. Advertising, industrial spokesmen maintain, is the major means by which they can present their side to the nation and thereby create a balanced picture of environmental affairs. Despite these protestations, there is little doubt that many major corporations have taken considerable liberty with the truth in their environmental presentations. Unless Congress or such agencies as the Federal Trade Commission enforce higher standards, there seems little prospect that environmental advertising will decrease in volume or improve in quality.

Beyond such general approaches, the philosophy and tactics of American business vary considerably according to the specific policies at issue. This matter we can leave to the chapters on policy that follow. An examination of the group structure of environmental politics would be incomplete, however, without briefly mentioning the activities of governmental bureaucrats. These interests are intrinsically important and have often been ignored in public interpretations of ecology issues.

THE BUREAUCRATIC STRUCTURE. It is difficult to estimate accurately the number of federal, state, and local governmental agencies with a strong interest in environmental politics. For instance, a recent federal study indicates that air pollution policy directly involves the Department of Health, Education and Welfare, the Department of Agriculture, the Environmental Protection Agency, the Department of the Interior, the Department of Transportation, the Coast Guard, and the Federal Aviation Agency; pesticide regulation vitally concerns four federal departments and the Environmental Protection Agency; the handling and transportation of hazardous materials affects four major federal departments and five independent commissions or agencies. To this list should also be added the multitude of state agencies with responsibilities within their own jurisdictions that would overlap those of the federal government. In short, any significant environmental issue is bound to engage the interest and activity of a great many governmental officials.

Administrators have many reasons for being concerned with environmental policy. They may be charged with the responsibility of implementing and enforcing environmental legislation enacted at federal or state levels. Thus, the Department of Agriculture's Forest Service and Interior's National Park Service are likely to have a vested interest and strong views about any contemplated change in land management of federal reserves; similarly, the "fish people"—the National Marine Fisheries Service (Department of Commerce) and the Bureau of Sports Fisheries and Wildlife (Department of Interior) —will be greatly concerned with water pollution control and water resource development. Moreover, bureaucrats are often creators and advocates of environmental policies, often working in conjunction with sympathetic private interests. In federal and state government, it is common to find that many legislative acts begin with, or are substantially shaped by, the work of administrative specialists in government whose expertise alerts them to the need for various environmental measures. Finally, most administrative agencies have developed strong political alliances with private interests involved in environmental politics and may be drawn into policy conflicts through such coalitions. Often, for example, foresters, fishery managers, fish-and-game officials, and water resource planners actively support the governmental policies advocated by the commercial interests with which such officials must deal constantly; sometimes, environmental groups have collaborated with insurgents within governmental departments wanting a major policy reform or change in traditional agency procedures. In any case, policy struggles among various private interests almost always draw various governmental agencies and their representatives into the fray. This is too common to be surprising, but it explains why an examination of governmental policy struggles must take account of these bureaucratic interests.

Environmental groups look with mixed emotion on the governmental agencies responsible for environmental programs. Environmentalists recognize that the expertise, experience, and cooperation of these bureaucracies are essential for environmental protection; ecologists frequently acknowledge that most bureaucrats attempt to discharge their responsibilities with reasonable good faith. Yet, environmental interests often assert that these administrators too often side with the *status quo* against new policies, identify too often with the private interests that cause serious environmental degradation, and use their influence to stifle innovation within their own departments. Thus, it seems to many environmental leaders that the established governmental agencies involved in environmental management and protection are, at best, fitful allies and frequent adversaries. However, it is a fact of environmental politics that ecologists need the collaboration of these agencies if environmental protection is to become a reality, and they must find a means of satisfying this large, important set of interests if new ecological policies are to be created.

SUMMARY: THE GROUP BASIS OF ENVIRONMENTAL POLITICS

We have witnessed in the last few years a transformation in the character of groups espousing environmental protection, a change that marks the end of the "conservation" movement and the onset of the "ecology" crusade. One manifestation of this has been a notable alteration in the political philosophy and tactics of groups concerned with environmental quality. In general, there has been a proliferation of new groups committed to explicit, wide-ranging political activity and a growing receptivity among older groups to more aggressive political action. Newer, militant political tactics have won growing acceptance within environmental groups; electoral action, environmental lawsuits, protest marches, and mass demonstrations, in particular, have proved popular and effective as new means of action. Moreover, environmental groups have considerably broadened their base of support and improved their political resources by enlisting the assistance of a large number of young people, a fact that has had much to do with the transformation to greater political militancy within the movement. All this has also been accompanied by a very ambitious definition of issues for which ecologists should work politically; the list of problems now embraces almost any matter that may affect the quality of man's environment. In short, the *mystique* of the movement is more political, more militant, more comprehensive in its social concerns.

At the same time, the group structure of the movement is not monolithic in its environmental priorities, its preferences for political strategies, or its militancy. It is divided internally on all these issues, so that one is likely to find a significant consensus on the existence of grave environmental problems but not on the proper remedies, tactics, or order in which the problems are to be solved. The group pluralism is hardly surprising—one does not find any major socioeconomic or ideological interests with a monolithic group structure—but it does point to serious internal political cleavages within the movement that are often neglected by observers.

Whatever its character, the long-range outlook for environmental protection will depend, in good measure, on the group structure of the ecology movement. Organized groups have been largely responsible for mobilizing discontent with environmental degradation, for proselytizing to increase the political strength of the movement, and for bringing sustained pressure to bear on governmental bodies to remedy environmental ills. The vigor, imagination, and dedication of these groups in political struggles of the future represent the most important political resource the environmental movement has at its disposal. All these resources will be severely tested in the battle to achieve and enforce environmental protection through government.

NOTES

1. Stewart L. Udall, "Total Environment: A New Political Reality," in Harold W. Helfrich, Jr., ed., *Agenda for Survival* (New Haven, Conn.: Yale University Press, 1970), pp. 10 and 11.

2. The political pressure generated by the Santa Barbara incident is described from an insider's viewpoint in Walter J. Hickel, *Who Owns America?* (Englewood Cliffs, N.J.: Prentice-Hall, 1971), chapter 4.

3. *New York Times,* March 8, 1972. For an interpretation of this "third-world paranoia" from an observer of the recent U.N. Conference on the Human Environment, see Robert Bendiner, "Third-World Ecology," *New York Times,* June 23, 1972.

4. This theory is most explicitly applied to the pollution issue in Matthew A. Crenson, *The Un-Politics of Air Pollution* (Baltimore: The Johns Hopkins Press, 1971), pp. 23 ff. The intellectual heritage, however, reaches into more general theories of elite structure in American society. See, for example, Peter Bachrach and Morton S. Baratz, "Two Faces of Power," *American Political Science Review,* December, 1962, pp. 947–52; and Theodore Lowi, "The Public Philosophy: Interest-Group Liberalism," *American Political Science Review,* March, 1967, pp. 5–24.

5. *New York Times,* September 12, 1971.

6. Thomas B. McMullen *et al.,* "Air Quality and Characteristic Community Parameters" (Paper delivered at the annual meeting of the Air Pollution Control Association, Cleveland, Ohio, 1967), Appendix. Cited in Matthew A. Crenson, *op. cit.,* p. 12.

7. See, for example, Rita James Simon, "Public Attitudes Toward Population and Pollution," *Public Opinion Quarterly,* Spring, 1971, pp. 93–99.

8. The difference between the current "ecology" and the earlier "conservation" viewpoint is best appreciated by reading a sampler of each ethic side by side. A good contrast would be a comparison between Alde Leopold, *A Sand County Almanac* (New York: Oxford University Press, 1940), and Gene Marine, *America the Raped* (New York: Simon and Schuster, 1969). In literary terms, Leopold's graceful prose is far superior to Marine's outraged, if eloquent, polemics, but the substance of the two books fairly represents the differences in the two movements.

9. Stewart L. Udall, *op. cit.,* p. 1.

10. Harvey Wheeler, "The Politics of Ecology," *Saturday Review,* March 7, 1970, p. 52; Daniel R. Grant, "Carrots, Sticks and Consensus," in Leslie

L. Roos, *The Politics of Ecosuicide* (New York: Holt, Rinehart and Winston, 1971), p. 104.

11. Frederick E. Smith, a Harvard ecologist. Cited in Fred Carvell and Max Tadlock, *It's Not Too Late* (Beverly Hills, Calif.: The Glencoe Press, 1971), p. 5.

12. Council on Environmental Quality, *Environmental Quality, 1970* (Washington, D.C., 1970), p. 6.

13. René Dubos, "The Human Landscape," *Bulletin of the Atomic Scientists,* March, 1970, p. 31.

14. Walter J. Hickel, *op. cit.,* p. 298.

15. Paul Ehrlich, "A Playboy Interview," in *Project Survival* (Chicago: The Playboy Press, 1971), p. 77.

16. Robert Rienow and Leona Train Rienow, *Moment in the Sun* (New York: Ballantine Books, 1967), p. 233.

17. Max Ways, "How to Think About the Environment," in Editors of *Fortune, The Environment* (New York: Harper & Row, 1970), p. 202.

18. *Man's Impact on the Global Environment: Report of the Study of Critical Environmental Problems* (Cambridge, Mass.: MIT Press, 1970), p. 232.

19. Charles R. Ross, "The Federal Government as an Inadvertent Advocate of Environmental Degradation," in Harold W. Helfrich, Jr., ed., *The Environmental Crisis* (New Haven, Conn.: Yale University Press, 1970), p. 173.

20. Barry Weisberg, "The Politics of Ecology," in Robert Disch, ed., *The Ecological Conscience* (Englewood Cliffs, N.J.: Prentice-Hall, 1970), p. 154.

21. Quoted by Peter R. Janssen, "The Age of Ecology," in John G. Mitchell and Constance L. Stallings, *Ecotactics* (New York: Pocket Books, 1970), p. 55.

22. Barry Commoner, "Beyond the Teach-In," *Saturday Review,* April 4, 1970, p. 63.

23. The purpose and philosophy of environmental lawsuits are fully discussed in Joseph L. Sax, *Defending the Environment* (New York: Alfred A. Knopf, 1971). The impact of citizen suits on judicial interpretations of the National Environment Policy Act are described in Frederick R. Anderson, *NEPA in the Courts: A Legal Analysis of the National Environmental Policy Act* (Baltimore: The Johns Hopkins University Press, 1973); and Council on Environmental Quality, *Environmental Quality: Fifth Annual Report* (Washington, D.C., 1974), and *Sixth Annual Report* (Washington, D.C., 1975), chapter 6.

24. *Wilderness Society* v. *Morton,* 495 F. 2d. 1026; 6 E. R. C. 1427.

25. Citizen groups in environmental politics are surveyed in Council on

Environmental Quality, *Environmental Quality: Fourth Annual Report* (Washington, D.C., 1973), chapter 8.

26. A typical socioeconomic profile of ecology enthusiasts may be found in Leslie L. Roos, *op. cit.* Evidence on the environmental degeneration of the inner city may be found in Council on Environmental Quality, *Environmental Quality: First Annual Report,* pp. 189 ff.

27. Quoted in Harold Sprout, "The Environmental Crisis in the Context of American Politics," in Leslie L. Roos, *op. cit.,* p. 46.

28. *New York Times,* May 7, 1976.

29. The group structure of the ecology movement is explored in Jeremy Main, "Conservation at the Barricade," in Editors of *Fortune, op. cit.,* pp. 167–80. Estimates of the Sierra Club's growth provided by Congressional Quarterly Service, *Man's Control of the Environment* (Washington, D.C.: Congressional Quarterly Service, 1970), p. 4.

30. Indeed, the public appears to see little else but industry as the environmental villain. See Hazel Erskine, "The Polls: Pollution and Industry," *Public Opinion Quarterly,* Summer, 1972, pp. 263–80.

31. Quotes taken from *New York Times,* November 2, 1974; December 8, 1975; April 6, 1975; and *Washington Post,* September 20, 1974.

32. *New York Times,* December 15, 1971.

33. Council on Environmental Quality, *Sixth Annual Report,* pp. 533–34

34. *Ibid.,* p. 155.

35. A detailed discussion of the emission control controversy is found in John C. Esposito, *Vanishing Air* (New York: Grossman Publishers, 1970), chapter 2.

36. This is fully described in J. Clarence Davies, *Politics of Pollution* (New York: Pegasus Press, 1970), pp. 46–48.

37. Matthew A. Crenson, *op. cit.,* p. 89.

38. *Gainesville Sun,* May 24, 1976.

4. The Pikes of Politicians: Setting Environmental Policy

The politics of ecology is ultimately a struggle to control the exercise of public power in the United States; in Washington, contending environmental interests converge in their efforts to exploit the authority of public agencies to their own advantage. Washington may not be the seat of the nation's environmental wisdom, but it is the only place where officials can create and enforce a national environmental policy; here, where the ambit of public power is greatest, the most critical policy decisions and conflicts occur. Ecologists know that their movement's energy will dissipate into a futile spasm of arrested reform unless the firm, continuing weight of federal authority is brought to bear on environmental protection. The nation's corporate managers, too, recognize that Washington sets the policy trend for all governmental levels in environmental affairs; if they are to shape that policy to their satisfaction, they must be effective in Washington.

Environmentalists commonly face the prospect of working with Washington's officialdom with varying degrees of wariness, frustration, and bitterness. "Perhaps I am a cynic," writes a veteran conservationist, "but in my lifetime I have seen too many potentially good leaders in the field of conservation come with high hopes to Washington only to be impaled on the pikes of politicians." To many in the movement, this is gospel: The pikes of politicians will impale not only good men but good policies, good agencies, and good intentions. Among conservationists, there is an unspoken conviction that something in the American political process is inherently inhospitable to environmental protection, that "politics" undermines sound environmental policies established in the public interest while nature's private exploiters profit. Many who do not share such pessimism still recognize they are operating in a milieu where the opposition has historically enjoyed the greater advantage and success. Under the most favorable conditions, environmentalists expect a hard, uncertain battle in an unfriendly arena before winning, if such is their luck, major environmental victories.

Ecologists, as we shall often note, have reason for disenchantment with past federal programs and grounds for reservations about the rewards of future effort. Why should this be so? And what, then, are the prospects for effective environmental protection through government? To answer these questions, one needs some acquaintance with the governmental process, together with an understanding of the particular problems this process poses for the environmental movement. Such an approach helps to explain not only what occurs in making environmental policy but *why* it happens.

ECOLOGY AND THE GOVERNMENTAL PROCESS

A customary style in the making of public policy in the United States, a recurring logic, marks the way in which our public institutions handle most policy issues. Although exceptions enough suggest that they are not locked into an immutable policy-making mold, powerful conservative forces inhibit most policy questions from departing very far from traditional procedures for their resolution. Most importantly, this decisional style is likely to have a significant impact on the making of environmental decisions.

The Bias of the Rules

In governmental policy-making, as economist Charles Lindblom suggests, it is important to know not only who makes policy but *what* makes policy.[1] Lindblom, like many analysts, suggests that the policy outputs of government are powerfully shaped by the principles and rules that govern decision-making—the "what" of the system. These principles include both the formal rules that dictate how decisions must be made and the informal understandings, or "rules of the game," that are shared by decision-makers and shape their relationships with one another. In any governmental system, these rules are biased in the sense that they will favor some policy decisions over others, will promote the consideration of some issues and encourage the neglect of others, and will generally "load" the governmental process in favor of some interests. The bias of decisional rules can be observed abundantly in Washington. The Congressional seniority system, which confers on southern interests an unusually large voice in legislative committee deliberations, or the electoral college's apportionment, which bestows such great influence on the populous states in Presidential elections, are garden-variety examples of "loaded" rules. Because decisional rules shape policy outcomes so strongly, it is understandable that those wanting to alter governmental policy often attempt to revise the rules by which decisions of concern to them are made.[2] It should also be apparent that a conflict over what rules shall prevail, for making decisions in governmental bodies is actually a contest to determine which array of interests will be favored by governmental decisions.

Despite the great profusion and complexity of decision-making procedures in American government, in the United States—as in other governmental systems—the rules tend to correspond with certain principles or values that are considered essential to the governmental process. Thus, the apparent diversity of rule-making procedures is undergirded by what has been called an "inarticulate ideology," an informal set of beliefs that provides a common logic to the many different decisional arrangements. This logic, of course, engineers a bias into the making of environmental policy as it does in other matters. Among the major components of this "inarticulate ideology," we shall briefly mention those that exert particular influence on governmental responses to the environmental movement.

INCREMENTALISM. Both formal rules and informal understandings among public officials promote public policy by "increments." Incrementalism favors the making of new policy on the basis of past experience, careful and prolonged consultation among all the major parties affected by decisions, bargaining and compromise among interested parties, and modest policy change rather than comprehensive or radical alterations in policy. Incrementalism also means that few policy problems are ever solved; indeed, final solutions are seldom expected. "In the United States," writes Lindblom, "policy-makers nibble endlessly at taxation, social security, national defense, conservation, foreign aid. . . . Political analysts assume that their problems are never solved, and hold themselves in readiness to return to them again and again."[3] A number of governmental arrangements encourage incrementalism or reflect a belief in its importance. Important policies in both the executive and the legislative branches cannot be formulated and ratified without consultation and eventual concurrence by numerous officials and agencies at many governmental levels. The division of powers among the three major branches of government forces bargaining, compromise, and time consumption in fashioning policy; the collaboration of numerous informal power holders (private interests) is usually essential if policy affects them. Moreover, the federal system puts brakes on rapid or radical policy innovation in favor of incremental changes engineered through consultation and the creation of consensus among differing governmental levels. This system does not wholly preclude major change, particularly in foreign and military affairs, where Presidential innovation often prevails. Still, radical or rapid policy change customarily occurs only under such extraordinary circumstances as depression, war, or other emergencies when decisive innovation may be necessary to meet urgent national needs.

An incremental system has several appeals for officials. In terms of policy planning, it concentrates their attention on a limited set of policy alternatives, reduces the complexity of factors they must consider, and permits them to draw on past experience as a guide for future decisions.[4] There are also political virtues. Once policy is fashioned, the coalition of supporting interests is likely to prefer an incremental change rather than a drastic revision that upsets established understandings, triggers more political bloodletting, and opens the possibility for undesirable new interests to gain some advantage. Incrementalism, additionally, seldom pushes change to the point where the public or major private groups balk at the new situation. Then, too, there is always the risk that constituents may react to drastic change by deposing the policy-maker or by altering the rules of decision-making to his disadvantage.

Thus, incrementalism is generally conservative in that it favors the perpetuation of the existing political framework, its dominant policies and interests. Since incrementalism places a drag on rapid or radical policy change, those who want major departures from the *status quo* will chafe under the restraints imposed by this system. Those excluded from the company of the elect who benefit from an incremental approach will view the system with equal prejudice. Especially for the reformer, incrementalism is frequently a cross to bear because the demand for reform is almost always a demand to alter the *status quo* in ways costly to vested interests. Not surprisingly, many ecologists believe that one of the most formidable pikes in the politician's arsenal is labeled "incrementalism."

ORGANIZED INTERESTS AND PUBLIC POLICY.   One explanation for Washington's incremental style is that public officials customarily engage in extensive consultation and negotiation with the major organized interests affected by a policy before any significant decisions are formalized. If many organized interests are affected, decision-making is likely to be protracted and contentious, with only those policies enlisting substantial support among most of the significant interests likely to prevail.

Although it has never been stated as an explicit doctrine, most political analysts recognize that governmental officials operate on the premise that major organized groups affected by public policy should have an important voice in both shaping and administering it. To many analysts, such as Theodore Lowi, this deference to interests has reached the stage where their control of public policy is considered legitimate and desirable. Today, he suggests, "The role of government is one of insuring access particularly to the most effectively organized, and of ratifying the agreements and adjustments worked out among the competing leaders and their claims."[5] Analysts who reject such a sweeping judgment would nonetheless find little quarrel with Grant McConnell's assertion that we have witnessed "the conquest of segments of formal state power by private groups and associations. . . . Although it would be impossible to state with any precision what portion of the power of American government has been taken possession in this way," he observes, "it is certain that the portion is substantial and that the control involved is considerable."[6]

Many arrangements illustrate how organized interests penetrate the governmental process at strategic points in ways sanctioned by law and custom. In the legislative arena, lobbying constitutes the most familiar exercise of group influence on public policy; the dominion of organized groups is further extended by the tendency of legislators to assume that important policy issues can be most satisfactorily clarified and resolved through the interaction of organized group spokesmen. Group influence is designed into the administrative branch in many ways. More than 1,400 "advisory committees"—usually dominated by representatives of major interests affected by agency programs— exist to give agency officials information on group reactions and preferences on policy;[7] thus, when the Environmental Protection Agency was created in 1971, President Nixon created a National Industrial Pollution Control Council, an advisory panel of big business executives, to give industry a voice in agency decisions. Some of these committees are merely ineffectual administrative decorations, but others exercise considerable influence on the actual decisions of public officials. Private groups also profit through the recruitment of their own members as administrators in many federal departments and agencies. Yet another enhancement of group influence is the creation of semi-public organizations that intermingle private group leaders and public officials with common policy concerns. One of the best examples of this is the Rivers and Harbors Congress, a private agency whose membership consists of public officials and group leaders concerned with water resource development; this organization's recommendations on water resource development have customarily been the agenda followed by Congress and administrative agencies in the water resource field.

This pervasive group presence has not always produced a group monopoly on policy to the exclusion of other sources of influence, but group activity at all governmental levels is so widely practiced and accepted that it has become, in effect, part of our constitutional order. This situation poses several problems for the environmental movement.

THE DIFFUSION OF POWER.   Authority and influence in the making and enforcing of public policy are parceled out among numerous agencies, governmental levels, and unofficial power wielders. This dispersion of power has been created by deliberate constitutional and legislative means and through the informal arrangements used by public officials and important group leaders to facilitate their negotiations in formulating policy. The division and subdivision of governmental power amounts to a fragmentation that is a basic structural trait of the American governmental process.

The Constitution ordains a fragmentation of governmental powers in two important directions. Federalism distributes power "vertically" among national, state, and local government levels, while the separation of powers within the federal government apportions authority "horizontally" among the three branches. In this era of vast federal power, federalism is often supposed to be an antique fiction disguising the actual poverty of power among state and local governments; however, in formulating and applying policy, all levels continue to exert considerable influence and to share major responsibilities. "It is difficult," writes a veteran observer of the governmental process, "to find any governmental activity which does not involve all three of the so-called 'levels' of the federal system."[8] As a result, no governmental level enjoys a monopoly of control over policy. "There has never been a time when it was possible to put neat labels on discreet 'federal,' 'state' and 'local' functions."[9] The separation of powers, as Richard Neustadt has aptly remarked, has not actually fashioned three institutions with separate powers but three separate institutions *sharing* powers. This shared power is readily apparent in such routine procedures as the enactment of legislation in which the President ordinarily proposes, Congress disposes, and— if legislation becomes law—the courts often interpret. The important point is that the vertical and horizontal divisions of power in government create numerous centers of authority that, whether in cooperation or in competition, disperse power in policy-making.

There is also a diffusion of power in other important directions— "inward" and "outward." A careful examination of Congress or the administrative branch of the federal government will reveal that power is internally divided so that there is an inward fragmentation of power and influence. This is most clearly revealed, in the case of Congress, by the committee system in both houses; committees are nuclear units of power within the Congressional system whose members can, and frequently do, wield influence independently of one another. Within the executive branch, the bureaucracy is an organizational constellation of units with different magnitudes of power and influence; departments, agencies, and bureaus acting alone and in differing combinations are capable of exercising considerable influence in making and implementing public policy. Finally, the outward distribution of influence relates to the influence that private interests customarily exercise in the governmental process—a matter discussed in Chapter 3. Public officials make a few important policy decisions without extending consultation outwardly to incorporate the major private interests in the process; few of these interests enjoy an absolute veto over policy proposals, but many enjoy the right to be consulted and to have their preferences honored in some degree before policy is formalized.

Fortunately, the fragmentation of power vertically, horizontally, inwardly, and outwardly seldom ends in paralysis, deadlock, or impotence in governmental responses to important policy issues. Major power holders in and outside government have stabilized their relationships, routinized decision-making, and reached numerous understandings that facilitate reasonable cooperation. Presidential leadership often serves as a catalyst to draw these disparate power centers into collaboration. In emergencies—wars, depressions, or international crises—the routine policy process can often be short-circuited and major decisions reached with great dispatch. However, the fragmentation of power has imparted several significant traits to the governmental process that affect the making of most policy. To begin, fragmentation encourages time consumption and incrementalism in policy-making. Moreover, extensive negotiation among many participants—the price of securing support for major policy in a fragmented power system—means that the policy that emerges is often the common denominator of many different preferences. Fragmentation of power gives a great tactical advantage to those who wish to defeat major policy initiatives; while the proponents of a policy must ordinarily struggle to coordinate and satisfy many interests throughout the government if they are to succeed, the opponents can often inflict a crucial defeat simply by withholding the support of only one power center. Thus, proponents of major policy change must often invest far greater resources, time, and political ingenuity in their efforts than need their opposition. Not least important, fragmented power frustrates comprehensive policy planning and implementation because it prevents the concentration of authority in the hands of a few individuals or agencies essential for continuity and deliberation in the unfolding of governmental policy. Without the goad of crisis, policy is customarily short-range, uncoordinated, and seldom possessed of the coherence that results from central direction and planning.

THE ADMINISTRATIVE STATE. The flow of the policy process does not necessarily follow the constitutional channels intended to guide it. The Constitution appears to vest the principal power to formulate public policy in Congress, while leaving the responsibility to see that it is "faithfully executed" to the President and his agents in the executive branch. Political realities are different. Public policy is *made* in both branches. "In many ways policy-making within executive agencies is indistinguishable from the process that takes place within legislative assemblies," writes one observer. "Agencies respond to group pressures by modifying existing policies or by developing new ones. Bargaining or the adjustment of conflicting interests is as constant a feature of administrative politics as it is of relations among legislators."[10] Policy is *implemented* and *enforced,* however, primarily within the executive branch (with judicial participation). In the last four decades, the administrative branch has burgeoned in responsibilities, manpower, and impact on the nation under the stimulus of increasing federal responsibilities for social needs. Once a modest enterprise of 600,000 civil servants in 1930, it is now a mammoth institution of more than 3 million employees distributed among 11 major departments, 27 independent regulatory agencies and boards and over 100 other specialized organizations. Today, any interest that wishes to influence the shape of public policy must be prepared to understand and cope with the administrative complexities of the policy process.

Why does the administrative establishment loom so large in the making of public policy? One reason is that Congress frequently enacts legislation only in broad outline, stating general purposes and guidelines while leaving administrators with the responsibility of filling in the details and eliminating the vagaries as their more technical training dictates. The delegation of authority to administrators is unavoidable and often wise, for legislation customarily deals with technicalities and complexities in which all likely contingencies cannot be anticipated or understood. The result of this delegated authority is to bestow on administrators many options in interpreting and applying general policies in particular cases—which amounts to making policy. Moreover, legislators often prefer to let administrators work out policy details and to negotiate among interests to arrive at an acceptable interpretation of policy; it may take some political heat off the legislators, satisfy important interests, or affect the nature of the policy in a manner legislators cannot achieve through legislative means.

Since policy is implemented in the executive branch, the actual scope and impact of any policy formulated by Congress will depend on how administrators handle it. In short, policy is not effective until it is administered; how it is administered will determine how effective it will be. This political maxim is lost least of all on the interests affected by public policy. The administrative apparatus in Washington is the focus of an intense interplay of group pressures on agency officials leading to a complex pattern of political understandings and relations among administrators and pressure groups. Those who want policy, those who hope to stifle it, and those who want its modification all invest considerable energy and resources in continuing efforts to affect administrators' interpretation and implementation of programs concerning them. The interplay of interest groups with administrative agencies is almost as old as the Republic and as fundamental to politics as the law of gravity to physics.

Since we shall extensively discuss the administrative process in environmental policy later, our purpose here is only to establish the importance of this process in policy-making. There are, however, certain implications that merit emphasis. First, because administration is crucial in policy-making, much of the actual policy-making process is remote, if not totally unknown and inaccessible, to many groups and individuals. As Francis Rourke observes, the bureaucratic policy process is often the least visible part of government.

> The environment of bureaucracy is a cloistered sanctuary as compared with the limelight of publicity in which a legislative assembly normally operates. . . . The meetings, conferences, negotiations, and agreements through which bureaucratic policy decisions are reached can only be dimly seen through the opaque exterior which an administrative agency presents to the outside world.[11]

This "opaque exterior," though seldom the result of a bureaucratic conspiracy, nonetheless often conceals or obfuscates the locus of important policy decisions from those vitally concerned with them. Groups lacking established bureaucratic influence or political expertise often experience extreme difficulty in knowing when and where decisions concerning them are made.

Second, given the importance of administration, it follows that policy battles apparently won in Congress may yet be lost in the administrative labyrinth; those vanquished in the legislative arena can, and often do, resort to the administrative forum where they successfully undercut the effectiveness of policy at the point where it is interpreted and applied. Thus, political logic dictates that both friends and foes of public policy must fight a two-front war if they are to be effective. Those favoring a public policy must take care that not only is it made in Congress but also "faithfully executed" administratively. The moral is that those who rejoice in the passage of legislation, confident that they have accomplished a major task in their quest for a public policy, are often deceived. In the end, a bill may become a law, but the law is still only a proclamation of possibilities, a declaration of intent that may or may not be realized. To be successful in Congress but ineffective in the administrative sphere is to be ineffective indeed.

Finally, this discussion suggests that vigilance over administration is the price of victory in the policy process, and that successful interests in the struggle are those that can create stable access and influence within the administrative branch. There are many ways to accomplish this. Groups may develop sufficient political weight to be able to offer agency officials desirable support and encouragement in the political in-fighting common to the bureaucracy—administrators always welcome allies. Groups may find formal or informal methods for placing sympathizers within the administrative process, perhaps through appointment or recruitment to administrative positions. Sometimes interests find that influence flows to them in administrative affairs if they can acquire and exploit Congressional or White House alliances. Whatever the technique, a strategy aimed at developing a measure of political power for the group within the administrative process is virtually a prerequisite for interests seeking long-range influence over the administration of policies vital to them.

Whatever else may be said of these procedures in making our public policy, they have often proved in the past to be the major stumbling blocks of sound environmental programs. At the same time, the character of the policy process is a "given" to the contemporary proponents of environmental protection, an unyielding reality that must be confronted and, if possible, surmounted in the present effort for a new environmental policy. In essence, the environmental movement places a set of demands on Washington policy-makers that the policy process has so far not been well adapted to meet. Environmental protection through the federal government largely depends on whether the policy-making apparatus is now capable of responding to these demands appropriately. Let us examine the most important of these and the particular stress they place on our policy process.

THE CHALLENGE OF ENVIRONMENTALISM

If Washington's efforts at environmental protection are to be something more than a charade, public officials need to find a method to respond affirmatively and effectively to some basic challenges posed to them by the environmental movement.

Protecting the Public Interest

Proposals to abate air and water pollution, to protect national resources, to reduce waste—indeed, most measures needed for environmental protection—are commonly considered public interest legislation. Those concerned with public policy have never reached a satisfactory agreement regarding what "public interest" means in general or in relation to some specific policy domain. However, as a practical matter, public interest policies are understood to be those intended to benefit a great many people or the entire public—this in distinction to policies whose benefits are rather narrowly distributed among a relatively small set of groups or economic interests.[12] Theoretically, most measures enacted and implemented in public agencies are supposed to be in the public interest but actually benefit a rather limited public. Nonetheless, environmental protection measures clearly fall into the category of policies whose benefits are presumed to flow to the public at large in the form of a safer, more enjoyable environment; these are collective benefits in the sense that "they must be available to everyone if they are available to anyone."[13]

Those who, like environmentalists, promote public interest policies confront formidable obstacles in their efforts to have such policies legislated and enforced. First, public interest legislation poses many political difficulties because, as a rule, the benefits are often intangible, long-range, and distributed among a very large public, while the costs are often very tangible, immediate, and imposed on a specific set of organized interests. Pollution abatement measures are an excellent example. Benefits from cleaner air and water will presumably accrue to each member of the public in some important but intangible manner, but the immediate expense, a very tangible one exceeding several hundred billion dollars, will be borne almost entirely by industry. The numerous private interests absorbing the immediate cost of these measures are likely to belong to existing political organizations with great influence, skillful leadership, and long experience in the political process. They also benefit, as we have observed, from some basic traits of the process itself. They enjoy many opportunities to modify or defeat such legislation, as they usually attempt to do, because the policy process "deals in" organized private interests at most strategic points and assumes that their voice should be important in policy decisions. Moreover, the diffusion of power within government allows wide latitude for such interests to delay or defeat public interest proposals by playing centers of power against one another or by occupying a crucial "veto point" among the many power centers that must be brought into the policy-making process. Thus, when public interest proposals create diffuse public benefits and specific group costs, they are likely to stimulate an intensive and extensive group mobilization that usually works against the broad objectives of a policy's supporters.

The task of securing effective public interest legislation is further compounded by the fact that groups promoting "public" measures are at a tactical disadvantage in organizing their support. Such groups are often *ad hoc* organizations that lack a continuing structure and an established access and reputation among policy-makers; it is, moreover, an arduous task to keep large segments of the public mobilized, vigilant, and active in support of such measures even if they are enacted into law. Interest wanes, the details and complexities of politics demoralize or bore many; often the "benefits" that the public expects to derive from policy are not sufficiently tangible or immediate to keep enthusiasm and political pressure strong. Then, too, the diffuse publics that often support public interest legislation can often be satisfied too easily with policies that give them largely symbolic reward but actually deliver few tangible, desired benefits; in effect, this can amount to buying off the public through "symbolic legislation." This might happen, for example, when the legislature declares that there will be a balanced use of publicly owned resources to ensure that environmental protection is not sacrificed to commercial demands, but fails to provide operational standards for enforcing the rule. Supporters of environmental protection might be mollified by such a symbolic gesture, while the the private interests seeking to exploit the resource largely for commercial advantage may still determine its actual use by their political influence in administrative agencies.[14]

According to an old political maxim, "money can wait." Organized special interests unsympathetic to public interest policies can often defeat them legislatively by outlasting the patience and interest of the mobilized public. Or the policies, once legislated, may be quietly frustrated within administrative agencies where the public is often uninformed or unconcerned about policy decisions. Often, notes one analyst, administrators charged with protecting the public interest discover that "the public interest must usually be identified without the constructive assistance of an organization representing the public. The organized public which eventually secured the passage of regulatory legislation quickly evaporates leaving only an inchoate, unorganized mass."[15] Thus, while environmental leaders have tried to make those concerned with environmental protection into a "constituency of conscience," such a constituency is quite vulnerable to impotence or slow dissolution.

Not least important, these policies often suffer a vagueness that leaves administrators without clear guidelines to follow in protecting the public interest. As in Gifford Pinchot's famous instructions to the Forest Service—"The public good comes first"—administrators are often given a mission to protect the public interest but not much assistance in determining what decisions are to be made, and in what manner, to this end. Not all administrators are set adrift in such a sea of ambiguity as Pinchot's directive suggests, but administrator's often find it difficult or impossible to create a satisfactory operational definition of the public's interest in a particular policy matter. In such cases, it often happens that administrators, for many reasons, must rely on the competing claims of private interests to arrive at a formulation of acceptable policy. This is especially true when administrators representing agencies with relatively weak political support must negotiate with politically potent private interests. What often happens under such circumstances is that an agency may be "captured" by the interests it is supposed to regulate for some public purpose. This has been the typical situation in the independent regulatory commissions: "Left largely to its own resources . . . a commission will probably be guided by dominant interests in the regulated industry in its formulation of the public interest. Thus the public interest may become more private than public."[16]

The capture of agencies charged with environmental programs has been frequent in the past. Over a considerable period, the Forest Service's stewardship of the federal government's public lands has come to be dominated in many respects by the commercial lumbering interests with which the service must deal; the Army Corps of Engineers has, in large measure, yielded any independent control of water resource development in favor of active collaboration with numerous private interests and Congressional leaders in the development of projects desired by these groups. The fate of the Forest Service and the Corps is perhaps an extreme illustration of public agencies whose public responsibilities have been subverted to largely private ends, but they symbolize a persistent trend in governmental affairs that environmentalists consider pernicious.

Concentrating Environmental Authority

If a "clean environment" is to be more than an official piety, it requires public officials to achieve substantial changes in the content and organization of policy-making. Such innovation, while not impossible, is difficult in our typically incremental decision-making system. It is, in general, a demand that moves in two directions. In the case of air and water pollution, it is a quest for new administrative agencies with broad, potent policies to deal decisively with problems that government has largely ignored in the past. In the case of other environmental issues such as resource use, land use, waste management, and pesticide control, the objective is to reinvigorate the agencies responsible for these matters with a sense of mission—to resurrect, especially, a concern for the public interest—while providing new resources and powers to agency officials. Both goals are difficult because they represent an effort to advance policy content and procedure well beyond the *status quo* and thus generate the inherent resistance to change that is part of the incremental system.

Probably the greatest single impediment to administrative innovation, regardless of where or when it is attempted, is the strong bureaucratic resistance to major change resulting from the "sunk costs" built into existing policy and procedure. These sunk costs have mounted over a long time in an agency's bureaucratic history and have produced some very crucial rewards that are not easily or willingly jeopardized. As Anthony Downs explains:

> . . . bureaus have a powerful tendency to continue doing today whatever they did yesterday. The main reason for this inertia is that established processes represent an enormous investment in time, effort and money. . . . Years of effort, thousands of decisions (including mistakes), and a wide variety of experiences underlie the behavior patterns a bureau now uses. Moreover, it took a significant investment to get the bureau's many members and clients to accept and become habituated to its behavior patterns.[17]

Nonetheless, sound environmental protection appears to require a sacrifice of some sunk costs as the price of administrative innovation.

Several innovations appear particularly imperative. The need for *comprehensive planning* and *comprehensive authority* for environmental use and protection is very great; broad environmental planning is largely a futile enterprise unless planners have enough power to implement their programs. The need for comprehensive environmental planning arises from the interdependence of environmental problems themselves; the environment, as ecologists emphasize, is a unity in which problems and solutions are all related. In governmental terms, this means that policy arrangements ideally should ensure that various environmental programs are coordinated through some agency or

agencies with a broad view of environmental problems and an awareness of how individual programs interrelate. Comprehensive authority would then be the necessary complement which ensures that
planning will be implemented.

Achieving a comprehensive governmental approach to environmental management is a formidable task, for environmental policies
have been neither comprehensively planned nor controlled. Rather,
planning and authority have been fragmented into a bewildering
mosaic of different agencies and levels of government, producing
frequent confusion, contradiction, and frustration in environmental
management. Planning has often proceeded by fits and starts owing
to the diffusion of power within the system; incremental change was
the easiest to engineer and, hence, the common element in most
environmental programs. Both federalism and fragmentary authority
within the national administration impede comprehensive environmental planning. The distribution of authority over most major environmental programs among national, state, and local agencies has
commonly produced inconsistency or failure in the planning effort. As
the President's Council on Environmental Quality noted, independent
local governments, each exercising its own tiny ration of authority,
cannot attack water degradation adequately:

> ... their focus is often too narrow to cope with the broad environmental
> problems that cut across many jurisdictions. Agencies dealing with
> water pollution, for example, typically do not have jurisdiction over the
> geographical problem—the watersheds. Control is split, instead, among
> sewage districts, municipalities, and a multitude of other local institu-
> tions.[18]

Not only the authority but the will to enforce effective water pollution
controls is often absent at local levels. Upstream polluters, whether
private or municipal, seldom feel the need to abate water degradation
as urgently as do the recipients of the pollution downstream; communities competing for industry are often reluctant to initiate stringent
water pollution controls that might discourage business from settling
in their area.[19]

Congress's penchant for delegating authority over water pollution
abatement to state and local governments has aggravated the planning
problem. The U.S. Comptroller General's 1969 study of all federal

grants to upgrade state water treatment facilities between 1957 and 1969—a $1.2 billion program involving 9,400 grants—illustrates how the planning that Congress had encouraged failed to materialize. According to the report, the states, rather than planning for the best funding of facilities, commonly listed all municipalities needing funds in alphabetical order, left the initiative for seeking such funds to the local governments, and failed to encourage local planning for sewage treatment. Congress again showed its preference for decentralized authority over comprehensive planning in the important Water Quality Act of 1965, which left to each state such important decisions as the most desirable use for its waters and acceptable pollution levels within its jurisdiction.

A more promising approach to air and water pollution abatement would be the creation of regional authorities with comprehensive control over whole watersheds or "airsheds." This, however, would require that state and local governments relinquish some authority to regional agencies—a proposal they stoutly resist. Currently, only five river-basin authorities exist in the United States—none with very impressive credentials. The Ohio River Valley Water Development Authority, often considered the best of these regional entities, has seldom initiated proceedings against major water polluters mainly because action requires virtual unanimity among the many representatives of the eight states constituting the authority; similar requirements for near consensus on action have hampered other regional agencies.

While decentralization of authority obstructs comprehensive environmental planning, it is usually favored by major industries and other interests that bear a major cost for environmental clean-up. Industrial influence is especially strong at local and state levels; hence, business can exert considerable influence in shaping environmental policy when state and local governments are empowered to do this task. Also, state and local governments have less sophistication and fewer resources to deal with industry than has the federal government; often, in fact, major industries are better equipped with technologists and resources in the pollution control area than are governmental units. Thus, the decentralization of environmental planning authority through federalism generally works, intentionally or not, to the advantage of major polluters, while frustrating extensive planning.

At the federal level, efforts at comprehensive planning have usually been grounded in the past by the dispersion of environmental authority within Washington's bureaucracy. Many environmental problems fail to respect organizational charts and cut instead across the jurisdiction of several agencies that seldom approach solutions through coordinated efforts. Agencies with one primary environmental mission—commercial fishing, water resource development or forest management, for instance—often work zealously within a narrow view of their task that desensitizes them to the wide-ranging ecological consequences of their endeavors. Additionally, some agencies have acquired an operational independence that insulates them from the influence of attempted comprehensive planning. The need for centralized federal environmental planning has long been recognized by administrative analysts, but their exhortations were largely ignored until recently. In 1971, President Nixon responded to the mounting gravity of environmental problems by proposing in his Environmental Message that a cabinet-level Department of Natural Resources be established to plan and coordinate federal resource programs and, thus, to end the welter of existing agencies and departments sharing environmental authority. The lack of this authority has resulted in some of the following situations:

• The 1969 Santa Barbara oil spill was the responsibility of three different agencies within the Interior Department: the Bureau of Land Management (which issues federal land oil leases), the U.S. Geological Survey (which oversees the technical aspects of federal oil leases), and the Federal Water Pollution Control Administration. The Federal Water Pollution Control Administration stayed out of the crisis to avoid further confusion, and Secretary of the Interior Hickel, irritated by the lack of action in the other agencies, finally intervened directly in the crisis.

• A gypsum company requested a permit to dig into four miles of Los Padres National Forest in California, basing its request on a claim bought in 1963. The nesting grounds of the rare California condor were threatened. While the Department of the Interior's Land Management Bureau could issue mining exploration permits, the forests were under the jurisdiction of the Department of Agriculture's Forest

Service. The Forest Service could only advise the other bureau on issuing the permit but would have to supervise any regulations issued by Land Management. Further, the U.S. Geological Survey had at least a technical oversight of the mining efforts. The agencies could not agree upon issuing the permit, and consultation continues.

• The Environmental Protection Agency must share authority for any regulation of airplane noise with the Federal Aviation Agency, may set general levels of radiation for environmental safety but must accept the Nuclear Regulatory Commission's decision on how much radiation individual nuclear power plants may emit, and must "clear" all major pesticide regulations with the Department of Agriculture.

Disagreements over environmental policy would undoubtedly persist in federal agencies regardless of the degree of centralized environmental planning and authority achieved in Washington; better planning arrangements would, however, reduce the instances of deadlock, confusion, and contradiction now common with agency policies.

Even should greater centralized planning and authority be accomplished within government, such innovations—like other purely administrative alterations—would hardly be more than cosmetic touches in the name of ecology unless there also takes place some transformation in the nature and priority of administrative values among those concerned with environmental protection. Obviously, to wait until administrators acquire a set of values certified as ecologically acceptable would be to wait forever. However, a significant advance in environmental protection does seem to require that some *relative* rearrangement of values occur. Most analysts suggest that environmental protection requires at least the following changed priorities among those responsible for decisions affecting the environment:

1. *Greater emphasis on long-range environmental consequences of decisions, less on the short-range economic consequences.* For many reasons, administrators have customarily been guided in environmental decisions by short-range economic considerations. Local officials confront almost irresistible pressure to "develop" land and other resources to increase jobs, expand employment, broaden the tax base,

and satisfy local interests benefiting from economic growth. State and federal officials have often sanctioned resource development and exploitation because of short-term economic advantages—especially in creating dams and canals and in leasing rights to public land by private interests. Pollution controls were often minimal and minimally enforced out of concern for consequences. A new environmental ethic would require a greater "balancing" of interests if not an absolute priority to long-run environmental values.

2. *A devaluation of the growth ethic.* "The most primordial fact of American culture," notes one observer, "remains its emphasis upon production." Production, or "growth" in all its economic dimensions, has been an orthodoxy of American business and public officials; it is imbedded in the logic of American public policy at all levels and, with few exceptions, in the cultural outlook of most Americans. The environmental movement, however, demands that growth no longer be viewed as an unqualified good or a goal to be approached as speedily as possible—though never fully attained. Instead, wise resource use and environmental protection appear to require some restraint on growth and very thoughtful reflection on its proper course and dimensions; unless these constraints are created by public officials, resource use is likely to proceed at a pace so rapid and unguided that irreversible environmental damage and dangerous resource depletion will occur.

3. *Less emphasis on the politics of compromise.* Public officials cannot long function effectively unless they are able to routinize and stabilize their relationships with the important private interests and other governmental agencies with which they must deal. We have seen that our governmental process encourages bargaining and compromise among these competing interests, with the result that administrative policies usually represent a moderate mid-position among the contending sides of a policy issue. However, this process of seeking the middle ground in policy conflicts often works against sound environmental policy. Effective environmental protection may require that administrators advocate and enforce politics that do not belong in the mid-range of options—that they find, in brief, means to push ahead without resorting to the politics of compromise as the primary tool of administrative decision-making.

Many administrative experts would regard these prescriptions as a counsel of perfection unsuited to the harsh realities of administrative politics in Washington. It is an intriguing question whether such changes can be achieved and to what extent. What is important, however, is that most of these alternatives are implied by any significant proposal for environmental protection—that is, genuine environmental protection seems to demand both changes in substantive policy and alterations in the way decisions are made. This is one reason the environmental movement constitutes a major challenge to Washington's decision-making apparatus.

Enforcing Administrative Responsibility

Environmental administrators are rarely deliberate assassins of the public interest in a wholesome environment. They are usually conscientious, reasonably diligent, and well-intentioned individuals trying to fulfill their mission under circumstances that have often contrived to produce undesirable environmental policy. Without impugning the integrity of most administrators, however, it seems imperative that new policies aimed at environmental restoration be attended with greater emphasis on ensuring accountability and reasonable faithfulness with the administrative branch in the implementation of these policies.

The need for increasing accountability arises from the field of political forces in which administrators operate in making environmental decisions. Our earlier discussion amply illustrated the considerable advantage that private interests enjoy in pressing their claims in environmental matters upon administrators. Additionally, legislators are also major participants in the administrative process, often exerting pressure to sway administrative decisions in directions incompatible with the intent of environmental legislation. A former commissioner of the Federal Power Commission describes how legislators often collaborate with important constituents to submit administrators to the "hard sell":

> . . . if it becomes necessary, industry can turn to its true friends, those representatives or senators who understand the role of government and business. For the hard sell, discreet phone calls from distinguished

senators from the "oil patch" or the current impoverished area as to the status of a particular case usually are informative enough for a good political regulator or administrator to get the message. Or possibly someone in government needs more money which can be obtained from bonuses for offshore oil and gas concessions. There is even the possibility that upon leaving government you can secure a good consulting contract for your new firm with either industry or the local, state or federal agencies—if you are a good boy. It is tempting.[20]

To these persuasive influences must be added the administrator's frequent vulnerability to outside pressure. This situation is most often created by the ambiguity of the goals he is supposed to achieve and the absence of effective group support for decisions more consonant with environmental protection.

Faced with these conditions, administrators often cope by resorting to strategies that environmental lawyer Joseph Sax calls "nibbling" and "suboptimizing"—strategies used quite often, without conscious intent, to defeat sound environmental management. "Nibbling," suggests Sax, is a process whereby administrators continually make little compromises with their environmental responsibilities by allowing the intrusion of wrong values into their decisions. "It is so easy for an administrator to adopt the position that this is the last intrusion to be permitted, that no bad precedent is being set, and that the line will be drawn at the next case."[21] But the line is often never drawn decisively, with the result that serious environmental responsibilities are compromised severely. "Suboptimizing" is a strategy for making a decision when "all the many constraints, pressures and influences at work are taken into account."[22] This is often decision by common denominator; the policy that best satisfies the most demands is made, and, in the process, the administrator often responds most readily to whatever combination of interests can generate the most compelling pressures upon him. Such approaches to decision-making, of course, can represent a willful effort to subvert policy intended to protect the environment, but, probably in most cases, they represent simply the best approaches administrators feel they can use and still function in their own milieu.

The point is not to judge the motivation of adminstrators but to suggest why concern for accountability in environmental affairs arises so often in discussions of sound environmental management. There are many procedures through which greater accountability might be obtained. One is vigorous legislative oversight of administrative decisions, an exercise of authority well within Congress's power to investigate and monitor administrative activity. How much this would accomplish would depend on many factors: the will and ability of Congress to conduct such oversight and the dedication of legislators to sound environmental use. Based on past experience, most environmentalists do not consider such a procedure the most promising means to achieve administrative accountability. Yet another procedure might be the creation within the administrative branch of an administrative unit with the specific responsibility for reviewing the conduct of environmental policy; alternatively, a new super-agency for environmental affairs might be established and staffed with administrators at the top level who would assume comprehensive authority over most environmental programs, together with sweeping planning powers. This last suggestion, in effect, is an effort to make a new start toward environmental management with a new administrative institution and personnel lacking the vested interests and established political alliances of older agencies.

Many environmentalists, however, believe a more promising approach lies in enabling environmental groups to use the courts as an instrument to enforce accountability—a procedure that might at first seem doomed to failure since it has worked poorly in the past. In general, the federal courts have so far been reluctant to review thoroughly or overturn administrative decisions relating to the environment, partly because judges did not consider themselves sufficiently knowledgeable in the frequently technical problems involved in environmental policy and partly because, following well-established legal precedent, judges viewed such determinations as policy issues that should not be resolved in the courts.[23] The practical effect of this judicial stance was to make it difficult, and usually impossible, for ecologists to challenge administrative decisions on environmental matters through the initiation of suits. Many ecologists now believe judicial methods to enforce administrative accountability may be more promising. They cite the government's growing ecological concern, which may incline judges to greater interest in environmental affairs, the enactment of new legislation—much of which we shall discuss in Chapter 8—that encourages citizen suits against administrative agencies to enforce environmental protection, and the enactment of bills that charge administrators with detailed, specific environmental responsibilities.[24]

Regardless of which strategies, if any, prove effective in securing a significant measure of administrative accountability in the handling of environmental policy, the issue will remain of utmost importance in the long-range effectiveness of current governmental efforts at environmental restoration.

No response yet made to the environmental crisis by the federal government has greater potential significance than the enactment of the National Environmental Policy Act of 1969 and the creation of the Environmental Protection Agency. They represent the most sweeping attempts yet to deal with environmental degradation at the level of the federal government and to solve the policy-making problems that, as we have seen, could obstruct or defeat sound environmental policy. While it is far too early to assess the impact of these measures, their unusual promise and influence on the course of all major environmental policy issues sets them apart for special emphasis.

THE NATIONAL ENVIRONMENTAL POLICY ACT OF 1969

The National Environmental Policy Act of 1969 (NEPA), an unprecedented bill, declared the federal government's commitment to a broad range of environmental protection goals and measures; it is the most thorough and comprehensive statement of environmental protection policy enacted by Congress.[25] Borne through Congress on a peaking tide of public environmental concern, NEPA encountered relatively little opposition, receiving the massive legislative support usually given only to measures of the utmost gravity or triviality. Far from trivial, NEPA set in motion a series of events that would have caused many Congressmen apprehension had they anticipated the consequences soon to be evident.

NEPA begins with a very general and generous federal pledge to environmental protection. The opening section declares:

... it is the continuing policy of the Federal Government, in cooperation with State and local governments, and other concerned public and private organizations, to use all practicable means and measures ... to create and maintain conditions under which man and nature can exist in productive harmony, and fulfill the social, economic, and other requirements of present and future generations of Americans.

Congress then pledged itself to assure healthy and pleasing surroundings to citizens, to avoid degradation of the environment, to preserve historic cultural and natural aspects of our national heritage, to achieve a balance between population and resources, and to enhance the quality of renewable resources, among other specific goals. Toward these ends, the act required the President to deliver an annual Environmental Quality Report to Congress. The cutting edge of NEPA, however, is its provisions requiring "impact statements" for all federal actions affecting the environment and its creation of the Council on Environmental Quality.

The Environmental Impact Statement

The provision in NEPA that has had the greatest immediate impact on governmental policy is its requirement of an "environmental impact statement," set forth in Section 102(2)(C). This section declares that all federal agencies must accompany "every recommendation or report on proposals for legislation and other major Federal actions significantly affecting the quality of the human environment" with a detailed report that describes:

1. The environmental impact of the proposed project
2. Any adverse environmental effects that cannot be avoided should the proposal be implemented
3. Alternatives to the proposed action
4. The relationship between local short-term uses of man's environment and the maintenance and enhancement of long-term productivity
5. Any irreversible or irretrievable commitments of resources that would be involved in the proposed action should it be implemented

These "EISs" must ultimately be made available to the public and filed with the President's Council on Environmental Quality; according to guidelines established by the Council on Environmental Quality, initial drafts of these statements must be available to the public and other agencies at least ninety days prior to the contemplated action, and final statements—taking account of comments from public and private agencies—must be available to the public at least thirty days in advance of the action. After "EISs" are properly filed with the council, it may advise the President or the concerned agency about the desirability of the proposed action in light of its environmental impact.

The requirement for impact statements had a number of clearly important purposes. It was an effort to force agency administrators to make a careful, searching appraisal of the environmental effects of their activities, to give the President and his advisers a comprehensive view of the environmental impact of federal activities, and to open federal actions to challenge on grounds of environmental impact—all of which was to apply categorically to *all* federal agencies and *all* activities that might effect the environment. Moreover, the rather exacting language of the requirement left administrators with fairly clear guidelines to follow in their appraisal. If these purposes are achieved to any important degree, the act would clearly represent a major attack on many of the policy-making problems that would seem to interfere with effective environmental protection.

The impact statement has been a unique challenge to federal administrators. Administrators long accustomed to the role of advocate for their particular agency projects were now expected to engage in self-criticism and searching examination of the ecological value of their efforts. In the beginning, ambiguity and confusion reigned. The specific procedures that agencies had to follow to produce a satisfactory impact statement were unclear. The meaning of critical words and phrases in the law had to be interpreted through administrative and judicial rulings. Many agencies lacked the technical resources to prepare the required statements. Some agencies delayed and balked at the new procedures; others overwhelmed the White House with an avalanche of EISs. Gradually, the broad picture of the law's effect is emerging; it has been shaped, in large part, through case law in which judges have defined the substance and scope of its authority.

Today, eleven major federal agencies routinely prepare EISs. As they have gathered experience and developed organizational arrangements for EIS preparation, the volume of paperwork has declined through more efficient procedures. An idea of the volume of work involved can be gathered from Table 2, which monitors major agency preparations through 1975.

During the first few years of NEPA, many administrative delays resulted from impact statement preparation, including delays in licensing vital projects such as power generating plants and in constructing federal facilities. These delays have largely disappeared, although EIS preparation undoubtedly extends somewhat the time of some administrative decision-making. To a great extent, EIS preparation has now become a routine and accepted—if not universally admired—Washington procedure.

Of more importance, what has been the impact of the EIS procedure? The Council on Environmental Quality cautions that "the impacts . . . are often elusive, and it is often difficult or even impossible to credit NEPA with specific agency actions."[26] There have been

TABLE 2. Draft Environmental Impact Statements Filed, by Agency, 1970–74 and Estimated 1975

Agency	1970	1971	1972	1973	1974	Estimated 1975	January 1– June 30, 1975
DOT	61	1,293	674	432	360	205	108
COE	119	316	211	243	303	332	147
USDA	62	79	124	166	179	259	110
DOI	18	65	107	119	109	117	38
AEC	32	22	65	28	36	–	–
ERDA	–	–	–	–	–	10	4
NRC	–	–	–	–	–	23	11
HUD	3	23	26	22	21	52	37
DOD	5	27	24	19	21	44	11
GSA	3	34	6	24	26	34	12
EPA	0	16	13	26	14	40	13
All others	16	75	135	66	68	64	39
Total	319	1,950	1,385	1,145	1,137	1,180	530

SOURCE: Council on Environmental Quality, *Environmental Quality: Sixth Annual Report* (Washington, D.C., 1975), p. 641.

some documented instances in which EIS preparation has changed agency determinations:

- The Interior Department's preparation of an EIS for the 800-mile trans-Alaskan pipeline prompted numerous design changes; among other things, these minimize disruption to animal migratory routes and encourage greater protection against oil spills on the vulnerable permafrost.

- The Corps of Engineers decided to drop or abandon work or more than a dozen projects because NEPA procedures revealed significant environmental damage.

- The General Services Administration abandoned its plan to construct the Kennedy Library and Museum immediately adjacent to Harvard Square when the EIS indicated major environmental disruptions to the area as a result.[27]

Moreover, many agency plans never reach the stage requiring a formal EIS because preliminary work indicates that the environmental costs would be so substantial that plans are abandoned. There is little doubt, then, that the requirement for EIS preparation has caused some changes in administrative behavior. EIS preparation, however, is far from satisfying to the law's proponents in several respects. Many agencies continue to mystify, bore, or confuse those outside the agency, particularly ecologists and the public, with their EISs—sometimes deliberately—rather than enlighten them on the ecological implications of decisions. "Too many statements," complains the Council on Environmental Quality, "have been deadly, voluminous, and obscure and . . . have often been inordinately long, with too much space devoted to unnecessary description rather than to analysis of impacts and alternatives."[28] Moreover, it has become clear as judicial interpretation of NEPA grows that agencies will seldom be *compelled* to make decisions in line with the environmental costs and benefits described in EISs; although agencies must prepare EISs and administrators must consider them, no agency, apparently, can be bound by the recommendations in an EIS—it is, in the judicial view, an *advisory* document. Thus, when the Secretary of Transportation tentatively approved in 1976 a permit for SST jets to land in New York and

Washington, this was done in spite of an EIS that described the environmental problems likely to result, including especially high noise levels. The dominant judicial view of the NEPA was summarized in a 1971 ruling:

> An EIS leaves room for a responsible exercise of discretion and may not require particular substantive results in particular [administrative] determinations. . . .
>
> Perhaps the greatest substantive importance of NEPA is to require the Atomic Energy Commission and other agencies to *consider* environmental issues just as they consider other matters within their mandates.[29]

The Council on Environmental Quality

A second major provision of the NEPA created the President's Council on Environmental Quality (CEQ), the highest-level advisory body to the President on environmental affairs. The CEQ is part of the Executive Office of the President and thus shares a formal status equal to that of the President's Council of Economic Advisers and other bodies that are top-level staff arms of the Presidency. The council, appointed by the President with the advice and consent of the Senate, consists of three members (one of whom is designated the chairman) serving at the pleasure of the Chief Executive.

The National Environmental Policy Act assigns many potentially important functions to the CEQ. It is expected to advise the President in the preparation of the annual Environmental Quality Report, gather "timely and important information" regarding environmental problems and transmit it to the President, review federal programs for their environmental implications, recommend legislation to the President, create independent environmental studies, and review environmental impact statements from the other federal agencies. In later legislation, Congress added to the CEQ a small professional staff, the Office of Environmental Quality, to assist it in discharging these responsibilities. The CEQ's actual influence will largely depend on how the President chooses to use the council. Like other White House advisory groups, the CEQ has the prerogative to inform, advise, and warn the President, but it has no right to be heeded and no operating authority over other agencies; it has no constituency of its own, nor funding for more than a modest level of independent activity. To its inherent weakness caused by a lack of political or administrative strength is added its dependence on the President to define what role it should play in the decision-making process. Since President Nixon had opposed the council's creation and Congress appropriated very limited funds for it, its initial prospects did not seem bright. Nonetheless, the council has taken the initiative in creating detailed specifications for impact statements, for reviewing them and advising the President on federal programs in the light of these statements. Moreover, the council appears to have largely shaped the President's 1973 and 1974 legislation proposals on the environment, and its advice was cited by President Nixon as a major reason for his unprecedented decision to halt the Cross Florida Barge Canal because of its detrimental environmental impact. From the viewpoint of environmental specialists, the council's annual reports constitute a very important source of data and policy information on environmental affairs.

THE ENVIRONMENTAL PROTECTION AGENCY

In December, 1970, President Nixon officially created the Environmental Protection Agency (EPA) with the concurrence of Congress and thereby initiated the most imaginative, sweeping federal effort to restructure and revitalize the making of pollution control policy. The EPA, now the most important "action" agency in Washington's attack on pollution, has rapidly acquired great attention and exposure nationally because it is usually the organizational arena for major pollution policy conflicts.

The EPA represents an effort to combat the decentralization and fragmentation of power in the field of federal pollution control; it is intended to provide a framework in which long-range policy planning and policy coordination can be achieved. To centralize the administration of pollution control in Washington, the EPA absorbed five major pollution programs that had previously been parceled out among various agencies. Specifically, it acquired authority over (1) water pollution policy formerly administered by the Federal Water Quality Administration in the Interior Department, (2) air pollution policy supervised by the National Air Pollution Control Administration in the Department of Health, Education and Welfare, (3) solid waste management programs that had been part of Health, Education and Welfare, (4) the setting of standards and guidelines for radiation control previously done by the Federal Radiation Council, and (5) the registration of pesticides and standard-setting for other toxic substances previously under the jurisdictions of the departments of Agriculture, and Health, Education and Welfare. Unlike the Council on Environmental Quality, the EPA is a "line agency" with great operating authority and resources. Not only has it acquired the authority and responsibility for pollution problems that were previously bestowed on the agencies it supplanted, but it is likely to have operational authority over most new federal pollution policies. With a budget of $5.2 billion in fiscal 1975 and more than 9,000 employees, the EPA has more fiscal and manpower resources than any other regulatory agency and several Cabinet departments. It runs the nation's largest public works program—the funding of municipal waste treatment facilities under the 1972 Water Pollution Control Act Amendments—and spends about $2 million daily on all its activities. It is responsible for the difficult and essential job of writing the regulatory guidelines that implement the nation's major air and water pollution control laws; it has produced, in this task, more than 2,000 pages of regulations so far.

Since the effectiveness of federal pollution control will largely depend upon the aggressiveness and initiative of the EPA, the long-run political status of the agency is crucial. Under its first two administrators, William D. Ruckelshaus and Russel E. Train, the agency usually adopted a firm, and sometimes tough, stance toward its regulatory responsibilities and quickly earned a reputation for being less amenable to influence from regulated interests than other regulatory bodies have been. Especially because the Nixon and Ford administrations were unsympathetic to the agency's major regulatory objectives, the agency has operated through most of its brief history without strong White House support and often in conflict with Presidential preferences on ecology issues. The agency has been under continuing pressure to relinquish many of its regulatory responsibilities back to the agencies from which the authority was originally derived—environmentalists charge that regulated industries have been abetting this pressure because they believe they will get a more sympathetic hearing from the older agencies. In 1973, for instance, the nuclear power industry won a victory when President Nixon instructed the EPA to defer to the Atomic Energy Commission's definition of safe radiation levels for nuclear power plants. Generally, these pressures have been ineffective; the EPA remains embattled but largely in control of the original authority with which it was invested. Although Congress has often been critical of the EPA, it has generally protected the agency's authority to regulate most environmentally important economic activities.

It is the fate of all regulatory agencies to satisfy no one. Regulated interests commonly charge that they are unfairly and excessively burdened by agency actions; those supporting regulatory policies are likely to interpret any compromise as a "sellout," any delay as deliberate obstruction, and most agency dealings with regulated interests as subversive to the public interest. Thus, regulatory bodies are in a constant cross fire of criticism; so it has been with the EPA. The auto industry, for example, has repeatedly charged the agency with excessive zeal and inflexibility in its formulation of auto emission regulations. Environmentalists have criticized the EPA's delay in enforcing auto emission controls. In fact, as we shall observe in the next chapter, the EPA has been charged with the enormous responsibility of creating both the scientific foundations and the detailed implementing procedures for environmental programs that have no precedent; consequently, almost all its activities move into untried and unproven directions. Although the agency is too new to have established a clear reputation, it has generally identified itself with the broad values of the ecology movement and, in these respects, does not appear to have been "captured," as most other regulatory bodies are, by its regulated interests.

SUMMARY: ECOLOGY AND THE POLITICS OF PROCEDURE

It should now be apparent why the creation of a truly operative policy of environmental protection is an arduous task, though not an unattainable goal. The struggle must proceed at two levels. At the policy level, it is a drive to ensure that the stated ends of policy and its actual substance are compatible with environmental protection. At the procedural level, it is a struggle to ensure that the way in which policy decisions are implemented will be conducive to the principles of environmental protection to which policy is ostensibly committed. The procedural issue, as we have seen, has been a formidable impediment to environmental protection in the past, for the design of the policy process has been one of those pikes upon which sound environmental policy has been impaled, a structural feature of our basic policy process that environmentalists cannot easily design out of the governmental system. In effect, there is a "politics of procedure" in American government, a distribution of advantage and influence ordained by the architecture of our traditional decision-making system that has worked, and may well continue to work, to the disadvantage of ecology.

The creation of the National Environmental Protection Act and the Environmental Protection Agency indicates the stirring of efforts to break out of traditional decision-making forms. Yet, there is no assurance that these acts may not in the end become "symbolic legislation" that fails to deliver the real rewards of environmental protection desired by the environmental movement. What seems apparent, in any case, is that both substantive and procedural changes must take place in Washington policy-making if the federal government's very uneven record of past ecological achievements is to be improved. Whether this can be accomplished, and to what extent, will largely be written in the record of Washington's attack on particular environmental problems. Let us turn, then, in the remaining chapters to a number of specific environmental issues in an effort to ascertain what has been accomplished, substantively and procedurally, in dealing with these issues.

NOTES

1. This point is made in summary form in Charles E. Lindblom, *The Policy-Making Process* (Englewood Cliffs, N.J.: Prentice-Hall, 1968), chapter 1. Its elaboration, from which much of the subsequent discussion is drawn, may be found in Charles E. Lindblom, *The Intelligence of Democracy* (New York: The Free Press, 1965).
2. This point is made cogently in David B. Truman, *The Governmental Process* (New York: Alfred A. Knopf, 1960), chapter 9.

3. Charles E. Lindblom, *op. cit.,* p. 26.
4. *Ibid.,* p. 27.
5. Theodore Lowi, "The Public Philosophy: Interest-Group Liberalism," *American Political Science Review,* March, 1967, p. 18.
6. Grant McConnell, *Private Power and American Democracy* (New York: Vintage Books, 1968), p. 162.
7. The role of advisory bodies in administrative decisions is usefully summarized in Harold Seidman, *Politics, Position and Power: The Dynamics of Federal Organization* (New York: Oxford University Press, 1970), pp. 237–68; the figure cited is taken from this discussion.
8. Morton Grodzins, "The Federal System," in Aaron Wildavsky, *American Federalism in Perspective* (Boston: Little, Brown and Co., 1967), p. 257.
9. *Ibid.,* p. 260.
10. Francis E. Rourke, *Bureaucracy, Politics and Public Policy* (Boston: Little, Brown and Co., 1969), p. 103.
11. *Ibid.,* p. 113.
12. This is certainly the sense in which it is commonly discussed among academic social scientists. See, for example, Glendon Schubert, *The Public Interest* (Glencoe, Ill.: The Free Press, 1960).
13. Matthew A. Crenson, *The Un-Politics of Air Pollution* (Baltimore: The Johns Hopkins Press, 1971), p. 137.
14. This argument is suggested by Ted Caldwell and Leslie L. Roos, Jr., "Voluntary Compliance and Pollution Abatement," in Leslie L. Roos, Jr., *The Politics of Ecosuicide* (New York: Holt, Rinehart and Winston, 1971), p. 243. Federal policy guaranteeing multiple use of the national forests might be considered a case of such symbolic legislation. See chapter 7 for a discussion of this issue.
15. Marver H. Bernstein, *Regulating Business by Independent Commission* (Princeton, N.J.: Princeton University Press, 1955), p. 156.
16. *Ibid.,* p. 154.
17. Anthony Downs, *Inside Bureaucracy* (Boston: Little, Brown and Co., 1967), p. 195.
18. Council on Environmental Quality, *Environmental Quality, 1971* (Washington, D.C., 1971), p. 15.
19. Local views are nicely summarized in J. Clarence Davies, *The Politics of Pollution* (New York: Pegasus Press, 1970), pp. 130 ff.
20. Charles R. Ross, "The Federal Government as an Inadvertent Advocate of Environmental Degradation," in Harold W. Helfrich, Jr., ed., *The Environmental Crisis* (New Haven: Yale University Press, 1970), p. 182.
21. Joseph L. Sax, *Defending the Environment* (New York: Alfred A. Knopf, 1971), p. 55.

22. *Ibid.,* p. 53.

23. The argument for a judicial approach is most carefully presented in *Defending the Environment* by Joseph L. Sax, noted above. A summary with a slightly different emphasis may be found by the same author in "The Search for Environmental Quality: The Role of the Courts," in Harold W. Halfrich, Jr., *The Environmental Crisis* (New Haven: Yale University Press, 1970), pp. 99–114.

24. Some early results of this philosophy are analyzed in Walter A. Rosenbaum and Paul A. Roberts, "The Year of Spoiled Pork: Comments on the Role of the Courts as Environmental Defenders," *Law and Society Review,* Fall, 1972, pp. 33–60.

25. Public Law 91–190, January 1, 1970.

26. Council on Environmental Quality, *Environmental Quality: Sixth Annual Report* (Washington, D.C., 1975), p. 626.

27. These examples are cited in *ibid.,* p. 628 ff. See also Frederick R. Anderson, *NEPA in the Courts: A Legal Analysis of the National Environmental Policy Act* (Baltimore: The Johns Hopkins University Press, 1973), particularly ch. 7.

28. Council on Environmental Quality, *Sixth Annual Report,* p. 632.

29. *Calvert Cliffs Coordinating Committee* v. *U.S. Atomic Energy Commission,* 449 F. 2d. 1112 (1971). For a detailed analysis of this judicial viewpoint, see Walter A. Rosenbaum, "The End of Illusion: NEPA and the Limits of Judicial Review," in Stuart S. Nagel, ed., *Environmental Politics* (New York: Praeger Publishers, 1974), pp. 260–77.

5. "You've Got to Hit Them with a Two-by-Four": Regulating Air and Water Pollution

In his brief tenure as Secretary of the Interior, Walter J. Hickel learned a lesson. Before the President permanently benched him from the Nixon team for "personal disloyalty" in 1970, Hickel had earned the respect of many ecologists for his progressively tough stand against environmental degradation, a surprise to many who initially considered him a weak conservationist. One incident that nourished Hickel's disenchantment with federal environment regulation was the aftermath of the 1969 Santa Barbara oil spill. Convinced that the California incident arose from corporate negligence toward safety regulations and weak bureaucratic enforcement, Hickel ordered an inspection of 7,000 oil rigs in the Gulf of Mexico that revealed hundreds lacking the federally required safety chokes; immediate prosecutions were ordered. Reflecting upon that incident, the Secretary propounded what might be called Hickel's Law for dealing with pollution violators: "You've got to hit them with a two-by-four to make them believe you."[1]

Until recently, Hickel's Law did not inspire the federal government's approach to pollution control. Past attempts were indecisive, reflecting a general weakness of federal pollution regulations that were encumbered with vague or unenforceable standards, irresolute leadership, and fragmented authority. The federal government's historically crabwise approach was abruptly ended in the early 1970's when mounting evidence of environmental degradation and the conspicuous failure of past abatement policies forced Washington to break with its past incremental approach to air and water quality management. Responding to what seemed a massive public demand for more incisive measures, Congress ordained new programs moving so suddenly and ambitiously beyond past approaches as to introduce a new scheme of air and water quality management in the United States. With this new approach came unprecedented and unexpected problems but also opportunities, for the first time, to make significant advances in pollution control.

From the beginning, Washington's approach to air and water pollution abatement has been based upon a "standards and enforcement" approach. Before examining how this policy was evolved, it will be helpful to briefly describe its underlying philosophy.

STANDARDS AND ENFORCEMENT

Only a relative handful of Americans are likely to understand much about the intricacies of pollution control policy. Americans may be pardoned for their ignorance. The design of federal policy-making on air and water pollution seems extraordinarily convoluted and complex, abounding with technicalities and bristling with an esoteric vocabulary—a situation that easily confounds the layman and deflates the resolve of even the well-motivated investigator. The complexities, however, are not necessarily as forbidding as they may appear. Once one understands the architecture of this system and its technical vocabulary, both the logic and the problems inherent in federal pollution abatement are revealed.

Essentially, the standards-and-enforcement method of pollution abatement involves a series of five phases through which pollution policy must pass before it is fully operative. Leaving aside for a moment the matter of which governmental officials will make and implement the policies at each phase, we can briefly describe the system in broad outline.[2]

Goal Setting

In theory, the first step in pollution abatement begins with a determination by public officials of the ultimate objectives they seek to accomplish through air and water pollution management. In the case of water pollution, for example, this may consist of a set of different uses to be assigned various water bodies; some might be designated for recreational use, others for navigation or commercial traffic, still others for industrial purposes—many categories and combinations are possible. In the case of ambient air, the goal may be to prevent the creation or aggravation of various respiratory illnesses, to eliminate smog, or to reduce crop damage. Logically, the specification of goals is the necessary first step in pollution abatement because it establishes the target for abatement policy. In practice, goals are sometimes vague or unspecified; there may be scant information available concerning what pollution levels are compatible with various goals or, especially in air pollution matters, officials may be content to pledge themselves to achieve the maximum abatement possible with existing technology.

Criteria

Criteria are technical data, commonly supplied by research scientists, that indicate what pollutants are associated with environmental damage and how different levels and combinations of pollutants will affect the environment. The practical purpose of criteria is to give public officials some operational concept of what pollutant levels they must achieve if various "goals" for air and water purity are to be realized. If, for instance, officials are pledged to reducing the danger of respiratory illness from ambient air in industrial centers, they will need to know what effect varying levels of sulfur oxide may have on humans. In a similar vein, if officials want to protect a river for a recreational use such as fishing, they will need to know how much organic waste can be tolerated before its biochemical oxygen demand (BOD) robs sport fish of necessary oxygen; officials may also want data concerning what BOD levels are desirable for various types of sport fish. Such criteria must be established for each pollutant.

Creating criteria for major air and water contaminants is extremely slow, laborious, and costly. Until the 1960's, little such research had been conducted. Only in late 1971 did the Environmental Protection Agency begin the first large-scale survey of industrial wastes discharged into the nation's waterways; although the Council on Environmental Quality estimates that more than one hundred different indexes of environmental quality should be studied, little data have been assembled. With adequate funding (which is not always dependable), reliable data take years to accumulate, and even then may be extremely contentious. Arguments arise not only among scientists who may disagree about the reliability of the data, but also among scientists, public officials, and the principal interests affected by pollution abatement. Although criteria are supposed to be only "advisory" to public officials, once scientists create such a standard for a given pollutant it is often regarded as a final verdict. Thus, if researchers advise that a given concentration of particulates seems likely to create chronic smog, officials may treat this as the particulate level to be recommended for smog control. Understandably, those interests who think they will suffer from such a decision are likely to attack the actual pollutant criteria.[3] In any case, these measures for major air and water contaminants are clearly essential for effective, rational pollution control. Although public officials have often been forced to set air and water quality standards without adequate criteria, as more refined criteria become available they should form the basis for policy decisions.

Quality Standards

Goals and criteria are a prelude to the critical business of establishing air and water quality standards—the maximum levels of various pollutants that will be tolerated in bodies of water and ambient air. As a practical matter, creating air and water quality standards amounts to defining what the public, acting through its officials, will consider pollution to be. An adequate set of quality standards should specify which contaminants will be monitored, what the maximum tolerable amounts of the contaminants will be, and what variation, if any, in levels and combinations of pollutants will be accepted if differing qualities of air or water are to be created.

An illustration of air quality standards can be drawn from the National Primary Ambient Air Standards issued by the EPA to define "that level of ambient air quality which is requisite to protect public health." In Table 3 are listed, in terms of parts per million (ppm), the quality standards for the six pollutants concurrently covered.[4] Maximum concentrations are not to be exceeded more than once a year for any named pollutant.

Emission Standards

Air and water quality standards are only a statement of aspirations unless they are accompanied by appropriate emission standards that describe the acceptable level of pollutants from important sources of air and water contamination. Emission standards are the cutting edge of pollution abatement; a successful program of pollution control needs emission standards as an essential ingredient. If emission standards are to be effective, they must clearly indicate the limits of tolerable pollution from all important sources and should be devised so that they are related to the air or water quality goals set by policy-makers. Because air or water quality standards are almost impotent by themselves, proponents of stringent pollution control have always insisted that tough, explicit, and thorough emission controls accompany all abatement programs.

Emission controls are often bitterly controversial. Scientists and economists have often encountered extreme difficulty in determining how much of a pollution "load" within a given body of water or air can be attributed to specific sources; this, in turn, often compounds the problem of apportioning the responsibility for pollution abatement equitably among a large number of polluters.[5] Moreover, the technology of emission measurement is still relatively primitive. Businessmen commonly balk at strict emission management, frequently arguing that they are forced to accept responsibility for sometimes severe emissions cutbacks when their actual contribution to a pollution problem remains problematical. They often assert that "premature" emission standards saddle them with a heavier burden of capital investment for pollution control equipment than more careful research would justify. Not infrequently, they argue that the technology required to achieve various emission standards is unavailable or prohibitively expensive. Public officials, exposed to the full weight of this industrial backlash, are often sorely pressed to yield ground. They not only have to contend with the ire of influential businessmen but also have to face a shortage of trained pollution abatement personnel and

TABLE 3.   National Primary Ambient Air Quality Standards
Established by the U.S. Environmental Protection Agency, 1971

Substance	Primary Standard
Sulfur dioxide (SO_2)	80 macrogm/m^3 (0.03 ppm) 365 microgm/m^3 (0.14 ppm) maximum in 24 hours
Particulates	75 microgm/m^3 annual geometric mean 260 microgm/m^3 maximum in 24 hours
Carbon monoxide (CO)	10 milligm/m^3 (9 ppm) maximum in 8 hours 40 milligm/m^3 (35 ppm) maximum in 1 hour
Photochemical oxidants	160 microgm/m^3 (0.08 ppm) maximum in 1 hour
Hydrocarbons (HC)	160 microgm/m^3 (0.24 ppm) maximum in 3 hours, 6 a.m.–9 a.m.
Nitrogen dioxide (NO_2)	100 microgm/m^3 (0.05 ppm) annual arithmetic mean

often a lack of sophisticated equipment for the essential monitoring
of factory emissions; it is easy, as well as expedient, for them to
rationalize vague or weak emission requirements or to sanction long
delays in setting the requirements while "further study" is undertaken. Whatever the real or alleged obstacles of effective emission

controls may be, setting quality standards for air and water without a viable emission control system will be largely an exercise in futility.

Enforcement

A great diversity of enforcement procedures might be used to ensure that air and water quality standards are achieved; adequate enforcement measures, as Hickel's Law implies, must carry enough force to command the respect of those subject to pollution regulations. Satisfactory enforcement schemes have several characteristics: They enable public officials to act with reasonable speed (and very rapidly, in case of emergencies) to curb pollution, they carry sufficiently strong penalties to encourage compliance, and they do not enable public officials to evade a responsibility to act against violations when action is imperative. It is desirable, moreover, that officials have a range of enforcement options that might, at one extreme, consist of little more than gentle prodding to secure compliance, all the way to court action and criminal penalties for severe, chronic, or reckless violations. Flexible, rigorous enforcement must be a component of sound pollution abatement, but abatement—like other regulatory policies—still depends heavily on voluntary compliance. It is impossible to initiate enforcement proceedings against all suspected violators or to guarantee compliance only through the threat of enforcement proceedings. Enforcement, in short, is considered the last resort in pollution abatement, not the everyday working method for the system.

The effectiveness of these procedures depends upon how rigorously they are followed, upon who implements them, upon bringing technical and scientific resources to the tasks, and upon the will to make them work.

PRESSURE POINTS: THE POLITICS OF ABATEMENT

"What people get from government," Murray Edelman reminds us, "is what administrators do about their problems rather than the promises of statutes, constitutions or oratory."[6] It is the business of the EPA to translate the "promises" of a standards/enforcement scheme into specific policy. This translation of law into policy triggers the administrative struggle over pollution control. It would be a relatively simple matter to make this translation if the law were unambiguous in its meaning, clear in its objectives, precise in details, and free of organizational confusion. However, pollution laws, in common with most legislation, are often written with cloudy language and inconsistent approaches, with deliberate ambiguities and convenient silences to conceal Congressional inabilities to reconcile conflicting viewpoints. Moreover, it is impossible for Congress to legislate without leaving to the law's administrative stewards a great freedom to interpret and define key terms; this is so because pollution control legislation embraces a multitude of highly technical and complex procedures about which most Congressmen are relatively ignorant. They must trust the expertise of the bureaucracy to flesh out the bare bones of the law with the necessary professional judgments and procedures to make it work.

The catalyst to the political struggle over pollution abatement is *administrative discretion*—that is, the ability of the administrator to decide when, where, and how to interpret the law. Political pressure flows to points in the implementation process where discretion exists; here, administrative behavior is most sensitive to influence. From opening line to closing paragraph, pollution control laws are permeated with administrative discretion. As a commonplace example, we can consider a section of the Federal Water Pollution Control Act Amendments (1972), which authorize EPA's administrator to control "toxic pollutants:"

> The Administrator shall . . . publish . . . a list which includes any toxic pollutant or combination of such pollutants for which an effluent standard shall be established. . . . The Administrator in publishing such list shall take into account the toxicity of the pollutant, its persistence, degradability, the usual or potential presence of the affected organisms in any waters, the importance of the affected organisms. . . .
> If after a public hearing the Administrator finds that a modification of such proposed standard . . . is justified, a revised effluent standard (or prohibition) for such pollutant or combination shall be promulgated immediately.[7]

Stripped of its legal jargon, this section authorizes the administrator to decide what pollutants will be considered "toxic," to decide what levels will be tolerated from pollution sources, whether the pollutant will be completely prohibited or only limited, whether it may be advisable to revise the original decision, and—in doing all this—to consider such things as the persistence of the poison, how rapidly it disappears naturally, and what organisms are affected by it. Perhaps hundreds of major industrial plants will be affected by such decisions.

It is the business of lobbyists for industry and environmentalists to know who exercises discretion and to influence it when possible. Among the points where discretion occurs, the following are common:

1. *When words, phrases, or policy objectives are vague.* Congress may deliberately shift responsibility to administrators for settling disputes between interests in conflict over how a law should be phrased; sometimes the law is vague because legislators themselves do not know how to interpret it. This amounts to tossing the bureaucracy a "hot potato." The Federal Water Pollution Control Act, for instance, requires the EPA to regulate spills of oils and other hazardous substances in "navigable waters" of the United States. Defining this term amounts to declaring where regulation shall occur. But this phrase is extremely unclear. This fuzziness, notes one expert, "bears all the earmarks of deliberate ambiguity designed to paper over irreconcilable disagreements among [legislators] over the desired scope of federal jurisdiction."[8] Nonetheless, the administrator is expected to decide. At this point, partisans for all sides with something to gain or lose by the definition are bound to gravitate to the point where the decision is made in hope of obtaining an interpretation congenial to their interests.

2. *When technical standards must be created.* Current air and water pollution law requires the EPA to define standards for major pollutants, to prescribe the necessary control technology, to decide whether compliance deadlines are appropriate or (in some cases) whether to relax them, to decide if a regulated interest is doing all it can technically to control its pollutants. Legitimate arguments often arise between experts concerning what decisions should be made. Often there will be no consensus among experts; sometimes there is no information available to inform the participants. In the absence of definitive technical information, administrators must nonetheless

make these decisions by selecting from among alternatives. For example, the American Smelter and Refining Company, producing 8 per cent of the nation's copper, objected when the Puget Sound Air Pollution Control Agency decided to impose upon the company a more stringent control standard for arsenic trioxide than the company was achieving on its stacks. The company asserted that it might have to close the plant if new controls were required; moreover, it noted that evidence was lacking to prove that arsenic trioxide was a significant health hazard.[9] Since local officials were acting under authority of the EPA, the agency faced decisions. Although there were no federal standards for arsenic trioxide, should the EPA conclude it was nonetheless a hazardous substance? Could it defend the decision scientifically? Did it have sufficient data to insist that the company could better control its pollutants? Whenever technical data do not overwhelmingly support an administrative ruling, a political conflict almost inevitably erupts. The regulated interests can force the issue into years of deliberation and litigation. Following this strategy, the Minnesota Reserve Mining Company, an industrial giant, delayed enforcement of an EPA order to cease dumping taconite into Lake Superior for seven years. At a cost of $6 million in legal fees, it succeeded in challenging the technical data supporting the EPA position until, in 1976, the federal courts finally ended its appeals.[10]

3. *When compliance deadlines are flexible.* Air and water pollution legislation bristles with explicit compliance deadlines for various programs. But administrators are also given discretion to extend them. Legislation is particularly generous in granting the administrator authority to extend compliance deadlines when, in his opinion, economic hardships or other inequities will result from strict enforcement. Thus, the Clean Air Amendments (1970) instruct the EPA to create standards for pollution control on all new pollution sources but "to take into account the cost of achieving such reduction" by the required deadline. A compliance deadline may also be relaxed, in many instances, if the EPA determines it is beyond the technical ability of a polluter to install the proper controls in the required time. Deciding whether a given deadline works an economic hardship or whether a type of pollution control is technically possible involves a great freedom for judgment on the part of the administrators.

4. *When enforcement is discretionary.* Few provisions in current air and water legislation *compel* the federal government to stop a polluting activity. Most often, enforcement actions depend upon an official judgment, as in Section 112 of the Clean Air Amendments, which instructs the administrator to regulate any pollutant from a stationary source when, "in his judgment," it "may cause or contribute to any increase in mortality or an increase in serious irreversible or incapacitating illness." Even when an enforcement action is initiated, officials are commonly given options in enforcement methods; these may range from seeking an informal understanding that certain pollutants will be controlled to asking the courts to issue a fine or injunction against an offending party.

Looking at these diverse points in the administrative process at which political struggles develop, it is obvious that few aspects of air and water pollution control are free of political conflict. More importantly, all these points of political sensitivity mean that implementation customarily becomes bargaining between government officials and regulated interests to determine how discretionary judgments will be made. Because there often is no inherently "correct" decision—or, at least, no authoritative rule exists when decisions must first be made —administrative determinations will often be shaped by the play of competing interests. This is particularly true in current air and water pollution policy because, as we shall observe, it permits an uncommonly large number of discretionary judgments.

FROM INCREMENTAL TO SPECULATIVE POLICY

For twenty years prior to 1970, Congress experimented with different variations on the standards/enforcement approach to pollution abatement. Building incrementally upon each other, these laws slowly expanded the role of federal agencies in the task of air and water quality management but never produced vigorous federal action. Congressional legislation was flawed in several ways. To begin, the laws placed almost all the responsibility upon the states for initiating pollution abatement procedures, for defining standards and enforcing controls. Moreover, federal standards meant to guide state action were vague, often ambiguous, and commonly so hedged with qualifications as to be almost meaningless. Further, enforcement procedures were tortuously complicated and cumbersome; they intimidated nobody. Finally, much authority granted to federal officials to obtain some compliance with the law was highly discretionary and seldom used.[11]

The Clean Air Act (1963) and the Water Pollution Control Act (1956)—the first significant Congressional efforts to define a role for Washington in pollution abatement—were alike in their insistence that pollution abatement was a "uniquely local problem" in which a "partnership" between federal and state was most appropriate for action. This deference to the states was continued in other provisions of the bills, which, for example, permitted federal officials to intervene in pollution abatement only at state request. Such reliance upon state authority was virtually a prescription for inaction. Few states would voluntarily write or enforce stringent pollution controls. Quite the contrary, the states—eager to lure industry and vulnerable to industry's threats to move elsewhere or to close plants—would engage in a tacit competition to avoid pollution policies that offended major industry. Local governments were often willing to become "pollution havens" if it appeared to promise an economic boost to the community. Thus, concludes Clarence Davies, a major impediment to effective pollution management has been "the existence of local governments, each jealously guarding its prerogatives and each diligently ignoring or working at cross-purposes with its neighboring governments."[12] Aside from largely empty admonitions to the states to begin pollution abatement procedures, this early legislation was distinctive for providing some modest financial assistance for local waste treatment facilities, for appropriating some funds for federal research, and, as we shall observe, for creating an enforcement process that almost never worked.

By the mid-1960's it was apparent that the states were doing little to abate air and water pollution. Having exhorted the states, Congress now moved a bit more vigorously to prod them into action. In the Water Quality Act (1965) and the Air Quality Act (1967), essentially amendments to earlier legislation, Congress ordained that the states should establish definite air and water pollution control jurisdictions, should create pollution standards and control procedures, and should meet explicit compliance deadlines. In the Air Quality Act, for instance, the Secretary of HEW was authorized to create "air quality regions" for which the states would create air quality standards. Once standards were set with federal research assistance, the states would submit for federal approval their "implementation plans" to achieve the standards. Essentially the same approach was used in water pollution policy: The states were to set water quality standards, to produce implementation plans, and to enforce them.

The new procedures, however, were riddled with ambiguities and constraints on federal action to enforce their provisions. Nowhere in the Clean Air Act or its amendments was the crucial term "air pollution" defined; as a result, no firm statutory standard existed for state guidance.[13] In neither air nor water pollution abatement did federal officials insist upon a state "nondegradation" policy—that is, upon a policy that prevented substantially clean air or water bodies from being polluted to some degree. The Water Quality Act applied only to *interstate* bodies of water; consequently, almost 80 per cent of the nation's waterways were excluded from the law's ambit. State "implementation plans" were often written without provisions for effective effluent controls from major polluters of air and water. Although both new laws contained compliance deadlines for the creation of state implementation plans, the states seldom met them. By late 1971, four years after the statutory deadline, less than thirty states had water quality standards and implementation plans approved by Washington as required by the 1965 legislation; in 1970, no state had a federally approved implementation plan for air pollution control—in part because Washington itself had been slow in designating the "air quality regions" to be affected.[14]

No element in federal pollution legislation of this period was more ineffectual than its enforcement provisions. Federal officials could seldom initiate any enforcement action unless requested to do so by the states—an invitation that seldom came. Although the 1965 Water Quality Act did authorize federal abatement action when water pollution appeared an imminent danger to public health, the basic enforcement mechanism was the "conference" system. Used in both air and water pollution abatement, this system required federal and state officials to show adequate "reason to believe" serious pollution existed. Then they (1) ordered a "conference" of all parties involved in the pollution at which "recommendations" for abatement were made which (2) federal officials pondered and (3) followed with a "hearing" if the pollution persisted and (4) continued with court action if the hearing did not produce significant results. At this point, the court might, or might not, decide to order a cessation of the pollution. Since each step might be repeated and years could elapse between steps the system proceeded at a glacial pace and was seldom invoked. From 1956 through 1971, only fifty-one conferences were ordered on water pollution, only four reached an advanced stage, and only one ended in court. Only two court actions resulted from this system: an order to the city of St. Joseph, Missouri, to control its waste water (this took fifteen years from first step to court order) and an air pollution abatement order against a chicken rendering plant in Bishop, Maryland, whose air emissions were so foul that they sickened investigating officials.

In short, there appeared to be neither a will nor a way for federal officials to act incisively against pollution. "With unbounded discretion as their only reed, federal agency officials engaged primarily in cajoling with little regulatory significance."[15]

The only tangible results in pollution abatement were achieved by the Motor Pollution Control Act (1965). By the early 1970's, the average American buying a new car paid about $50 for pollution control equipment required under the act—a modest penance, indirectly ordained by Congress, for the privilege of owning the most proficient air polluter. Since almost two-thirds of the total volume of air pollutants released yearly result from internal combustion engines, advocates of federal pollution control had long pressed Congress to legislation on emission controls for trucks and automobiles. The Motor Pollution Control Act ordered the Secretary of HEW to establish emission standards for new motor vehicles; the first regulations, to apply to new vehicles in the 1968 model year, were intended to reduce hydrocarbons and carbon monoxide emissions by 90 per cent each. Beginning in 1968, manufacturers were expected to secure a "certificate" from Washington, indicating that new models complied with the federal emission standards, before the vehicle could be sold.

The End of Incrementalism

By 1970, neither federal air nor water pollution policies had achieved any notable results—with the exception of modest gains in auto emission controls. Congress, in a striking reversal of form, became convinced that only vigorous federal authority combined with stringent standards and rigorous enforcement provisions would be likely to reverse the progressive deterioration of the nation's air and water. Thus, between 1970 and 1973, federal legislators rewrote the nation's air and water pollution policies through creation of the Clean Air Amendments (1970) and the Federal Water Pollution Control Act Amendments (1972), which ostensively "amended" earlier legislation but in effect created a whole new approach to the standards/enforcement procedure.

Essentially, Congress ordained policy goals, standards, and control procedures that leaped well beyond proven technical capacities, existing scientific research, and past abatement experience.[16] The key to this approach was a determination to "press technology"—to force pollution control research and techniques to reach levels required to implement the law. Additionally, the laws set explicit, demanding compliance deadlines for each phase of the programs. In both laws, Congress asserted a vigorous federal role and enlarged federal authority enormously in carrying out pollution abatement. Compliance procedures were to be rigorous and credible. And all this was done without the customary long, accommodating negotiations with the regulated interests. This, in Charles O. Jones's apt description, was "speculative" policy.

> The [policy-making] processes were not constrained, as expected, by confirmed scientific, organizational and technological capabilities; nor was policy escalation checked by those economic interests to be regulated. As elected officials sought to satisfy the public interest, policy was augmented beyond normal incrementalism.[17]

Although such legislation was indeed unprecedented, it was by no means visionary, since the goals and procedures, as many experts have attested, were theoretically attainable. The story of federal air and water abatement policy since 1970 has been the tale of hard struggles to make speculations into accomplishments.

AIR POLLUTION

The nation's air pollution abatement policy has been largely defined since 1970 by the Clean Air Amendments. Passed with Congressional unanimity despite opposition from the Nixon administration and most major industries, it attempted to give the federal government a firm, potentially decisive role in shaping pollution policy. Achieving the ambitious goals of this law has been difficult because of technical obstacles, uncertainties in the meaning of the law, and intense opposition from powerful segments of the American industrial community.

The Clean Air Amendments

Though long and complex, the Clean Air Amendments (1970) had clear objectives.[18] Essentially, the legislation was intended to prevent the deterioration of existing clean bodies of ambient air, to achieve levels of ambient air quality sufficient to protect public health by 1975, and to achieve thereafter a level of air quality preventing any adverse effects on any environmental, man-made, or aesthetic processes. To achieve this, the federal government, through the EPA, was given broad authority to set guidelines and compliance deadlines for states to implement these objectives. The major features of the amendments included the following:

1. *National air quality standards.* The EPA was ordered to establish national air quality standards for all the major pollutants designated in the bill; this ended reliance upon the states to set such standards on a region-by-region basis. The standards were to be (1) *primary standards* to protect public health by 1975 and (2) *secondary standards,* to be achieved "within a reasonable time" to protect the natural and man-made environment from any adverse air pollution effects.

2. *State implementation plans.* Each state was responsible, after public hearings, for creating plans to implement the air quality standards set by the EPA. These implementation plans, to be submitted to Washington by January, 1972, were to describe the procedures each state would use to control all air pollution emissions and to achieve

the air quality levels for each pollutant by the deadline dates ordered by the EPA.

3. *Deadlines for new auto emission controls.* Giving special attention to auto emissions, the act required auto manufacturers to reduce their carbon monoxide and hydrocarbon emissions by 90 per cent of the 1970 levels by 1975; a 90 per cent reduction in nitrogen oxide emissions (by 1970 standards) were to be accomplished by 1976.

4. *Hazardous pollutants and new sources.* The amendments authorize the administrator to establish emission standards directly applicable to any source, wherever located and of any type, that emits a substance the administrator determines to be hazardous. Additionally, the EPA is authorized to establish "standards of performance" for classes and categories of new sources that "contribute significantly to air pollution or contribute to endangerment of public health or welfare."

5. *New enforcement procedures.* Once air quality standards have been established and state implementation plans created, the federal government may notify a violator and require compliance. If compliance is not obtained, the federal government can either order compliance or initiate a civil suit against the violator. A fine of $25,000 per day and a year in prison are provided; additional violations can result in $50,000-per-day fines. When air emissions appear to constitute an immediate threat to public health, the EPA may order an immediate cessation of the pollution.

Such legislation seems unusually bold in light of the political influence and enormous technical complexity of the industries and activities to be regulated. In effect, the new law ordained a major reorientation in the economic and physical development of America's major industrial sectors.

The Regulated

The weight of federal pollution policy rests heavily on three sectors of the American economy. Almost half (42 per cent) the total volume of air pollutants comes from automobiles and trucks, a fifth (21 per cent) from electric generating sites, and a substantial remainder (14 per cent) from industry; together, these sources pour more than three-fourths of the yearly pollution load into the nation's atmosphere. The volume of the five most significant pollutants created by these sources is indicated in Table 4.

TABLE 4.   Sources of Air Pollution in the United States, 1968 (Percentages by Weight)

Source	Carbon Monoxide (100 million tons)	Sulfur Oxides (33 million tons)	Hydro-carbons (32 million tons)	Nitrogen Oxides (21 million tons)	Particulates (28 million tons)
Fuel burning for transportation	63.8%	2.4%	51.9%	39.3%	4.3%
Fuel burning in stationary sources	1.9	73.5	2.2	48.5	31.4
Industrial processes other than fuel burning	9.6	22.0	14.4	1.0	26.5
Solid waste disposal	7.8	0.3	5.0	2.9	3.9
Miscellaneous*	16.9	1.8	26.5	8.3	33.9

*Includes forest fires, agricultural burning, coal waste fires, and gasoline marketing.
SOURCE: John Holdren & Philip Herrera, *Energy* (San Francisco: The Sierra Club, 1971), p. 145.

THE ELECTRIC POWER INDUSTRY.   The electric wire has become the umbilical cord of American society. We depend heavily on electric power: Industry consumes about 41 per cent of the available power, residential users about 32 per cent, and commercial enterprise an additional 23 per cent. The demand for electric power in the United States—power without which almost all industrial, scientific, domestic, and commercial activities would cease—is escalating rapidly; projections indicate that national demands will quadruple between 1970 and 2000. The present 3,400 generating plants in the country must be supplemented by at least 255 additional plants to meet this demand; not surprisingly, the electric utilities are the fastest-growing major industry in the United States.

This insatiable appetite for electricity is ominous because electric generating plants are extremely "dirty" environmentally. Particulate matter and nitrogen oxides are two hazards, but the most dangerous emission is sulfur oxides—an acrid yellow gas emitted in great volume from plants burning fossil fuels (oil, gas, and coal) and responsible for most of the reported respiratory ills associated with the presence of electric generating plants. Large plants disgorge huge quantities of this potentially lethal gas: Chicago's Consolidated Edison produces 420,000 tons of sulfur oxides annually. However, this is only a sniff alongside the volume that will arise from the controversial "Four Corners" project currently under way in the open desert where New Mexico, Arizona, Utah, and Colorado meet; only partially complete, the project when constructed will be the largest power generation complex in the United States, daily producing 1,280 tons of nitrogen oxides, 240 tons of fly ash, and 1,970 tons of sulfur oxides; existing generators at the site produce a thick smoke trail 215 miles long—big enough to be observed from Gemini 12 more than 170 miles away from earth. At the moment, controlling these emissions is difficult and expensive. The most effective approach is to reduce the sulfur content in the fossil fuels used by the generators by switching to low-sulfur fossil fuels; limited success has been achieved through the utilization of expensive hydrostatic "scrubbers" and electrostatic devices that remove some sulfur oxides before they leave the stacks. Such techniques are still experimental and do not guarantee the removal of all dangerous sulfur oxide emissions.

AUTOMOBILES AND THE FUEL COMPLEX. Automobiles and trucks pour 180 billion pounds of contaminants into the air annually; almost two-thirds of the carbon monoxide and half of the hydrocarbons released are traceable to internal combustion engines, which also cause the chronic smog found in Los Angeles, New York, and other metropolitan areas. Spurred by massive governmental expenditures for highways and encouraged by automakers' pervasive advertising, Americans have fully embraced the automobile as a fundamental of their life style and show no inclination to change their ways. Almost 100 million automobiles and trucks now exist in the United States, supplemented annually by 10 million new vehicles.

It would be difficult to overstate the economic and political importance of the automotive industry in the United States. General Motors, the largest industrial corporation in the world, currently has an annual sales volume approaching $20 billion, which exceeds the gross national product of all but a few nations. The automobile industry employs about 810,000 individuals, sustains numerous service industries, and consumes many raw and manufactured products, including steel and other metals, crude rubber and finished rubber products, and a great diversity of other materials. Any significant change in the technology or economic structure of the automobile industry brought about by governmental controls on air pollution is bound to have enormous direct and indirect effects on this most important sector of the economy. The intense political involvement of the industry's leaders and lobbyists in air pollution policy has brought the weight of one of the world's most powerful corporate structures to bear upon this issue.

In good part, air pollution policy must be fuel policy. Any effort to control air contamination affects the volume and content of fuel used for energy production in all sectors of American society. The nation's coal, gas, and petroleum industries have a substantial stake in air pollution policy and have been deeply implicated in the policy process associated with air pollution abatement.

The fuel industry is interlocked with the power and automobile industries technologically, financially, and structurally. The link between petroleum and the automobile is rather obvious: The internal combustion engine is the principal consumer of gasoline, the most expensive of fuels distilled from crude oil and the backbone of the petroleum market (about 80 billion gallons of gasoline are annually poured into America's automobiles). A less familiar but instructive example of interdependence between fuel producer and consumer is the relationship between coal producers and the electric power industry. This relationship stands out in sharp relief when the problem of sulfur oxides is raised.[19] Currently, more than half the electric power generated in the United States is produced by medium- to high-sulfur coal, which will probably cease to be a generally acceptable fuel when federal and state sulfur-oxide emission standards are firmly established. Although there are, or may soon be, some alternative methods of converting high-sulfur coal into a form more acceptable for use when sulfur-oxide emission standards are enforced, the coal industry is understandably concerned with how severely the emission standards will limit the present market for existing high-sulfur coal. Many of the coal companies own large reserves of high-sulfur fuels; clearly, the strength of the market and its potential income will depend on the sulfur emission standards. Moreover, many coal companies, having negotiated thirty-year contracts with electric companies, are heavily committed to specific electric utilities. In some instances, electric utilities (such as the General Public Utilities Corporation, a large eastern holding company) have built "mine mouth" generating stations on the coal mining sites as an alternative to transporting the coal long distances to generating plants; such companies, dependent in the most fundamental manner on existing coal sources, cannot easily find new coal supplies. Further, many electric plants would have to convert boilers and accept higher fuel costs in order to switch to low-sulfur coal. None of these is an insurmountable problem—in fact, many East Coast utilities have already turned to new low-sulfur coal sources or have converted to other fossil fuels with moderate sulfur content—but the economies of electric power and coal, like the economies of other fuel users and fuel producers, are so intertwined that both will be vitally affected by air pollution policy. In many cases, any change in fuel use can only be accomplished by rather massive changes in both consumer and producer relationships.

HEAVY INDUSTRY. Although the nation's heavy industry ranks third among the leading producers of air pollution, this still amounts to 85 billion tons of pollutants contributed to the atmosphere annually —about 300 pounds for every citizen. No major industry in the nation is innocent of air pollution; Table 5 lists the leading industries and their principal pollutants. The greatest volume of these pollutants is discharged in the Northwest and in the Great Lakes region of the Midwest, around large cities generally, and in the Southwest; in recent years, however, the spread of heavy industry across the United States

TABLE 5.   Leading Industries and Their Principal Pollutants

Industry	Principal Pollutants	Annual Average Volume, in Billion Pounds
Petroleum refining	Particulates, sulfur oxides, hydrocarbons, carbon monoxide	8.4
Smelters (aluminum, copper, lead, zinc)	Particulates, sulfur oxides	8.3
Iron foundries	Particulates, carbon monoxide	7.4
Kraft pulp and paper mills	Particulates, carbon monoxide, sulfur oxides	6.6
Coal cleaning and refuse	Particulates, sulfur oxides, carbon monoxide	4.7

SOURCE: John C. Esposito, *Vanishing Air* (New York: Grossman Publishers, 1970), p. 70.

and increasing urbanization have almost done away with areas free of significant air contamination. Since American heavy industry produces almost half of the nation's gross national product, the economy is very dependent on its continuing operation and profitability.

It now seems clear that Congress and the EPA had not anticipated realistically the difficulties in bringing so massive a segment of the American economy into compliance with the law. Political opposition from the regulated interests was one obstacle. Another was the lack of scientific data, technical facilities, and experience with the new pollution procedures. Some progress has been made in achieving the bold intent of the law, but it is far short of expectations.

ACHIEVEMENTS: "A NEED FOR IMPROVEMENT."   Summarizing the impact of the 1970 amendments after five years, the Council on Environmental Quality concluded in 1976: "Air pollution control programs appear to be stemming pollution growth. The estimated nationwide emissions of particulates and carbon monoxide have been reduced significantly, and the other major regulated pollutants have remained near 1970 levels."[20] The CEQ could claim that roughly three-quarters of the "stationary sources" of pollution (primarily power generating plants and industrial sites) had met state or federal emission standards or were scheduled to do so; auto emissions had been reduced by 67 per cent of levels in 1970. A more comprehensive picture of achievements nationally is presented in Figure 3, which depicts changes in major pollution levels from 1970 through 1974. A glance at the figure shows, as the CEQ suggests, that the principal achievement of the 1970 amendments to date has been the prevention of further significant deterioration of air quality rather than an impressive improvement in ambient air.

If one examines the record of the individual states, their achievements are not particularly impressive. Only a third of the nation's "air quality regions"—the 247 areas that constitute the basic units of air quality control—had fully met the ambient air standards for the public health protection in 1976. Moreover, by 1976—four years after the statutory deadline for state submission of implementation plans to Washington—no state had a plan fully approved by Washington, and consequently in most states the procedures for pollution abatement had yet to be fully implemented. Looking at the five-year record, the CEQ concluded: "There is a need for improvement."[21]

Why had accomplishments fallen so far below expectations? Environmentalists were likely to assert that the major reason—if not the only one—was a lack of political courage on the part of Congress, the EPA, and the states in enforcing the letter of the law. This explanation is too simple. Clearly, governmental agencies are sometimes loath to grasp the nettle by enforcing the law with its politically painful consequences. But technical problems caused by the speculative nature of the law and the need for judicial clarification of many statutory prescriptions were also responsible.

"WAFFLING" THE LAW. In administrative jargon, to "waffle" is to blunt the impact of the law by various procedures qualifying and hedging its original intent. Congress, the EPA, and the states have all demonstrated an aptitude for waffling; the result has been a delay in many enforcement deadlines in the Clean Air Amendments and, in some cases, a change in the law's objectives. This has happened in several important ways.

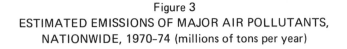

Figure 3
ESTIMATED EMISSIONS OF MAJOR AIR POLLUTANTS, NATIONWIDE, 1970–74 (millions of tons per year)

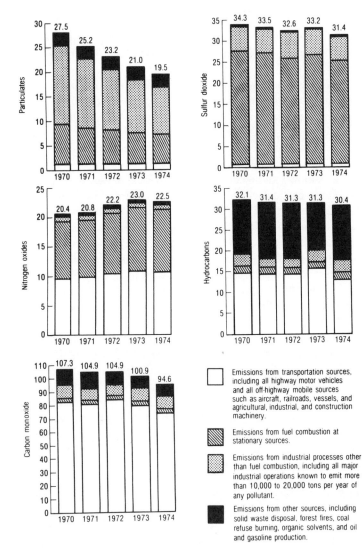

The legend shown:

Emissions from transportation sources, including all highway motor vehicles and all off-highway mobile sources such as aircraft, railroads, vessels, and agricultural, industrial, and construction machinery.

Emissions from fuel combustion at stationary sources.

Emissions from industrial processes other than fuel combustion, including all major industrial operations known to emit more than 10,000 to 20,000 tons per year of any pollutant.

Emissions from other sources, including solid waste disposal, forest fires, coal refuse burning, organic solvents, and oil and gasoline production.

SOURCE: Council on Environmental Quality, *Environmental Quality: Sixth Annual Report* (Washington, D.C., 1975), p. 306.

First, the EPA and the states have not rigorously enforced the nondegradation provision of the 1970 amendments. The 1970 law clearly intended to protect existing clean air bodies by preventing the states from setting air quality standards below the prevailing quality of such regions. Thus, Congress insisted that when an air quality region contained high-quality air, it could not be "degraded" by allowing it to reach a lower quality even if the lower quality were the highest federal standard. Nondegradation is intensely objectionable to many states and most industries; they insist that such a policy will, in effect, prevent polluting industries from moving into such areas. In 1971, the EPA's guidelines to the states for implementing pollution plans did permit degradation; the Sierra Club succeeded in obtaining a judicial ruling to prevent such a policy. Subsequently, the EPA's new directives still appeared to allow some air quality deterioriation, and the issue was again thrown into the courts. With the matter in the hands of the judges, the states have taken no steps to implement further a nondegradation policy until a definitive court ruling emerges. In the meantime, no action has been taken against polluters who may be guilty of violating the law if a nondegradation policy is to prevail.[22]

Second, Congress has amended the 1970 legislation to relax some compliance deadlines and air quality standards. In particular, Congress passed legislation in 1974 that prevented the EPA from insisting that the states control automobile parking in order to regulate auto emissions in urban areas. Another 1974 bill delayed the deadline the states were expected to meet in controlling "indirect" sources of air pollution, such as shopping centers or entertainment complexes, which contribute materially to air quality problems. A third 1974 enactment permitted power generating plants and industries converting from oil to coal as an energy source to delay until 1979 their compliance with air emission standards originally intended to apply in 1977. The effect was to grant a grace period during which significant pollutants might still be emitted from the affected sources. Moreover, Congress has consistently underfunded the EPA's air programs since their inception; this effectively reduces the regulatory resources available for pollution abatement.

Third, deadlines for auto emission controls have been continually liberalized. The EPA first extended by three years the 1975 and 1977 deadlines for emission controls originally written into the Clean Air Amendments—this extension was permitted under the law itself. Then, acting under additional authority granted by Congress in 1974, EPA's administrator further extended the deadlines for achieving emission controls on hydrocarbons and carbon monoxide for an indefinite period. Calling it "the most unhappy decision EPA has had to make since I've been here," administrator Russell Train cited technical problems as the reason for the deadline extension. In effect, reduction of hydrocarbons and carbon monoxide was required to meet an "interim standard" significantly below the 90 per cent reduction level set originally in the law.

Furthermore, Congress appeared willing to grant still more concessions to the auto makers in response to their assertion that they could not meet even these more relaxed emission control deadlines. In late 1976, legislation passed both houses of Congress in which the date for achieving emission controls on carbon monoxide, hydrocarbons, and nitrogen oxides was extended to 1982 from the 1978 deadline originally in the law. Additionally, under the new legislation, the specific reduction in nitrogen oxides required by the Clean Air Amendments would be abandoned in favor of permitting the Administrator of EPA to set the standard. Although Congress adjourned before the House and Senate versions of this legislation could be reconciled in conference, there was little doubt that some extension of the compliance deadline would be forthcoming.

Finally, the EPA and the states have often permitted control of emissions from industry and power generating plants through shutdowns and cutbacks during periods of poor air quality, by the use of tall stacks to diffuse the pollutants in the upper atmosphere and other "intermittent control systems." Environmentalists argue that this approach amounts to an "out of sight, out of mind" attitude toward regulation, in contrast to an insistence that emissions be regulated at their source through stack controls—which, they insist, follows the intent of the law.

These events, a few of many that have delayed the achievement of the law's original objectives, have collectively perpetuated many of the nation's pollution ills. Defenders argue that the situation is unavoidable because scientific knowledge and control technologies are often limited persently; moreover, they assert, regulation must be "reasonable," and this implies some accommodation to the regulated states and industries. Ecologists, in rebuttal, assert that such waffling amounts to a political capitulation to the regulated interests which is neither necessary nor justifiable. In any event, difficulties in achieving the law's intent are often compounded by very real technical obstacles. At times, failures to comply with the law result less from deliberate waffling than from the lack of technical resources or adequate skills in achieving the goals.

TECHNICAL PROBLEMS. It has become increasingly apparent that many regulatory procedures ordained in the 1970 amendments are difficult, or impossible, to implement as intended and that some legislative goals may be technically impossible to achieve by the deadlines mandated. It is often difficult to determine whether a procedure cannot work or whether there is no will to make it work. However, several aspects of the law seem clearly beyond existing technical resources to implement.

One area in which major technical problems have arisen is auto emission controls. It has been discovered that the catalytic converters used presently to control auto emission may, in turn, create serious sulfur oxide emissions that outweigh the benefits of controlling hydrocarbons and carbon monoxide. This, a quite unanticipated problem, has been instrumental in causing the EPA to delay the original compliance deadlines for the auto industry to control its major air pollutants. Further, the experts disagree upon solutions. Thus, in 1974, a study by Harvard, MIT, and Columbia experts warned that it was an "unwise gamble" for the auto industry to adopt the catalytic converter to meet emission control deadlines in the late 1970's. The next year, another gathering of experts (the National Research Council) asserted that they saw no reason to delay enforcement of the strict standards because the sulfur oxide emissions could themselves be controlled.[23] Moreover, it became apparent that the catalytic converter reduced fuel economy; the auto industry has argued since the "energy crisis" of 1974 that the new catalytic converters were fuel wasters whose advantages did not compensate for their cost in lost energy.

Equally important, it appears that even full compliance with the law may not achieve the intended results. EPA engineers have esti-

mated, for instance, that even with full pollution controls on all
stationary air pollution sources and a 90 per cent reduction in auto
emissions, there will be such concentrations of cars in urban areas that
the nation's ten largest cities cannot meet federal air quality standards
without limiting auto use in the cities. In Los Angeles, according to
EPA estimates, this auto reduction would have to amount to eliminating 85 per cent of all the automobiles used daily in the metropolitan
area. Arguments continue about the efficiency of "scrubbers" as a
control upon industrial and power plant stack emissions; critics of
EPA regulations assert that scrubbers often cannot achieve the levels
of control expected under the law. Indeed, as we have observed, the
efficacy of many existing pollution control procedures has yet to be
demonstrated.

In short, many delays in achieving the objectives of the 1970
amendments cannot be assigned entirely to a lack of political courage
or the absence of administrative integrity in Washington or the states.
It is quite possible—perhaps inevitable—that such a speculative approach to regulation as that embodied in the 1970 legislation will
sometimes founder on the shoals of scientific ignorance and technical
limitations.

THE JUDICIAL LABYRINTH.   Most important parts of any regulatory law will be subjected to prolonged litigation; those interests who
fail to achieve their purpose through legislative or administrative
means can always resort to the courts in yet another effort to shape
the law to their taste. The result is that an authoritative declaration
of the law's intent often comes from judges, but only after prolonged,
expensive litigation. So it has been with the 1970 amendments. The
EPA's review and approval of state implementation plans, as required
by the Clean Air Amendments, has alone been challenged over a
hundred times in the courts; industrial interests filed more than three
times as many of these actions as environmental groups. The EPA's
definition of primary standards for major air pollutants, its ruling on
the nondegradation issue, its definition of technical standards for
pollution control equipment required by the law, and most other
major administrative interpretations of the law have been, and continue to be, grist for the judicial mills. This contributes to the delay
in implementing the law and often fosters official inaction until the
courts define for officials their responsibilities.

Litigation is particularly disruptive in the enforcement phase of pollution control because regulated interests, often handsomely endowed with the cash to underwrite elaborate legal defenses, can delay pollution controls for years and sometimes force governmental agencies to settle for less than success in order to avoid protracted legal wrangling. Although the EPA has initiated more than a thousand enforcement actions against air pollution violators since 1970, it usually has its greatest success with the small companies; the largest industrial polluters, such as U.S. Steel, often resist fiercely any abatement actions, and consequently their contribution to air quality deterioration is among the last to be abated.[24]

In short, the many obstacles to rapid implementation of the Clean Air Amendments have caused, and will continue to cause, considerable delay in approximating—if possible—the objectives of the 1970 amendments. Many of these obstacles are inherent in any regulatory program, for, as we shall see, they reappear in the water pollution program as well.

WATER POLLUTION

Washington's current approach to water pollution control, contained in the Federal Water Pollution Control Act Amendments (1972), follows the same philosophical design as the earlier Clean Air Amendments. There is the same insistence on strong federal leadership in setting standards and deadlines for state compliance, a similar emphasis upon explicit compliance deadlines for achieving general goals, the same ambitious objectives, the same effort to "press technology" by moving boldly beyond existing pollution abatement research and resources. In short, Congress continued the "speculative" approach to abatement that it first embraced in the Clean Air Amendments, and, not surprisingly, many of the same problems have arisen.

The Federal Water Pollution Control Act Amendments (1972)

A brief review of the major programs and objectives in the FWPCAA will readily reveal its broad scope and ambitious objectives. The principal features of the law include:

1. *The abatement of all significant national water pollution by 1985.* Congress has declared its intent "that the discharge of pollutants into the navigable waters be eliminated by 1985" and that "wherever attainable, an interim goal of water quality which provides for the protection and propagation of fish, shellfish, and wildlife and provides for recreation in and on the water be achieved by 1 July 1983." In effect, this amounts to a commitment to make all the nation's navigable waters "swimmable and fishable" by 1983 and wholly free of pollutants in 1985.

2. *A national permit system for all municipal and industrial effluent discharges according to national standards established by the EPA and Congress.* The permit system is an interim measure, serving as a means to control effluents until the deadlines for abatement in 1983 and 1985 are reached. Under this provision, the federal government will establish broad guidelines that the states must follow when issuing permits for industry and municipalities to discharge pollutants into navigable waterways. If state guidelines prove unacceptable or the states are unable to administer the permit system, the EPA is authorized to assume control of the state permit system. Permits will define the nature and volume of effluents that may be discharged into waterways.

3. *Industrial and municipal pollution discharges must meet minimum technical control standards.* The 1972 amendments declare that all industrial dischargers must establish the "best practicable" technology to control pollution by 1977 and the "best available" technology by 1983. All municipalities must achieve at least "secondary treatment level" for their effluents by 1977. These technology standards must be taken into account when the states, or the EPA, issue discharge permits; they define the minimum acceptable control levels to be achieved by specific compliance deadlines.

4. *State implementation of federal standards.* Unlike previous approaches to pollution abatement, Congress establishes in the FWPCAA that the states must implement their water pollution controls within the water quality standards, technological control standards, and compliance deadlines set by Washington.

5. *A federal construction grant program of $18 billion to assist the states in building municipal waste treatment facilities to meet the goals defined in the law.* This, the largest single public works project ever authorized by Congress, authorizes the federal government to finance

75 per cent of the cost to municipalities for constructing waste treatment facilities required to meet the effluent standards created in the law.

6. *Creation of toxic standards.* The amendments authorize the EPA to establish effluent standards for any substance that may cause death or "disease, behavioral abnormalities, cancer, genetic mutations, physiological malfunctions . . . or physical deformities." If necessary, the EPA may prohibit the discharge of any pollutant determined to be "toxic" under definitions of the amendments.

Behind these and other provisions of the new law appeared to be a steely Congressional logic: "This legislation," commented its Congressional architects, "would clearly establish that no one has the right to pollute—that pollution continues because of technological limits, not because of any inherent right to use the nation's waterways for the purpose of discharging of wastes."[25]

This new legislation has had its greatest impact upon the nation's municipalities and major industries, which together create the largest volume of water effluents.

THE REGULATED. More than 21,000 American municipal treatment plants were brought within the ambit of regulation under the FWPCAA. Of these, only about 3,400 could meet the law's effluent standards in 1974. More than 16,000 had to be improved, usually at considerable cost, to comply with the law; another 1,500 cities had no treatment facilities at all. In addition, uncounted thousands of tiny communities, too small to be identified as "municipalities," must now treat their wastes to avoid becoming violators of national effluent standards.[26] Estimates by the EPA suggest that the initial $18 billion authorization to assist the nation's cities in meeting the new municipal effluent limits will barely nudge standards upward; full compliance may cost in excess of $400 billion. Major cities have pressed Congress continually since 1972 concurrently to relax the 1977 deadline for achieving "secondary level" treatment of their effluents and to appropriate many more billions of dollars to assist them in the mammouth task of upgrading their water quality.[27]

Industry constitutes the other major economic sector heavily affected, and politically active, in the water pollution abatement process. The industrial demand for water and the volume of pollutants dumped into the nation's waterways is growing. American industry, now using ten times the volume of water consumed by municipal sources, will probably require sixteen times the municipal demand by the year 2000. No complete inventory of pollutants discharged into the nation's waterways is yet available; when the inventory is complete, the volume and variety of contaminants from major industry will be extremely large. Some idea of the water contaminants from industrial sources can be gained from the steel industry, which is, as one recent study notes, "the king of the manufacturing consumers":

> The steel industry [uses] upward of four trillion gallons of this precious fluid a year. Steelmakers need water to cool and condense hot metal . . . and to "scrub" bases before using them for fuel; they also blast finished sheets of steel with a high-velocity water spray to knock off the waste scale clinging to the steel surface. The average steel plant produces one million ingot tons of steel each year. For each ingot ton a plant puts out, it also generates 125 pounds of suspended solids, 2.7 pounds of lubrication oils, 3.5 pounds of free acids (like sulfuric acid), 12.3 pounds of combined acids (like metal sulfates), eight ounces of emulsions, and between one and two ounces of such poisons as phenol, flouride, ammonia and cyanide. Each ingot ton produced raises the temperature of the water used for cooling by 10°.[28]

By far the largest portion of pollutants currently found in the nation's waterways comes from industry. More than 80 per cent of the water pollutants, measured by their biological oxygen demand, originates in industry; among its many environmental hazards, this organic waste is responsible for the "dying" (eutrophication) of lakes and streams when it reaches a concentration that robs higher life forms, such as fish and shellfish, of dissolved oxygen, thus suffocating them. This organic waste is seldom treated; practically all the industrial wastewater containing more than three-quarters of the biochemical oxygen demand is directly emptied into streams, rivers, or lakes in its raw condition.

In recent years, scientists have become increasingly apprehensive about two other sources of water pollution closely related to industrial processes: oil spillage and thermal pollution. Oil discharges in the Santa Barbara channel in February, 1969, which released 235,000 gallons of crude oil into the Santa Barbara harbor, and a year later in Tampa Bay (10,000 gallons of crude oil from a grounded Greek tanker) dramatized the urgency of the oil pollution issue. More than one thousand oil spills involving more than one hundred barrels of crude oil were reported in the United States in 1969; these discharges contaminate sea water and nearby estuaries and often mar beaches, causing considerable cost to public officials for clean-up. Thermal pollution is caused when water, heated from use as a coolant for industrial equipment, is released in large volume into cooler waterways; the subsequent alteration in water temperature can extend for many miles from the source and may drastically transform the ecology of the water bodies it affects. The major cause of this pollution is electric power generation, which produces more than 80 per cent of thermal heat released into the nation's waterways. With the great expansion in electric power generation anticipated in the next decades and the growing use of nuclear power equipment (which produces 50 percent more thermal pollution per unit of power than conventional generators), the thermal pollution problem threatens to become increasingly severe.[29]

Considering the enormous regulatory task in bringing this diversity of interests and activities within the reach of the law, it is not surprising that the job has been demanding and that results have been uneven.

RESULTS—"SERIOUS PROBLEMS REMAIN." Water pollution abatement since 1972 is a tale of intermittent achievement palled by delay and impasse—a narrative of technical and political obstacles in the way of grand designs. Many regulatory aspects of the program are operational: Twenty-four states had assumed responsibility for their effluent permit program, the EPA is managing the rest, and together they have issued permits for almost 80 per cent of the nation's major industrial polluters. Some of the nation's worst water pollution problems have clearly diminished, particularly in the Great Lakes and in major rivers such as the Mississippi and Colorado. Most major municipalities have begun, with federal assistance, the job of upgrading their effluent treatment processes. Numerous major waterways have shown improvement, ranging from moderate to major, in control of organic wastes and coliform bacteria—two common and troublesome contaminants.

Nonetheless, it was obvious by 1976 that almost none of the interim compliance deadlines and intermittent goals established by the 1972 law had been achieved; consequently, achievement of the 1985 goal of "zero discharges" into the nation's waterways seems visionary. The National Commission on Water Quality, created to evaluate the impact of the FWPCAA, described some major deficiencies in the program after three years:

• *Water quality.* Most lakes studied in the eastern states are suffering some degree of accelerated eutrophication.

• *Industrial permits.* The permit program is generally behind schedule; too many exemptions have been permitted by the EPA and the states. Establishing control technologies has lagged to a degree that neither the 1977 nor the 1983 goals of the law can be met.

• *Municipal treatment facilities.* About 60 per cent of the permits for these sources have been written in a manner that prevents the achievement of "secondary treatment" levels by 1977 as required by the law. Moreover, the initial $18 billion Congressional appropriation for municipal waste treatment plants will be inadequate to achieve treatment levels required by legislation.[30]

The reasons for this situation are substantially akin to those we have observed in the air pollution program. The difference appears to lie in the far greater technical and scientific difficulties encountered in water quality management.

TECHNICAL PROBLEMS—AGAIN.   Looking back with the wisdom of hindsight, a Congressional subcommittee responsible for the original legislation concluded that the authors of the 1972 law had "underestimated the tasks to be done and overestimated the results that could be achieved."[31] Among the many technical problems encountered, government officials have found it particularly difficult to describe the treatment technologies that had to be applied by industry to meet the requirements for the "best practicable technology" by 1977 and the "best available technology" by 1983. To cite a single illustration, the law required that the EPA make these determinations with consideration for "the total cost of application" and in "relation to the effluent reduction benefits to be achieved." Often, no standards existed to define what were "best practicable" or "best available" technologies—the range of technologies, their performance characteristics, and their availability were often unknown or only sketchily defined. The economic impact of such technologies, in addition, often could not be easily estimated. Further, the industrial processes within even a single industry, such as aluminum smelting, were so varied that the impact of a single pollution control device could not be readily ascertained. In light of such ignorance, defining the economic costs and benefits of control systems was difficult and sometimes impossible by the deadlines contained in the law.

Another technical problem that continues to bedevil federal officials is the job of setting effluent limits for a whole class of industry such as paper and pulp manufacturing. Setting such a broad standard for any single industry may be impossible in light of the complexity of industrial processes involved. Similar arguments arise when proposals to define and limit a "toxic substance" are considered by the EPA. It is often difficult to know whether a "toxic" can be eliminated from an industrial process and whether the benefits outweigh the economic costs across the range of an industry's national operations.

But perhaps the most enigmatic of all tasks posed for the EPA is the law's requirement that the agency see to it that states control "non-point" pollution sources—that is, pollution that arises from sedimentation, from fertilizer drainage into water, or from any other source that does not originate in a single "point." Difficult as it may be to control pollution from an industrial outfall pipe or from a city's waste treatment plant, officials at least know where the pollution originates and can measure its volume and constituents. Controlling non-point sources, however, means identifying the nature of pollutants that might originate in thousands of separate places—if, indeed, sources can be identified. "No one," concludes one authority, "seems to know how to achieve this."

Illustrations of these technical issues can be indefinitely multiplied. Though many aspects of the law are not so handicapped, the bill abounds with technical barricades to implementation so often that surmounting them, when possible, will greatly delay enforcement. In a political perspective, technical difficulties are weapons in the arsenal of regulated interests seeking to frustrate abatement procedures. Administrators, working with limited knowledge and technical resources, are constantly challenged by these regulated interests through administrative procedures and the courts to justify decisions sometimes made with meager information. Often, officials feel compelled to bargain with the regulated parties to achieve some acceptable compromise where technical problems prevent agencies from confidently defining and enforcing the law.

DISCRETION AGAIN.   Faced with the technical problems inherent with the 1972 amendments, the EPA has felt intense pressure from regulated interests to exercise its discretion, when permitted by the law, to extend compliance deadlines and to grant exemptions to the law. The agency has frequently yielded to such pressure, usually citing technical difficulties as the reason. Quite often, environmentalists—convinced that it is usually political influence and not scientific problems that prevent enforcement—have judicially challenged such determinations, and protracted litigation ensues to further delay pollution abatement.

Three discretionary determinations, in particular, have undoubtedly slowed improvement in the nation's water quality. First, the EPA has permitted the states to allow some degradation of high-quality bodies of water; this has been justified because the law appears to permit such deterioration if it is "necessary for social and economic development." Second, the agency has granted exemptions to over 400 major industries in meeting requirements that they install "the best practicable" pollution control technology in their plants by 1977. Among these are many of the nation's more proficient water polluters. Some of these exemptions have been given on grounds that new controls "might result in severe economic and employment disruption." In one stretch of the Mahoning (Ohio) River, for instance, plants of U.S. Steel, Youngstown Sheet and Tube Co., and Republic Steel were exempted on this basis. In other cases, exemptions were granted because the new limits were being challenged by the industries in the courts. Finally, the agency has issued many industrial permits that set effluent standards substantially the same as those already achieved—in effect, no significant improvement is required—because officials assert that better treatment technology is not yet available. Environmental groups have challenged all these rulings in the courts. Until a definitive judicial decision is made, the EPA's interim judgment will stand.

SUMMARY: THE LIMITS OF SPECULATIVE POLICY

It is increasingly evident that it will take decades, not merely a dozen years, to achieve the lofty goals of high air and water quality attempted in the 1970 and 1972 pollution laws enacted by Congress. It is quite conceivable that such goals, if attainable at all, will not be reached in this century. The problem, as we have seen, arises because the existing scientific, technical, and resource limits now experienced by governmental officials in achieving the "speculative" goals of the law have, quite unintentionally, aided the opponents of regulation in their political struggle against regulation. Under these circumstances, the discretion given to government officials in interpreting and applying the law—a discretion that must be granted in so complex an undertaking—is often exercised to create delay and compromise in achieving incisive pollution abatement. When disputes over the meaning of the law must, in addition, run their long and costly course through the judicial system, yet more time elapses between writing the law and achieving its purposes.

NOTES

1. Walter J. Hickel, *Who Owns America?* (Englewood Cliffs, N.J.: Prentice-Hall, 1971), p. 110.
2. The standards-and-enforcement procedure is more completely analyzed in J. Clarence Davies, *The Politics of Pollution* (New York: Pegasus Press, 1970), chapters 7 and 8; and in John C. Esposito, *Vanishing Air* (New York: Grossman Publishers, 1970), chapter 7.
3. An example of such a battle is the one that erupted over sulfur oxide criteria initially formulated by federal officials in the early 1970's. This is fully described in J. Clarence Davies, *op. cit.,* pp. 163–69; and in John C. Esposito, *op. cit.,* chapter 10.
4. Cited in 40 C.F.R., Part 50, 36 Fed. Reg. 22384 (1971).
5. Many of the problems arising from emission controls, together with a comparison of other pollution abatement methods, may be found usefully

summarized in George Hagevik, "Legislating for Air Quality Management: Reducing Theory to Practice," in Leslie L. Roos, Jr., *The Politics of Ecosuicide* (New York: Holt, Rinehart and Winston, 1971), pp. 311–45.

6. Murray Edelman, *The Symbolic Uses of Politics* (Urbana, Ill.: University of Illinois Press, 1964), p. 51

7. Section 307(a)(1) and (13), Federal Water Pollution Control Act Amendments (1972), Pub. L. 92-500.

8. Robert Zener, "The Federal Law of Water Pollution Control," in Erica L. Dolgin and Thomas G. P. Guilbert, eds., *Federal Environmental Law* (St. Paul, Minn.: West Publishing Co.), p. 690. The "buck passing" approach to environmental legislation is carefully explored in Edwin T. Haefle, *Representative Government and Environmental Management* (Baltimore: The Johns Hopkins University Press, 1973).

9. *New York Times,* May 25, 1975. The technical problems associated with enforcement, together with the discretion that results, are discussed in Clarence Davies, *op. cit.,* chapters 6–9; and in Allen V. Kneese and Charles L. Schultz, *Pollution, Prices and Public Policy* (Washington, D.C.: Brookings Institution, 1975), chapters 2–6.

10. The saga of Reserve Mining is told in Wade Greene, "Life vs. Livelihood," *New York Times Magazine,* November 24, 1974, pp. 17 ff.

11. The history of federal air and water pollution legislation is summarized from Clarence Davies, *op. cit.;* David Zwick and Marcy Benstock, *Water Wasteland* (New York: Grossman Publishers, 1971); and John C. Esposito, *op. cit.*

12. Clarence Davies, *op. cit.,* p. 130.

13. Thomas Jorling, "The Federal Law of Air Pollution Control," in Erica L. Dolgin and Thomas G. P. Guilbert, *op. cit.,* p. 1061. This article is an excellent summary of the Congressional experience with air pollution prior to 1970.

14. There is little debate over the adequacy of enforcement procedures; even responsible federal officials recognize the weakness. See, for instance, the assessment of the Council on Environmental Quality, *Environmental Quality, 1971,* pp. 12–13. The most critical examinations are found in John C. Esposito, *op. cit.,* chapter 6, and David Zwick and Marcy Benstock, *op. cit.,* chapter 6. One of the few case studies of voluntary compliance problems is found in Ted Caldwell and Leslie L. Roos, Jr., "Voluntary Compliance and Pollution Abatement," in Leslie L. Roos, *op. cit.*

15. Thomas Jorling, *op. cit.*

16. This "leap" in policy logic is carefully explored in Charles O. Jones,

Clean Air (Pittsburgh: University of Pittsburgh Press, 1974); and in Charles O. Jones, "Speculative Argumentation in Federal Air Pollution Policy-Making," *Journal of Politics,* May, 1974, pp. 438–64.

17. Charles O. Jones, "Speculative Argumentation," p. 459.

18. Clean Air Amendments of 1970, Pub. L. 91-604, 42 U.S.C. 1857 *et seq.* The principal features of the law are summarized in Thomas Jorling, *op. cit.,* and Charles O. Jones, *Clean Air.* A useful résumé of the clean air programs may be found in U.S. Environmental Protection Agency, *The Clean Air Amendments of 1970: Highlights* (Washington, D.C., 1971).

19. This interlock is discussed in John C. Esposito, *op. cit.,* chapter 5. The legal implications of this relationship are usefully explored in Association of the Bar of New York, Special Committee on Electric Power and the Environment, *Electricity and the Environment* (St. Paul, Minn.: West Publishing Co., 1972).

20. Council on Environmental Quality, *Environmental Quality: Sixth Annual Report* (Washington, D.C., 1975), p. 305.

21. *Ibid.,* p. 59.

22. The nondegradation issue is fully discussed in Thomas Jorling, *op. cit.,* and Council on Environmental Quality, *Sixth Annual Report,* pp. 50–52.

23. *New York Times,* October 18, 1974; June 5, 1975.

24. Many of the enforcement problems are carefully explored in Bruce A. Ackerman, *et al., The Uncertain Search for Environmental Quality* (New York: The Free Press, 1974).

25. Quoted in Robert Zener, *op. cit.,* p. 694. The most complete history of the FWPCAA is found in U.S. Library of Congress, Congressional Reference Service, *Legislative History of the Federal Water Pollution Control Act Amendments of 1972,* vols. 1 and 2 (Documents No. 93-1).

26. Council on Environmental Quality, *Sixth Annual Report,* pp. 444–45.

27. Current problems in cost expansion of treatment facilities are reviewed in U.S. Environmental Protection Agency, *Review of the Municipal Waste Water Treatment Works Program* (Washington, D.C.: U.S. Environmental Protection Agency, 1975).

28. David Zwick and Marcy Benstock, *op. cit.* p. 44.

29. The thermal pollution problem is analyzed most informatively in Richard Curtis and Elizabeth Hogan, *Perils of the Peaceful Atom* (New York: Ballantine Books, 1969), chapter 8.

30. *New York Times,* September 28, 1975.

31. U.S. Congress, House Committee on Public Works and Transportation, Subcommittee on Investigations and Review, *Interim Staff Report on the Federal Water Pollution Control Act Amendments of 1972.*

6. Earmuffs for Alligators: The Politics of Water Resources

Alan C. Stewart was a dedicated man, candid to the point of indiscretion, quick-tempered and vastly impatient with the environmentalists who disliked his airport. For a quarter century, as director of the Dade County Port Authority, he had tenaciously campaigned for big aviation in Miami. But for the environmentalists, he would have succeeded. In 1968, the Federal Aviation Agency announced the first planning grants for one of the world's largest jetports to be located near Miami. Rising in the green wilderness forty-five miles from the city, embracing an area larger than Miami itself, the runways alone would have exceeded the total size of the four largest ones existing in the nation; two six-mile runways, the site showpieces, would launch more than 200,000 commercial flights yearly. "It's not fantasy," Stewart had burbled. "No matter how big they build the monsters of the airlines, we'll have space for them."[1]

But conservation killed the Great Miami Jetport. A broad alliance of environmental groups launched a furious campaign against the project because it appeared to threaten the ecology of the vast Everglades National Park adjacent to the future runways. Skillfully using the media, ecologists cited expert evidence indicating that aircraft noise and airport congestion would drive rare birds from their nesting, that a continual drizzle of jet fuel would drive away or poison numerous park animals, and that the combined inroads of aviation and commerce might eventually despoil one of the nation's great natural adornments. Finally, in January, 1969, government officials agreed to seek an alternate site less menacing to the unique Everglades wilderness.

168

Seldom indulgent toward conservationists, Stewart grew bitterly caustic as his jetport evaporated. In his lexicon, they had always been "butterfly chasers"; now he suggested to the press that all conservationists protected were "yellow bellied sapsuckers." Why not, he asked, build an astrodome next to the runways where the conservationists could chase their butterflies unmolested? When told that conservationists expected the jet noise to disturb the Everglades alligators, he reportedly quipped that he would buy the alligators earmuffs. All this further mobilized environmentalists and brought many previously disinterested citizens into the fray on the side of the butterflies. Alan Stewart, in the end, contributed in no small measure to a significant environmental victory.

In retrospect, most of Stewart's remarks were counterproductive and silly. To many ecologists, however, he was the incarnation of a resource ethic that had dominated American government for more than a century. Earmuffs for alligators and a stadium for butterfly chasers could be dismissed as the indiscretions of an embittered man, yet such flippancy also betrayed a callousness toward environmental values that conservationists had long perceived, less crudely stated, among other public officials with resource responsibilities. To many conservationists, the airport battle became one of those rare occasions in which the traditional official indifference toward environmental values had been blatantly declared and publicly exposed. In sparing the alligators their earmuffs, many conservationists believed they had achieved both a material and symbolic triumph over a long-standing resource ethic in official circles.

Despite the jetport decision, altering governmental attitudes toward natural resources is still a difficult task. To begin, it requires a transformation in a pervasive attitude found among most governmental officials and policy-makers with resource responsibilities. Federal officials have frequently genuflected to environmental protection in the past, but environmental values customarily took second place in their approach to resource use. Washington adopted two methods for dealing with major resources. In some cases, it has used a *laissez-faire* philosophy, leaving many resources largely open to appropriation by private interests without significant federal opposition. In the case of most resources now considered nationally important, Washington asserted control over resource use, but the policy-making process has been organized in a manner very responsive to the interests of those using the resources for personal or corporate gain. Grant McConnell's description of federal land policy generally characterizes Washington's past resource policy: "The persistent success of demands for private exploitation has become a tradition, conferring a degree of legitimacy on a wide variety of actions that give control of land and land policy to limited groups, within the general population."[2] Such a procedure amounted to promoting resource use with little concern for environmental consequences.

Once corporate interests gained their access, they customarily created a strong, resistant political structure to protect and enhance their objectives, usually with considerable indifference to environmental amenities. Commonly, large national trade associations representing the major corporate users, formed in conjunction with state and local counterparts, gained entrée and influence among Washington officials charged with resource regulation. Eventually these interests became the clientele groups for their regulatory agencies, and the pattern of cooperative accommodation between regulated interests and their governmental regulators developed, as it did in other areas of federal regulation. Thus, environmentalists who are determined to introduce a larger measure of concern into deliberations on resource use must confront both an official inattention to environmental values and a sturdy political structure resistant to major policy change. The problems these institutionalized obstacles pose for environmentalists can be illuminated by examining recent federal policy affecting water development.

WATER RESOURCE POLITICS

The federal government has promoted water resource development since George Washington's first administration, but the great expansion of federal effort, authority, and investment in these projects did not occur until the twentieth century. Congress set the administrative design for federal water resource development in the Federal Power Act of 1920. This legislation divided authority over water resource projects among the Army Corps of Engineers, the Interior Department's Bureau of Reclamation, and the Agriculture Department's Soil Conservation Service. Intense infighting had erupted between private groups and public officials partisan to each agency, in their struggle to ensure a major policy role for their respective administrative favorites, and Congress ended the conflict without resolving it. Each agency was given essentially similar responsibilities, although on different scales, a decision that precluded the possibility of a coherent, carefully planned national water resource policy and assured that the agencies would be chronic competitors for control of water resource policy and projects. Further, various Congressional committees exercised jurisdiction over the water agencies to further confound systematic planning. However, this situation conformed to the political realities of water resource planning: It assured that client groups of each major agency would have some voice in water resource decisions. In general, water resource development has more often responded to the field of political forces surrounding it than to good principles of administrative or environmental management.

Among the three water resource agencies, the Bureau of Reclamation and the Army Corps of Engineers are clearly dominant in size, responsibilities, appropriations, and political influence. Since its major reorganization in 1923, the Bureau of Reclamation has operated exclusively in the seventeen western states, Alaska, and Hawaii. Originally given development of irrigation projects as its principal responsibility, it has now broadened its work to include flood and navigation control, recreation development, power generation, and most other enterprises associated with water resource development. With 11,000 workers and appropriations averaging almost $500 million per fiscal year, the bureau controls 252 dams in the West, together with forty-eight power plants, 344 canals with a combined length of 6,781 miles, and impounds enough water to cover New York State to a depth of four feet.[3] Within its western dominion, the bureau is a major force in shaping water use but is still eclipsed by the Army Corps of Engineers as a water resource planner for the nation. The Corps is, and has been, the nation's major administrative agent in the politics and planning of water resources; it has been the focus of persistent, intense conflicts between federal water resource planners and conservationists. Most of the environmental problems inherent in current water resource planning can be identified by examining the relationship of the Corps and its political associates and the environmentalists.

The Corps and Pork-Barrel Politics

Few federal agencies boast a longer, more impressive, or more successful history than the Army Corps of Engineers. Created by Congress in 1802 with both civil and military responsibilities it was to be the principal engineering consultant and agent of Congress in the creation, operation, and maintenance of national navigation and flood control projects, together with related work.[4] During its history, unblemished by major scandal and adorned with praise for its professional competence, the Corps has compiled an honorable record of military accomplishments, but almost from its inception its greatest effort has been devoted to carrying out its civilian responsibilities. Although it has eight operational sections (including those responsible for nuclear activities, the space program, civil defense, and missile site construction), the bulk of its appropriation and personnel is devoted to civil projects.

Through continuous Congressional expansion of its responsibilities, today the Corps' authority touches every aspect of American water resource development. Its domain embraces the construction, operation, and maintenance of civil works projects for navigation, flood control, and related purposes including shore protection; additionally, the Corps may construct hydroelectric power generating facilities, manage municipal and industrial water supplies, assist in water quality control, and aid in fish and wildlife protection. Employing about 32,000 civilians directed by 200 military engineers who are among the army's political and intellectual elite, the Corps has amassed an impressive catalogue of achievements. By mid-1975, it had completed over 3,300 projects costing more than $11 billion; another 275 were under way for $13.5 billion more. Along the nation's shorelines, the Corps is presently constructing projects exceeding $1.8 billion in value; completed wetlands projects cost about $200 million in annual upkeep. The Corps' total finished work amounts to 25,000 miles of waterways, 350 reservoirs, 9,500 miles of levees and flood walls, 7,500 miles of improved channels, and 107 commercial port facilities. The Corps' civil works average $1.5 billion in yearly appropriations— about three-quarters of all federal money allocated yearly for water resource development. Accompanying such prosperity in appropriations and projects has been an administrative and political status almost unique among federal agencies. The Corps has been virtually autonomous within the federal administrative structure, free of most supervision or control by the President, the Secretary of Defense, and the Secretary of the Army, all of whom are administrative overseers of the Corps according to the organization charts. This autonomy is further enhanced by the great favoritism and protectiveness with which Congress treats the Corps. In short, the Corps has reigned among that tiny pantheon of administrative agencies almost untouched by the political hazards faced by other bureaus.

There are several circumstances that have both contributed to the Corps' favored status and, directly and indirectly, led to its conflict with conservationists; among these are the pork-barrel system in Congress, the Corps' own political astuteness, and the phalanx of private interests associated with the Corps.

PORK-BARREL POLITICS. To their critics, the Engineers are mercenary pork-barrel soldiers, a simplification that nonetheless recognizes that the Corps is one popular conduit for the heavy flow of pork-barrel appropriations that annually emerge from Congress.[5] Pork-barrel funds are moneys allocated by Congress for federal works at the state and local level—rivers and harbors projects, interstate highways, military bases, space installations, and other enterprises. Pork-barrel projects are extremely important to virtually all congressmen. In American political culture, senators and representatives are expected to produce a reasonable flow of pork-barrel appropriations for their constituents if they are to retain the favor of local political influentials. Pork-barrel projects infuse new federal money into constituencies, creating construction and service jobs, often producing large, continuing employment and payrolls, and frequently enhancing the civic ambience of communities; in depressed areas, pork-barrel spending may be the customary remedy for a sagging economy.

It is understandable that legislators, eager to discover and maintain projects in their districts for which pork-barrel appropriations can be made, should look toward flood control, water recreation development, hydroelectric sites, reservoirs, canals, and other projects under the authority of water resource agencies such as the Corps. Thus, political realities create a community of interest between Congress, with its appetite for political pork, and the Corps, with its aptitude for public works. This affinity has obvious benefits for the Corps. It disposes Congress to appropriate handsomely for the Corps' projects and to protect the Corps' autonomy within the administrative branch so that it will continue to be responsive to Congress without serious obstruction from administrative superiors less addicted to the pork barrel. But the Corps' unchallenged ascendancy among water resource agencies results, in addition, from almost a century's lead over its administrative competitors in building strong Congressional relations and its virtuosity at cultivating Congressional favor.

"AN UNCOMMONLY CORDIAL RELATIONSHIP." The traditional working relationship between Congress and the Corps can best be shown by examining briefly the planning procedures for water resource projects entrusted to the Corps. This planning involves five steps:[6]

1. Local interests request a member of Congress to propose a project. The legislator seeks, and commonly obtains, authorization for the Corps to undertake the study from the appropriate Congressional committee.
2. The Corps makes a preliminary examination to determine the project's economic feasibility.
3. If the preliminary study is favorable, a detailed engineering and economic study is made.
4. If detailed studies still justify the project, it is customarily authorized by Congress.
5. Congress appropriates funds for the project; contracts are let out and actual construction begins.

The procedure is extremely sensitive and responsive to congressmen and their constituencies. Legislators, in collaboration with local partisans of a project, initiate all Corps studies. While the Corps does not report favorably on all projects, its planning arrangements provide project promoters with many opportunities to influence agency planners and to advance their arguments effectively. During the early planning stages, for example, the Corps routinely arranges public hearings within the area affected by a proposal. Enthusiasts for the enterprise customarily appear in force to testify to its virtues, while the hearings often generate additional local mobilization for the project and further publicize it. According to one careful estimate, there are at least thirty-two points in this planning process at which groups may voice their views to the Corps or to Congress.[7] In cases where projects are unfavorably reported, an elaborate review and appeals system exists within the Corps structure, offering project promoters a chance to urge reconsideration and further study of a project's feasibility. In short, planning has been in good measure a system for representing and adjusting local group and Congressional sentiments on proposed water resource projects. Indeed, "the planning process appears to be specifically organized in response to the need for an adjustment of group interests at the several levels at which these interests may become articulate."[8] This orientation within the Corps not only provides numerous opportunities for the expression of group opinion but also—whether intentionally or not—gives prominent voice to those most likely to promote public works in the constituency.

This planning method also means that individual projects are normally considered in isolation from one another. With its bias toward local interests and their Congressional spokesmen, the Corps concentrates on solving the engineering and economic problems associated with the specific projects advanced by such interests, and it gives comparatively little attention to the cumulative effect of individual work on large areas or whole river basins. Such an approach allows the Corps great freedom to evaluate and respond to proposals for particular projects without the constraints imposed by a comprehensive water development plan into which individual projects would have to fit or perish.

In all its planning and project investigations, the Corps insists that it is merely the administrative arm of Congress, responsible for evaluating and implementing such projects as Congress may entrust to it and offering its professional opinion when solicited. The Corps has steadfastly refused to take significant responsibility for creating and recommending to Congress any comprehensive plans for national water development. It will neither initiate comprehensive national water resource planning nor advise Congress about how such planning might proceed. In holding to this philosophy, the Corps has resolutely resisted repeated efforts to bring it within the control of a comprehensive water resource planning agency in the executive branch. As a result, the Corps can continue to encourage and respond to individual Congressional proposals without the shackles of a comprehensive plan to impede the input. Such a passive stance prevents the inevitable conflict—with the loss of Congressional grace—that would develop between the Corps and Congress if the Corps had to reject proposals on the grounds of good planning principles.

This is not to suggest that the Corps' passiveness extends to those Congressional proposals it might initially reject on engineering or economic grounds. Rather, these projects are frequently restudied until the Corps believes it has solved the original problems and can recommend the development to Congress. Sometimes a project, approved by the Engineers, may lie dormant because of the lack of Congressional funding or because the Corps has other projects to which it has assigned higher priorities. Such proposals seldom languish long, because the Corps will usually take the initiative in soliciting Congressional action upon them. In short, the Corps extends itself considerably to make projects feasible, and, notwithstanding its rejection of many projects, its working bias has been to find a way to get a project under way if at all possible.

The Corps' accommodation to Congress is mirrored in Congressional protection and promotion of the group. Congress has vigorously and successfully fought to maintain or improve the conditions enabling the Corps to work diligently at public works. The most conspicuous example is the repeated Congressional efforts to protect the Corps from the control of any executive agency or the President himself. At various times, Presidents Hoover, Roosevelt, Truman, and Eisenhower attempted to reassign the Corps' civil functions to other agencies, to impose greater White House control over the Corps, or to bring the Corps within the influence of a comprehensive water resource planning agency.[9] In all instances, Congress was instrumental in preserving the Corps' independence. During one period, between 1934 and 1942, twelve major efforts by President Roosevelt to alter the Corps' administrative autonomy were rebuffed. As a result, the Corps' formal position as a subordinate agency in the Defense Department is largely fictional. In theory responsible to the Secretary of the Army, the Secretary of Defense, and, finally, to the President, the Engineers have reported directly to Congress from whence come their marching orders.

Congress has looked after the Corps in other ways. The Engineers have a blanket authorization to initiate projects costing less than $1 million without specific Congressional approval, as well as permission to spend up to $10 million by committee resolution alone, a situation enabling the Corps to construct a continual array of small projects and giving it considerable bargaining power with congressmen who covet many modest developments in their districts.[10] Once Congress has authorized a project study, the Engineers are free to continue it indefinitely and, should they find the project feasible, to then propose it for funding. Some current Corps undertakings have ripened for centuries. The massive Tennessee-Tombigbee Canal, now nearing completion at a cost of $1.5 billion, prevailed through twelve feasibility studies beginning in the late 1700's before it was finally authorized in the late 1960's; the Cross Florida Barge Canal, currently suspended by litigation, was first studied in 1842. Congress also retains the right to authorize projects in spite of economic unprofitability or environmental damage, as it did with the Tennessee-Tombigbee waterway.[11] Congressional hearings on Corps appropriations and favorable study reports have been predictably amiable and complimentary. Although Congress has required in NEPA that all Corps project proposals be accompanied by environmental impact statements, Congressional committees pay them slight attention. A few legislators have frequently voiced disenchantment with the Corps and have proposed its reorganization in the name of better resource planning, but they are a distinct minority, impotent to ruffle seriously what one representative observer has called "the uncommonly cordial" understanding between the Corps and Congress.

GROUP SUPPORT.   The Corps' legislative support is augmented by vigorous promotion of its programs by a great diversity of public and private groups with a stake in the Corps' endeavors. The Corps awards contracts to private firms for almost all its construction and service needs on individual projects; more than half a billion dollars in such contracts is annually dispensed to dredge-and-fill companies, concrete producers and purveyors of other building materials, land-clearing enterprises, general contractors, electric contractors, equipment manufacturers, and a host of other firms. Past recipients of such largess and those with hope of future reward are customarily sympathetic to the Corps programs. So, too, are the local chambers of commerce, small businessmen, tourist industries, hotel and restaurant proprietors, land developers, and recreational interests, all of whom expect an economic boost or new amenities from various developments. Thus, rejoiced one partisan of the Tennessee-Tombigbee project: "It will cause the port of Mobile to boom and become one of the South's great cities. It will boost other cities and towns all along the way. And it will provide thousands of new jobs in one of the poorest corners of the country."[12] Especially in areas economically depressed, "thousands of new jobs" has irresistible appeal.

Those to whom the Corps' largess flows so generously include commercial barge and ship operators using completed canals and landowners with property adjacent to waterway improvements. The federal government charges no user's fee to commercial traffic on improved waterways—in effect, this amounts to subsidizing such activity; property owners may reap enormous windfall profits as their land value increases from waterway improvements. The National Water Commission, appointed by President Johnson to evaluate national water policy, has recently joined many other resource policy panels in urging both a user's fee and restraints upon the "unconscionable windfall profits" associated with Corps undertakings.[13]

The most effective national pressure group allied with the Corps is the 7,000-member National Rivers and Harbors Congress (NRHC), founded in 1901 to promote national water resource projects. A group embracing in its membership the U.S. Congress (all of whom are honorary members) and all the Corps personnel engaged in rivers and harbors works (as *ex officio* members), it also has fifty state organizations and additional affiliations from state, city, and county governmental agencies, water and land development associations, business firms, and other groups. Members of Congress and the Corps take an active part in the NRHC, serving as officers, workers, and—on several occasions—presidents of the association.[14] This produces an unusual situation in which members of the legislative and executive branches with responsibility for formulating water resource policy are themselves members of a major pressure group in water resource politics; although some congressmen, Corps officials, and many conservationists have objected to what they consider the impropriety of this arrangement, it has not been significantly challenged or widely exposed and debated. The NRHC actively promotes a variety of river and harbor projects through its annual hearings and studies at its national meetings, organizes and coordinates the work of groups lobbying for such projects, and brings together within one organizational roof public policy-makers and private project promoters in a traditionally cordial atmosphere. The work of the NRHC fosters a common outlook and amiable working relations between public officials and lobbyists in water resource matters and further contributes to the Corps' high standing among interest groups concerned with its work. Besides the NRHC, a variety of regional water resource organizations also exist that usually concentrate on promoting government water development within their own geographic boundaries; among these, the Atlantic Deeper Waterways Association and the Ohio Valley Conservation and Flood Control Congress are also influential in the deliberations of Congress and the Corps on policies affecting them.

The Corps' group support rounds out the political profile of an agency that has successfully combined a remarkable degree of administrative autonomy with great finesse in Congressional policies to establish a control over national water resource development that pales its administrative rivals. Such a lofty position makes it logical and inevitable that environmentalists concerned with water resource policy should focus on the Corps.

CONSERVATIONISTS AND THE CORPS

"In the view of conservationists," writes John McPhee, "there is something special about dams, something—as conservation problems go—that is disproportionately and metaphysically sinister." To many, dams are the conservationist's evil incarnate:

> The outermost circle of the Devil's world seems to be a moat filled mainly with DDT. Next to it is a moat of burning gasoline. Within this is a ring of pinheads each covered with a million people—and so on past phalanxed bulldozers and bicuspid chain saws into the absolute epicenter of Hell on earth, where stands a dam.[15]

It is a rare conservationist, in any case, who does not consider many dams and other federal water resource developments to be among

Washington's most objectionable creations. Environmentalists have not been unappreciative of the valuable water resource projects sponsored by Washington, but they believe such benefits are increasingly overshadowed by the indiscriminate planning and building of federal projects with little intrinsic merit and enormous environmental cost —of which dams are the most obvious examples.

The "Engineering Mentality"

The conservationist's most fundamental criticism of the Corps is that it is insensitive to the environmental degradation it creates. Supreme Court Justice William O. Douglas, an arch-conservationist, once complained: "The Corps has no conservation, no ecological standards. It operates as an engineer—digging, filling, damming the waterways."[16] Conservationists argue that the Corps is captive to an "engineering mentality" that leads it to approach a project without regard to environmental amenities, aesthetics, or long-term ecological consequences; only technical problems and solutions matter. One indication of this, suggest the critics, is the Corps' "straight-line syndrome"; it seems compelled to straighten out the pleasing bends and curves in waterways and, in so doing, systematically obliterates a river's natural beauty and much of its original ecology. Moreover, the argument continues, the Corps has an aversion to free-flowing water; it must be dammed and impounded. "A free-flowing river is to any Army engineer what an unlicensed dog is to a dog-catcher," runs a variation of the complaint; "his first duty is to impound it or otherwise prevent it from running wild."[17] This environmental indifference often produces grave environmental degradation in the wake of Corps projects: Continual dredging and filling of estuaries destroy irreplaceable habitats, with their valuable wildlife and commercial fishing resources; deepening or widening rivers and constructing canals increase siltation to dangerous levels and often produce pollution of water bodies into which the streams and rivers flow.

Environmentalists have joined many resource planners and public administration experts in indicting the Corps for its failure to practice comprehensive water development planning and for its tendency to view individual projects in isolation from one another. This myopia, they maintain, prevents the Corps from using a sounder approach in which comprehensive development plans for whole river basins or watersheds would come first; then the utility and impact of individual projects could be better evaluated and, if necessary, the projects abandoned. Under the more or less piecemeal planning system used by the Corps, suggest these observers, there is too much duplication of, or counterproductivity among, projects and unanticipated environmental damage that might be avoided by more deliberate, area-wide thinking. Conservationists have pointed to many specific projects to illustrate their charges against the engineering mentality; among them are the following:

• *The Cross Florida Barge Canal.* When it was to be completed in 1974, the east-west canal through the upper Florida peninsula would have destroyed twenty miles of the Oklawaha River by straightening and dredging. The Oklawaha, one of the few "wild rivers" remaining in the United States, was then being considered for governmental protection. Moreover, the canal, by cutting into the Florida aquifer, the ground water system supplying all of southern Florida, was likely to alter its composition, possibly polluting it and changing major underground springs farther south.

• *The Libby Dam (Montana).* To be completed in 1972 at a cost of $428 million, the dam across Montana's Kootenai River has begun backing up water to an eventual length of 90 miles, creating a gigantic new lake. Erected to control flooding from the Columbia River, it has ended the popular cut-throat trout fishing in the Kootenai. Quite unexpectedly, the dam produced an infusion of so much dissolved nitrogen in water below the dam that major fish kills have occurred.

• *The Tennessee-Tombigbee Canal.* Begun in 1971, the waterway would be a 170-mile canal, dam, and lock project linking the Tennessee River at its southern end; estimated costs were $1.6 billion. Conservationists assert that little study was given to the consequence of linking two rivers with different ecologies, that large tracts of prime forest and agricultural land would be inundated, with a great loss of fish and game habitat—a consideration that did not appear to trouble the Corps.

In these instances, which environmentalists argue are typical of Corps project planning, environmental problems were given little, if any, attention until they actually occurred or until the projects were too far along to be stopped easily.

The Smell of Pork

Conservationists believe that environmental damage from such projects is greatly compounded by the Corps' tireless promotion of projects that will maintain its Congressional favor and bureaucratic prosperity. They point out that this unceasing quest for new undertakings not only disinclines the Corps to take account of environmental values but also encourages it to seek truly massive, "big water" projects with ill-considered repercussions. Many conservationists believe the Corps has become too indiscriminate in its desire to satisfy Congress with big water construction. They cite as an example the Corps' enthusiasm for the Ramparts Dam development. In response to Congressional authorization, the Corps studied, then proposed the damming of Alaska's Yukon River, the nation's fourth largest. Estimates in 1964 suggested that the project, costing possibly $20 billion, would create a dam 530 feet high and stretching 4,700 feet across the Yukon Valley; behind it would grow a reservoir larger than Lake Erie —an inland water body two hundred miles long and eighty miles wide. The primary purpose of the project was power generation; generally considered an excellent hydroelectric site, it would have produced 34 billion kilowatts of power. Although Congress initially viewed the plan favorably, conservationists and their Congressional allies stopped appropriations by arguing that the environmental damage would be massive: The U.S. Fish and Wildlife Service estimated that the *annual* wildlife loss would be 1.5 million ducks, 12,800 geese, 10,000 cranes, 20,000 grebes, 13,000 moose, 3.6 million commercial fur-bearing animals, and 400,000 salmon. Also, emphasized the opponents, by the time the electric power was available, there would be more economical means for generating what, in any case, would be energy vastly exceeding Alaska's needs for decades. Conservationists regard the dam's defeat as a major victory but hasten to point out that such proposals demonstrate the Corps' lack of restraint in its search for new undertakings.

More recently, the Engineers, in coalition with Texas' large Congressional delegation, have vigorously promoted the $1.6 billion Trinity River Project to dredge a canal between Dallas–Fort Worth and Houston. Although a public referendum in the affected counties soundly rejected the plan, the Corps has continued to advertise its virtues, which, the Engineers allege, include substantial recreational benefits and low-cost commercial barge traffic between the state's largest cities. This appetite for projects, ecologists assert, is often whetted because the salaries for the Corps' civil employees, the great bulk of its personnel, are always charged against a specific project and, thus, their continuing employment depends on a steady flow of new undertakings.

The pork-barrel system has also frustrated environmentalists by making the Corps almost impervious to change. Most of the indictments leveled against the Corps by environmentalists have been made, with slight variation, for at least a half century with little effect. While the Ramparts Dam incident, among others, demonstrated that conservationists, working with sympathetic public officials, have sporadically affected Corps policy, these occasional reversals produced no fundamental change in the Corps' philosophy. Remarked a former chairman of the Corps Environmental Advisory Board: "Only when monumental, countervailing, external political pressure was used have the Corps project directions been forced to change."[18] Such pressure—"monumental, countervailing, external"—is rarely generated.

The Benefit-Cost Formula

A project is seldom authorized unless the Corps can demonstrate to Congress that the undertaking has a favorable "benefit-cost ratio." Although Congress can, and occasionally has, authorized projects without a favorable b/c ratio, this calculation customarily becomes the standard for estimating a project's value. This formulation has been carefully scrutinized and often criticized by environmentalists, economists, planning experts, and even some Corps officials. To many environmentalists, the deficiencies that abound in the preparation of these cost estimates are a case of bad economics becoming the consort of poor ecology in the service of the Corps' need for political security.

Since 1936, Congress has usually required that any federal improvement of navigable waters should be undertaken only when "the benefits to whomsoever they may accrue are in excess of the costs."[19] The Corps, like other federal water resource agencies, prepares and presents to Congress a benefit-cost ratio for every project it studies; if, after complex calculations, the expected economic benefits over the life of the project (commonly estimated to be fifty years) exceed its total cost, the project is usually undertaken. In practice, this means that a project must have a benefit-cost ratio exceeding 1.0—that is, a return greater than one dollar for every dollar invested. Authorized projects usually have ratios of 1.05 or better. The Corps can include numerous possible benefits when assigning value to a project. In the case of a dam and reservoir, for instance, it can consider benefits in flood control, water supply, fish and wildlife enhancement, recreation, water quality, power production, transportation, irrigation, or general regional economic improvement, among many other items. Costs have traditionally included the equipment, material, and manpower for the job, the cost of land used for the undertaking, and the expense of relocating homes, communities, highways, and other structures affected by the system. Corps officials, in defense of their calculations, point out that they are sufficiently rigorous to result in the rejection of more than half the projects studied.

Environmentalists object not to the principle of a benefit-cost calculation but to the manner in which the Corps usually comes up with its figures. The Corps, they charge, will exaggerate benefits and unreasonably minimize costs to enhance projects, and it commonly manipulates the figures until it can produce a favorable ratio for a Congressionally important project. Since Congress seldom studies a favorable benefit-cost ratio carefully, the formulation too often becomes a formality to justify projects that have not been subjected to a truly rigorous economic investigation. "It's nothing but a ritual," charged a former colonel with the Engineers. "They come down the aisle swinging their incense and chanting 'benefit-cost.' You can adjust the b-c ratio to justify any project. I did it a few times myself."[20] Specifically, conservationists point to some of the following deficiencies in estimates of project benefits that economists have frequently noted:

1. *Overestimating transportation benefits.* The Corps commonly assumes a greater volume of water traffic for a project than actually develops.

2. *Misleading flood control benefits.* By a curious logic, the Corps often builds a dam in order to protect an area from flooding and then lists among its benefits the control of floods for residents who would not move into the area unless the dam were built. Flood control is often temporary, in any case, for dams frequently suffer quick siltation.

3. *Exaggerated recreational benefits.* Often, reservoirs and other impoundments that are supposed to provide extensive recreational opportunities soon silt up or develop aquatic weed and pollution problems to the point where they discourage recreational use. Also, in cases where such damage does not occur, actual use falls below anticipated levels.

4. *Overly optimistic economic gains for an area.* Too often, the Corps anticipates an influx of new business and a general rise in area prosperity that is difficult to calculate in advance or fails to develop after construction.

These inadequacies have largely surfaced only since NEPA has encouraged the courts to give b/c calculations searching scrutiny. During judicial review of the Corps' Trinity River Project, for instance, the court found that the Engineers had based their estimates for recreational use of the new project upon such dubious calculations as "increased urbanization, increased leisure time for the elderly and the large number of young people not in the labor force"; that the costs and benefits were not figured over the same geographic area; that the Corps' estimate of recreational use exceeded by five times those of the Fish and Wildlife Service and by three times those of the National Park Service. Noting this shaky logic, the judge ruled the b/c calculation inadequate.[21]

Among the inadequacies in figuring the costs of a project, environmentalists would put first the Corps' failure to calculate the toll of environmental damage that often accompanies a project. No estimate is provided, they note, for such effects as the destruction of game and fish habitat, the loss of timber and agricultural land, the loss of a stream's free-flowing character, or the transformation of a wildnerness area into commercial and recreational development following a project's completion. Moreover, they point out that other costs are often underestimated, so that large cost overruns are frequent. Cost overruns of 30 to 100 per cent are not rare; several recent projects have cost almost 400 per cent more than estimates.

Virtually all economists familiar with water resource planning have pointed to the "discount rate" used in benefit-cost calculations as the system's greatest weakness. In simple terms, the discount rate is the return the government might expect on the money it invests in a project if it invested the same money over a comparable period in another enterprise; it is somewhat analogous to an interest rate and should generally compare to interest rates common for major types of commercial investment. The lower the discount rate applied to a project, the higher the benefit-cost ratio will be. Low discount rates thus increase the prospects for producing a favorable cost ratio; conversely, as discount rates rise, a favorable cost ratio is more difficult to obtain. Until the late 1960's, Congress permitted the Corps to use a discount rate of 3⅛ per cent, far below what economists believed to be a reasonable figure. In 1974, Congress set a new rate that will eventually raise the discount to perhaps 7 per cent—still below that considered adequate by most experts; a "grandfather clause" also ensured that most projects authorized before 1969 would be planned and evaluated with the very low 3.25 per cent rate. The result of consistently low rates has been to produce a favorable benefit-cost ratio for many projects that could not have been justified with more realistic discounts; according to one estimate, the Corps would have had to reject nearly half of the 578 projects it had authorized in early 1972 if a discount rate higher than the conservative 5⅛ per cent had been used.[22]

In any case, environmentalists are correct in asserting that the Corps' benefit-cost calculations have produced numerous uneconomical, if not unnecessary, projects. After carefully studying almost 150 federal water resource projects constructed in the South after World War II, one economist concluded that almost half (63) had proved too poor an investment to have been justified; a comprehensive national study would probably reveal an equally substantial record of unwise investment elsewhere.[23] Until the 1970's, however, all these protestations availed conservationists very little, for the Corps and Congress showed little inclination to alter their approach to water resource projects and environmentalists lacked the political leverage to force a change. Then, in the early 1970's, came a swift succession of events suggesting that an environmentally sounder philosophy of water management may be forced upon the Corps.

THE CORPS AS ENVIRONMENTAL DEFENDER?

By an ironic twist of agency fortunes, the Corps has found itself, unexpectedly, in the unaccustomed role of environmental defender. A series of Congressional enactments has thrust upon the Engineers a new definition of their mission in which preservation and enhancement of the environment must be given major attention. An agency that has spent a century and a half fashioning its political success by largely ignoring ecological values does not easily reform; there is evidence, however, that the Corps is struggling to conform to the new ecological standards.

Regulating Dredging and Filling

The Corps has inherited a major responsibility for environmental management through three recent Congressional enactments. The Federal Waste Pollution Control Act Amendments (1970) now invest the Corps with the authority to issue permits for the disposal of any dredged material in the "navigable waters" of the United States; the Maritime Protection, Research and Sanctuaries Act (1972) expands this authority to "ocean waters." Together, these bills bestow on the Corps control of virtually all significant dredging operations in U.S. waters. Almost all development in the ecologically important coastal zones, estuarine land, riverfronts, and lakefronts of the nation require dredging and filling; control of these conditions, with its power also to prohibit such development, gives the Corps a potent role in shaping the ecological destiny of American wetlands. Traditionally, the Corps gave little attention to the ecological consequences of dredging and filling; its previous authority over such activity, when it was exercised, seldom impeded the developer's shovels. However, the Rivers and Harbors Flood Control Act of 1970 requires that the Corps consider "the possible adverse economic, social and environmental effects" of such operations. Essentially, the Corps is now expected simultaneously to control dredge-and-fill operations and to apply environmental impact considerations to the task.

These new responsibilities have abruptly altered the customary accord between developers and the Corps. Previously, the Corps facilitated development; now it must regulate it. One result has been that an adversary relationship has frequently emerged between the Corps and developmental interests. One striking illustration was the Corps' decision in 1976 to refuse a permit for the huge Deltona Corporation to dredge and fill 2,500 acres of Florida mangrove swamp on Marco Island, near Miami, for housing lots. The Corps' refusal, a pleasant surprise to ecologists, was based largely on its judgment that too much of the nation's rare and endangered mangrove swamps would be irretrievably lost. Predictably, Deltona has challenged the decision through the courts. As the Corps' authority over dredge and fill has expanded, so has the political pressure and counterpressure upon the agency from developers and ecologists attempting to influence the terms of permits. Once the Corps was a stranger to such political cross pressure; now it is in the middle.

The Impact of NEPA

No federal agency has felt the impact of the National Environmental Policy Act more directly than the Corps. Like all other federal agencies, the Engineers must prepare the impact statements required by Section 102 for all "significant actions affecting the environment"; this covers practically every project presently authorized, now under construction, or proposed by the Engineers. In the mid-1970's, the Corps was second only to the Department of Transportation in the volume of impact statements rolling from its bureaucratic mills; at an estimated cost exceeding $25 million yearly, the Corps was producing more than three hundred statements annually.[24] Equally important, Corps projects have been a favorite target of ecologists eager to challenge federal environmental policies on grounds of their incompatibility with NEPA. During the early 1970's, so many Corps projects were tied up by litigation that the agency's program schedule was seriously retarded.

Armed with Section 102, environmentalists initially challenged Corps projects because they allegedly lacked satisfactory impact statements. Like most other federal agencies, the Corps did not at first know what was required in satisfactory statements and was not anxious to find out. Regarding the impact assessments with a mixture of annoyance, confusion, and apprehension for the agency's future, the Corps failed to satisfy the courts. Thus, by 1972, more than fifteen major projects, including the huge Tennessee-Tombigbee Canal and the Cross Florida Barge Canal, were halted by court injunction until the Corps could produce satisfactory impact assessments for them. Gradually, the bureaucratic fog lifted. By the mid 1970's, the courts had clarified NEPA's murky language sufficiently to permit federal agencies to discern what, in general, they had to do to prepare satisfactory impact statements.[25] As the Corps slowly adjusted its organization and procedures to accommodate these new judicial constraints, projects were gradually freed from judicial injunctions based upon the agency's failure to produce satisfactory statements for them. Decades will elapse before the courts fully interpret NEPA's intent, but the Corps has largely routinized its impact statement procedures in accord with judicial guidelines to the extent that obvious errors in statement preparation are increasingly avoided.

What has NEPA's impact been upon the Corps? There is little doubt that the courts have forced the Corps to follow very careful and extensive *procedures* to assess the environmental impact of its activities. Among the major judicial rulings defining these procedures, the following have been particularly important:[26]

• The Corps must reassess all previously authorized projects (including those authorized before NEPA) with attention to their environmental impact as outlined in Section 102.

• The Corps must adopt new decision-making procedures, including new environmental impact measurements, when assessing environmental consequences of projects.

• The Corps must, in most cases, evaluate the uncompleted portions of projects already under way to determine their environmental consequences.

- Even very small projects are covered by Section 102. Thus, the Corps was required to file an impact statement for a proposal to condemn 250 acres of grazing land for flood control.

- The Corps' benefit/cost calculations must take careful account of the costs involved in the loss of ecological resources from any project construction.

This latter ruling, opening for the first time the previously sacrosanct benefit/cost calculation to full judicial inspection, is particularly noteworthy because it enables ecologists to challenge judicially the major justification for most Corps undertakings.

There is, however, another important aspect in the Corps approach to impact statements. Although the courts have clearly ordained rigorous procedures for preparation and consideration of impact statements, to ecologists there is a more vital issue: Do these procedures actually result in more ecologically sensitive decisions? The preparation and examination of impact statements can easily become an empty ritual, an agency game in which great motion produces little ecological meaning. There is no guarantee that following the correct procedures will necessarily lead to heightened environmental consciousness; numerous federal agencies have demonstrated an impressive ability to assess the environmental consequences of their policies with fine exactitude and then ignore the findings.

It is difficult to find unambiguous evidence that the new procedures have changed the quality of the Corps' stand in the Deltona case as evidence of a new ecological awareness. The Council on Environmental Quality, additionally, has cited at least a dozen Corps projects that have been dropped or abandoned because NEPA procedures revealed significant environmental damage. At the same time, the Corps has shown no aversion to promoting a number of projects, such as the Cross Florida Barge Canal and the Trinity River Project, from which extensive environmental losses would undoubtedly occur. In short, it is too early to tell whether the Corps has truly altered its historic indifference to environmental values or whether it has only experienced a momentary conversion that may not last the decade. Some ecologists are hopeful. In perhaps the most generous verdict on the Corps' behavior to date, one careful observer has congratulated the agency for changing "from a regulatory agency narrowly concerned with the enhancement of maritime commerce to a regulatory agency concerned with the general welfare, including environmental values."[27]

NOTES

1. *Miami Herald,* October 6, 1968.
2. Grant McConnell, *Private Power and American Democracy* (New York: Vintage Books, 1970), p. 196.
3. The history of the Bureau of Reclamation is summarized in George Laycock, *The Diligent Destroyers* (New York: Ballantine Books, 1970), pp. 85–87.
4. This summary of Corps history and functions is taken from Arthur Maass, *Muddy Waters* (Cambridge, Mass.: Harvard University Press, 1951), chapter 1; and *New York Times,* November 19, 1971.
5. The pork-barrel system is well documented. Two conservationist indictments may be found in Arthur E. Morgan, *Dams and Other Disasters* (Boston: Porter Sargent Publisher, 1971), chapter 4; and Elizabeth B. Drew, "Dam Outrage: The Story of the Army Engineers," *Atlantic,* April, 1970, pp. 51–62.
6. Arthur Maass, *op. cit.,* pp. 22 ff.
7. *Ibid.,* p. 51.
8. *Ibid.,* p. 37.
9. The chronology of this battle is summarized in Arthur Maass, *op. cit.,* pp. 72–119.
10. Arthur E. Morgan, *op. cit.,* chapter 4.
11. The Corps' relationship with Congress, particularly those aspects involving legislative authority to authorize projects, is carefully explored in Garrett Power, "The Federal Role in Coastal Development," and William A. Hillhouse III, "The Federal Law of Water Resource Development," in Erica L. Dolgin and Thomas G. P. Guilbert, eds., *Federal Environmental Law* (St. Paul, Minn.: West Publishing Co., 1974); pp. 792–843, 844–927.
12. *New York Times,* June 22, 1976.
13. United States National Water Commission, *Water Policies for the Future* (Washington, D.C., 1973), p. 157; see also pp. 113–21.
14. This relationship is explored in Grant McConnell, *op. cit.,* pp. 218 ff.
15. John McPhee, *Encounters with the Archdruid* (New York: Farrar, Straus and Giroux, 1971), p. 158.

16. William O. Douglas, "The Corps of Engineers: The Public Be Damned," *Playboy,* July, 1969, p. 19.
17. Paul Brooks, "Notes on the Conservation Revolution," in John Mitchell and Constance L. Stallings, *Ecotactics* (New York: Pocketbooks, 1970), p. 40.
18. Charles M. Stoddard, former chairman of the Corps Environmental Advisory Board, quoted in *New York Times,* July 24, 1971.
19. Flood Control Act of 1936.
20. Edwin R. Decker, formerly the Corps' St. Louis District Engineer. Quoted in *New York Times,* February 20, 1972.
21. Frederick R. Anderson, Jr., "The National Environmental Policy Act," in Erica L. Dolgin and Thomas G. P. Guilbert, *op. cit.,* p. 317. The case involved is *Sierra Club* v. *Froehlke,* 359 F. Supp. 1289.
22. Estimated by U.S. Office of Management and Budget and reported in *New York Times,* February 20, 1972.
23. R. H. Haveman, *Water Resource Investment and the Public Interest* (Nashville, Tenn.: Vanderbilt University Press, 1965).
24. Council on Environmental Quality, *Environmental Quality: Sixth Annual Report* (Washington, D.C., 1975), pp. 636–37.
25. The early judicial history of NEPA is carefully documented in Frederick R. Anderson, *NEPA in the Courts* (Baltimore: The Johns Hopkins University Press, 1973).
26. The cases, in order of their citation in the text, are: *Calvert Cliffs Coordinating Committee* v. *AEC,* 449 F. 2d. 1109; *Sierra Club* v. *Froehlke,* 359 F. Supp. 1289; *United States* v. *247.37 Acres of Land,* 1 ELR 20513.
27. Garrett Power, *op. cit.,* p. 821.

7. No More Limitless Horizons : The New Politics of Land Use

Back then, EXPANSION FOREVER! The America of the first half of my life was one of limitless horizons, soaring expectations, progress, productivity, prosperity, abundance, expanding forever and ever, amen. Despite its miseries, the Great Depression, which I weathered in college, was seen as but an embarrassing pause in a production miracle which would fetch each American family a spacious home, vacations abroad and two cars in every garage. . . .

Fletcher Knebel[1]

The American land has always had a deep and abiding capacity to stir men's imagination. Its abundance seemed inexhaustible. America's first recognition in English literature, a passage in George Chapman's *Eastward Ho* (1605), dwelt upon its richness. "And is it a pleasant country withal?" asks a character. "As ever the sun shined on," his companion replies. Those who first saw the United States as a lush continental wilderness struggled for comparisons. "Take foure of the best kingdomes in Christendome," wrote the governor of Virginia in 1611, "and put them all together, they may no way compare with this countrie either for commodities or goodness of soil."[2] Most Americans have always agreed with Thomas Wolfe's conclusion in his lyric celebration of the American soil, *Look Homeward, Angel:* "It is a fabulous land. The only fabulous land."

Yet it was Alexis de Tocqueville, that most astute French observer, who probably captured most perceptively the American attitude toward the land. "Fortune," he remarked, "has given an immense booty to the Americans." Americans have commonly professed affection for the land; they have seldom seen themselves as plunderers or spoken of nature as spoil. Nonetheless, Americans have loved the land more than they have respected it. In their passion to exploit its abundance and in their conviction that nature was neutral stuff requiring human "development," they often behaved as if the land were spoil and they were annointed with a special destiny to inherit it. We have seen that Americans consumed the nation's physical abundance with extravagant disregard for consequences. Long after the American frontier ended, Americans acted as if they could forever follow the sun westward to new resources. Only belatedly, as the environmental movement testifies, has the nation begun the arduous task of adjusting cultural and political institutions to the new imperative of resource management.

In nothing were the Americans more lavishly endowed than with open space. Because open space has been traditionally plentiful and land relatively cheap, the nation has been particularly tardy in recognizing the need to conserve its remaining unsettled areas. The use of land still remains the one major environmental issue to which the federal government has yet to address itself fully. The issue, however, has become insistent. Within the last decade, state and local governments—the historical arbiters of land use—have been embroiled in bitter disputes over land use arising from growing competition for open space. These conflicts cannot be adequately resolved, or a satisfactory national land use policy developed, without federal participation.

Land use controversies are particularly intense over the issues of urban growth management and the development of the nation's coastal zones. These issues merit attention not only for their intrinsic importance in the political system but also for their environmental significance. Moreover, the mosaic of groups and political forces illuminated by these issues serves well to illustrate the general political character of most land use problems.

THE CLUTTERED HORIZON

The appearance of the land seems to belie any suggestion of a land use crisis. More than half the nation's acreage is still agricultural; of the remainder, about half is ungrazed forest land. Less than 3 per cent of the nation's total area, a comparatively small 60 million acres, is currently classified as urbanized or otherwise intensively developed. However, if one examines the rate at which the nation is consuming open space and confines attention to that portion of the land desired for settlement, a more accurate portrait of land pressures emerges.[3]

Land Hunger

Open space across the United States is disappearing at the rate of 1,000 square miles a year; an area the size of New Jersey is being converted from open to urbanized land each decade. Transportation projects alone devour huge areas.[4] Each mile of interstate highway requires about 48 acres to build; presently, the interstate system accounts for 26 million acres of rural soil. More land is required in the average city to accommodate human transportation than to accommodate the people transported: About two-thirds of many urban areas is devoted to streets, roads, and parking. However, population growth and the tides of human migration across the continent, which continually intensify the nation's urban growth, are the major cause of land development. The impact of this growth is suggested in Table 6, which describes the nation's urban growth from 1920 through its projected impact in the year 2000.

In the "sunbelt states," this population pressure is particularly heavy. Subdivision growth in California has reached 100,000 acres yearly. In Florida, 200,000 new recreation and retirement subdivision lots have been created each year of this decade. Americans seeking a place in the sun have flocked to Houston at the rate of 1,000 new residents a week; riding high and happily on this population wave, Houston has become a sprawling megalopolis, the nation's fifteenth largest city.[5] Since most of the nation's population lives on 10 per cent of the land, it is urban land and its fringes where the heaviest competition for land use exists.

The nation's hunger for open space has moved concurrently in the direction of rural and coastal lands—the most desirable remaining open space, the land most accessible to the urban resident. Since half the nation's population lies in states bordering the Great Lakes, the Gulf of Mexico, and the oceans, the country's coastal zones have inevitably felt the pressure for development. The "rural fringe" on the

TABLE 6. Population and Land Area of Urban Regions: 1920–2000

	1920	1940	1960	1980[a]	2000[a]
Number of urban regions	10	10	16	24	25
Population					
millions	35.6	53.9	100.6	164.6	219.7
Percent of total U.S.					
population	33.6	40.8	56.1	73.4	83.1
Land area[b]					
Square miles	60,972	94,999	196,958	395,138	486,902
Percent of total					
U.S. land area[c]	2.1	3.2	6.6	13.3	16.4
Gross population density					
People per square mile	584	568	511	417	451

[a] Based on Census Bureau series E population projection (based on a fertility assumption of 2.1 births per woman)
[b] Excludes urban region of Oahu Island, Hawaii
[c] Coterminous U.S. excluding Alaska and Hawaii
SOURCE: Jerome Pickard, "U.S. Metropolitan Growth and Expansion 1970–2000 with Population Projections," prepared for the Commission on Population Growth and the American Future at the Urban Land Institute, Washington, D.C., December, 1971.

perimeter of the typical city, commonly agricultural land, is rapidly yielding to the developer's bulldozers. Estimates suggest that more than 1 million rural acres a year are converted to housing, transportation, or industrial use. Population pressures will not abate soon; projections indicate that the American population will expand by an additional 50 million individuals before the turn of the century. To a large number of Americans, including for the first time a significant portion of public officials, these growth statistics spell an ominous message: the loss of amenities that make urban and suburban life desirable, growing congestion and discomfort, lost cultural and historical treasures, visual ugliness, the devastation of ecologically brittle wetlands, and, in general, growth out of control. The ecologist, in addition, sees this rampant consumption of open space as a threat to the nation's environmental health. A concern with growth, in effect, has allied the environmental movement with a much larger constituency of citizens and public officials who share with conservationists an alarm at unfettered land consumption. The result is a broad, and increasingly powerful, movement seeking constraints on land consumption.

The Growth Backlash

It is a significant sign of the times that according to a recent survey, American civic officials considered "land use" and "growth" to be the two most urgent environmental problems confronting local government. Indeed, for many public officials, "growth management" is *the* major public issue.[6] One result of this evolving official awareness of growth problems is a new attitude and an angry new rhetoric. Only a few decades ago, it would be hard to imagine the governor of a major state speaking of growth in the terms used by Oregon's Governor Thomas McCall:

> We are facing a shameless threat to the whole quality of our life— unfettered despoiling of the land. We find speculators despoiling the waterless desert and embarking on shoreline construction projects in a process we now call "condomania." Subdividers are chopping and thrashing away, making hamburger out of the magnificent landscape of Oregon. . . .[7]

Oregon is exceptional in the vehemence of its governmental resistance to unconstrained population growth, but the concern, in less extreme form, is practically universal among the states. Forty-eight states have now enacted, or are seriously considering, legislation to expand the previously limited role of the state governments in regulating land use. In an oft-quoted passage, the Task Force Report on the Use of Land, a major study sponsored by the Rockefeller Foundation, spoke of a "new mood in America . . . that questions traditional assumptions about the desirability of urban development."[8] This "new mood," which now seems to include almost all development, urban or otherwise, is one of the most remarkable transformations in the policy orientation of American public agencies in this century.

The politics of growth management begins when the rhetoric about growth management ends and practical policies must be formulated. It is quickly evident that those who agree on the need to "manage growth" do not necessarily share an understanding of what growth is to be controlled, where it is to be restrained, who should wield the proper authority, or what long-range objectives should be followed. Also, those who oppose growth in one perspective—say, the uncontrolled use of coastlands—may be quite unmoved at the prospect of farms on the urban fringe becoming hamburger stands and condominia. In short, the political issues and alliances involved in growth management are complex.

The Political Perspective

The political struggle over growth management, wherever found, involves some broad common components. First, the issue facing public officials and their constituents is *where* to permit growth, not whether there shall be additional open space surrendered to population pressures. "The needs of the American population," the Rockefeller Task Force noted pointedly, "existing and projected, can be met only through continuing development.... With high incomes have come high levels of consumption—automobile ownership, recreation, travel, the purchase of bigger homes and even second homes...."[9] In light of this unyielding reality, talk about "no growth" in any significant portion of the American population or "no further" conversion of open space is wildly unrealistic for almost any American community.

Second, American governmental units at all levels, like most other American institutions, have virtually no experience in creating and implementing managed growth policy; thus, how to manage land use to control growth has become a perplexing matter in which experimentation is often the solution. Conflicts over growth management often turn upon the question of which strategy will work and what consequences are likely to follow. Moreover, any management policy must pass a series of exacting judicial standards of acceptability; what is considered politically desirable or feasible in a community or a state may turn out to be illegal.

Finally, growth management is a highly divisive issue politically; it often tends to fragment communities and states into a large number of conflicting social groupings far more complex than might at first seem likely. Ecologists often embrace a simplistic Devil Theory that attributes most problems in growth management to "developers." In fact, growth management is likely to create at least five major political cleavages whenever it is attempted:

1. *Between ecologists and "developers."* Often, those who object to the continuing settlement of open land are individuals and groups whose primary aim is to preserve ecologically significant sites, such as estuaries or swamplands, for their ecological value.

2. *Between social classes.* Growth management has a capacity to stir antagonism between middle- and upper-class individuals, for whom "limited growth" often means "no more people around," and the disadvantaged, who perceive growth management as a ploy to exclude them from communities.

3. *Between levels of government.* Many of the bitterest conflicts over growth management involve arguments between state, local, and federal agencies over their respective rights and authority in land use decisions.

4. *Between the courts and other governmental agencies.* In the political struggle over growth policy, the courts are usually asked to become the arbiters whenever questions about the legality of policies arise. Almost always, the losers in the political struggle will seek a redress of their grievances through court action. Quite often, governmental agencies find themselves at odds with judges over when and how growth management can be properly achieved.

5. *Between communities and between states.* It is common for one community to perceive in another's growth management some form of discrimination against its neighbors. This is particularly likely when adjacent communities, or states, disagree over the value of growth management. Often, one community will allege that another, in enacting growth controls, is attempting to use its neighbors as a "dumping ground" for excess population.

All these cleavages will become evident as we explore in greater detail the issues of controlled growth in urban areas and the problems of coastal zone management.

THE CITY—GROWTH, SLOW GROWTH, OR NO GROWTH?

Almost three of every four Americans live in a metropolitan area; half of these reside in the suburbs. Traditionally, civic officials and business leaders equated growth with "progress"; continual urban expansion since the nation's founding was considered both normal and beneficial. America's cities continue to expand vigorously, most often by transforming agricultural acreage into subdivisions and shopping centers. Three of America's major growth counties illustrate the general trend: Suffolk County, New York, has lost almost half its agricultural acreage since 1960; Orange County, California, has lost 60 per cent of its prime agricultural land since 1950; and Washtenaw County, Michigan, has lost almost 50,000 acres to development within the last twenty years.[10] This apparently relentless absorption of open space is now being questioned, not only for the first time in many communities, but usually by many of those who once would have deemed it "progress."

What Is Wrong with Growth?

The President's Council on Environmental Quality succinctly summarized the indictment against urban growth: "Citizens in many communities share the feeling that the development process is out of control, that decisions are made which benefit only the influential developer's interests, and that piecemeal changes are having an unpredictable cumulative effect on the quality of life."[11] Some citizens would apparently be pleased if miraculously they could stop all further expansion of their communities, but it is the "out of control" aspect that appears to trouble most current critics of growth. In this perspective, it appears to many Americans that many communities are having to accept the "unpredictable cumulative effects" of this unrestrained growth as a cost while only the developers reap a tangible benefit.

Several specific effects of growth are now commonly cited as undesirable. To begin, the amenities that make urban and especially suburban living attractive are often imperiled. Suburbia has usually been the last outpost in the middle-class quest for the good life. Suburbanites have sought quiet, a reasonably clean environment, an atmosphere free of congestion, perhaps some open space, and a more relaxed pace of living. As suburbanization intensifies, however, they have increasingly found themselves witnessing the backside of "progress": traffic congestion, noise, air pollution, subdivision crowding, the disappearance of the open horizon, and visual ugliness wrought by shopping centers, quick food shops, highways, and the often reckless disregard for aesthetics in community planning. Having moved to the suburbs, they discover they can't leave the city.[12]

Environmentalists also cite the ecological costs of increased suburbanization. Stormwater runoff, a common urban problem, is a major source of water pollution; capturing the debris of city life, it contributes significant amounts of solids, pathogens, bacteria, and BOD to urban water contamination. Suburbia, particularly in its typical sprawl of single-family, low-density units, is a prodigious energy consumer. Half the nation's energy consumption is attributed to transportation and residential dwellings. For most Americans, suburban living would be impossible without the ready availability of cars and roadways; heating and cooling the average family home accounts for most residential energy use.[13] As cities expand, they often place extreme stress upon indigenous water supplies. Many cities, having already exceeded the carrying capacity of local water sources, must now survive at the end of a pipeline transporting additional water from vast distances. The resort communities of St. Petersburg, Clearwater, Madeiria Beach, and others on Florida's populous west coast have largely exhausted their own wells and now draw 80 million gallons daily from surrounding counties.[14] Tucson and Phoenix, the epitome of sunbelt boom towns, will have to depend for future water upon the contemplated Central Arizona Project to tap Colorado River water hundreds of miles away. Urbanization sometimes proceeds through the destruction of ecologically fragile but extremely valuable coastal zones and estuaries; wetlands are dredged and filled, coastlines yield to "condomania," floodplains blossom into tract homes.

The ecological costs of suburbanization often escalate because growth is largely unplanned; city zoning and provision of services are often reactive—an effort to catch up with new developments rather than to anticipate them. Better planning, many experts argue, could reduce the ecological and fiscal cost of suburbanization. Recent studies suggest, for example, that a combination of "clustering" (concentrating housing units only in several portions of a large subdivision) and high-density use (putting multifamily units in place of single-family dwellings) can produce significant resource conservation. Among the benefits:

• High-density, clustered communities may reduce the cost of housing a given number of individuals to almost half the cost of putting the same number of individuals in single-family, single-lot homes.

• Higher-density developments require less energy for heating or cooling and less auto use than low-density, subdivision-type homes.

• A clustered community with high density may require a third less water consumption than an equal number of people living in the traditional suburban subdivision.[15]

Innovations like clustering and high-density housing may at first seem objectionable because they ignore the low-density, subdivision arrangement so beloved by most suburbanites. However, these newer arrangements often preserve generous open space surrounding dwellings and, when attractively planned, can be as appealing as today's typical suburban tract.

Not least important, many suburbanites assert that the financial cost of expanding communities is now disproportionately borne by the existing taxpayers. It is often argued that new residential units often fail to "pay their own way," that after a community reaches a certain size, new residents enjoy expensive services without paying an equal share of costs. A recent study in Palo Alto, California, for example, suggests that it would require adding an additional $17,000 to the value of a $45,000 home in that community to generate the additional taxes necessary to equal what the home actually costs the community in services.[16]

Thus, growing disaffection with unconstrained urban sprawl feeds upon a variety of grievances. In an effort to turn the growth tide, a number of communities—the shock fronts of expansion—have taken the initiative in seeking remedies. This, in turn, has precipitated a mounting legal and political battle over control and direction of policy.

Local Action

The first governments to take measures aimed at controlling community growth have been local ones. In response to citizen pressures, about one-fifth of the nation's local governments have imposed, or have attempted to impose, some sort of restraint upon additional housing and commercial and industrial growth.[17] Techniques of growth control are still highly experimental. Some of the most common include the following:

1. *Sewer moratoria.* Many communities have declared a permanent or temporary end to additional sewer services for new residents and business. In Ohio and Illinois alone, more than 160 communities have implemented such measures; in Florida, forty communities established similar strategies between 1970 and 1974.

2. *Building permit moratoria.* Like sewer hook-ups, the control of building permits draws upon the existing powers of local governments as a control device. Building permits may be entirely eliminated or, more often, restricted to certain segments of the community or "phased" over a period of years with limits on yearly numbers.

3. *"Down-zoning" and large-lot zoning.* A number of communities have attempted to inhibit growth by lowering the density of residents permitted in given geographical areas. Through "down-zoning," communities reclassify higher-density areas to lower through zoning changes, e.g., an area may be down-zoned from apartments to single-family dwellings. Large-lot zoning, in contrast, involves classifying new areas for very large lots—6 acres per dwelling, for example—which would effectively keep the density very low per acre.

4. *Population or housing unit "caps."* In some areas, local governments have set numerical limits on the maximum size of the community through population figures or dwelling unit limits. Thus, a community may decide it will not exceed 100,000 population or will not permit more than 500 new dwelling units to be constructed.

5. *Growth phasing.* Some communities have attempted to control the pace of their growth not by creating absolute limits on dwelling units or population but by controlling the rate at which new units appear and, in some cases, the areas that develop. Some cities have formulated growth plans for several decades; over a given period, limits are set on the numbers of individuals or housing units to be

permitted, although no "caps" may be established for ultimate community size.

6. *Development rights.* A few community governments have sought to influence land use through public purchase of valuable open space, through the acquisition by government of certain "rights" to private land which restrict the use of the land to stated purposes, or through a requirement that portions of subdivisions be donated to public purposes by the developers. Collectively, these are known as "development rights."

7. *Preferential land assessment.* Some state and local governments are currently experimenting with the preferential assessment of open space, particularly agricultural and wetlands, to encourage the owners to keep them out of development. By providing a lower tax rate for such properties, governments hope to persuade owners (who must otherwise often pay a very high tax on their property) to retain them in their original condition.

These measures appear in numerous places and many combinations throughout the nation. In Livermore, California, an initiative measure passed by local voters in 1972 ordered the local government to shut off further building permits if community facilities were inadequate to serve new residents. According to the legislation, community services would be deemed "overextended" if the schools were forced to double sessions, or if water effluent from the local treatment plant significantly deteriorated, or if water had to be rationed to the existing population. The St. Petersburg (Florida) City Council, beset by rapidly falling water tables and rapidly rising population, sought to control both by setting the city's maximum population at 235,000— a measure that, if it had prevailed, would have amounted to ordering the last 5,000 residents arriving in the city to move elsewhere. In Suffolk County, a study of the county's existing zoning plan revealed that by the year 2020 the area would have permitted at least a million more individuals to settle there than the area could support; some high-density areas in the county were then down-zoned.

However much these and other growth control measures reflect the dominant sentiments in a community, they have been immediately challenged politically and legally because, in some cases, they go too far in the view of some interests and because, to others, they are not sufficiently comprehensive.

GROWTH CONTROL: THE POLITICAL CONFLICT

At the core of the conflict over community growth management are issues of equity and control. Who shall bear the costs, in their many different forms, for growth controls? Who shall decide how costs will be apportioned? Characteristically, the competing sides in a growth management debate are likely to assert that they favor "balanced" growth but that the policies they oppose place an inequitable cost upon themselves.

Property Owners and the "Taking" Issue

"With no mountains or gorges, Florida has no natural impediments to man-made changes," notes a Florida planning official. "Florida is like a big bag of silly putty, and it is being reshaped irreversibly in the hands of the big subdivision developers."[18] The lash of criticism against unplanned community growth, as this quote suggests, is likely to fall first upon developers. Those who live by purchasing, clearing, and developing land, together with those institutions such as banks or savings and loan associations which underwrite construction, often feel community constraints upon growth directly and sometimes severely. Additionally, owners of undeveloped land will feel penalized if growth restraints appear to deny them the opportunity to sell their property for its most profitable use. Developers and property owners, together with national trade associations representing the developer, property owner, real estate agent, and others, are usually the first to join the battle against growth restraints. Environmentalists and others critical of growth are prone to believe that it is unalloyed avarice that motivates such objection; however, it often happens that those restrained from land development do pay a very steep price in lost income, and their objections are understandable. One may feel some empathy for property owners like this Aspen (Colorado) developer, whose modest construction business was severely curtailed by the community's new growth controls:

I have a great deal of sympathy for [the controlled growth] aims. . . . I was glibly going along, but suddenly I couldn't hardly do any work around here any more. It's horrid. The county board is now totally arbitrary . . . to the point of taking over the right to pick the color of the paint on the porch of your house.[19]

The most powerful weapon property owners and developers have currently wielded against growth controls is the "taking" issue. The Fifth Amendment to the Constitution states that "private property" shall not be "taken for public use without just compensation." Property owners have sometimes successfully persuaded the courts that growth control measures that prevent an individual from selling his land for its most profitable use have suffered an unconstitutional "taking" of some portion of the property. Thus, if a property owner's land, once zoned for high-density apartments, is rezoned to lower density, he may assert to the courts that he has effectively lost the difference between the income he would have received for the high-density land and the (usually) lesser amount he will receive for the lower-density land—in short, public agencies are "taking" part of his prospective income. The courts have always permitted local, state, and federal governments to impose some restraints upon land use; the state's power to protect public health, safety, or welfare can legally be exercised, under appropriate circumstances, to regulate land use without the need for compensation or other redress. It is only when the judges deem the taking to be "unreasonable" that the property owner is entitled to compensation or other redress.

When is a taking reasonable? The courts currently vary in the criteria they apply in determining the legality of taking, and, consequently, rulings are often inconsistent. Several examples illustrate this trend:[20]

The Petaluma Case.　Nestled in the Sonoma County foothills north of San Francisco, Petaluma was one of many small cities experiencing a land boom converting them into bedroom communities for nearby urban areas. After growing from 14,000 to 25,000 residents between 1960 and 1970, the community passed by referendum in 1972 a measure declaring a five-year moratorium on all subdivision annexation. Thereafter, the city would extend services to only 500 new subdivision units a year. The law was challenged by the National Homebuilders' Association in alliance with many other developmental interests; more than 250 other communities joined in the defense.

Petaluma's plan was first ruled unconstitutional by the federal circuit court but was subsequently ruled valid by the appeals court and the U.S. Supreme Court. In the governing opinion, the appeals court declared: "The concept of the public welfare is sufficiently broad to uphold Petaluma's desire to preserve its small town character, its open space, and low density of population and to grow at an orderly and deliberate pace."

The Southeast Case. The tiny town of Southeast, New York, in 1970 increased the minimum lot size required for a subdivision while the developer's application for building approval was still pending before local government. The city based its decision primarily on environmental and public safety considerations. The city argued that the proposed development was in a part of the community where sewer and water facilities would be difficult to install because of the topography and that, as a result, only wells and septic tanks could be used. These, it argued, would contribute materially to water pollution if the area's original high density were maintained. A lower density, however, would better safeguard local water quality. Despite the court's acknowledgment that a water pollution problem might arise from the original high density, it overturned the town's decision because it would impose upon the developer an additional expense exceeding $3,000 per lot. This was "significant economic injury," in the court's opinion, for which countervailing considerations (such as the pollution problem) were not sufficient.

The Sanbornton Case. The hamlet of Sanbornton, New Hampshire, with a resident population of 1,000, moved in 1970 to prevent the development of a 500-unit recreational home subdivision by increasing the minimum lot size required to 6 acres. The developer appealed the decision to the courts. The federal circuit court upheld the town ordinance as a "stopgap" measure to prevent a population influx overwhelming the community's existing services. At the same time, however, the court warned that the ordinance appeared to spring from a desire "to keep outsiders, provided they wished to come in quantity, out of town." This, the court suggested, could not stand as a continuing justification for further growth restrictions.

It is still difficult to discern what broad guidelines the judiciary may design for determining when governments may restrain land use without violating the constitutional prohibition against taking. Apparently, the courts prefer to leave it to state and local governments to decide when land use may be regulated, provided the judges can find a legally defensible reason for this preference. Generally, the courts will permit such governmental action when there is a clear indication that state or local legislative authorities "have reached a considered judgment on the public interest and the private equities involved" in land use controls. This means that such constraints must be based upon a clear, explicit balancing of interests by such authorities and must also arise from reasonable grounds—that is, there must be some plausible justification (such as stress on community resources) for the limits imposed. Further, the courts now seem more willing than previously to consider carefully such matters as environmental costs, general community welfare, the preservation of open space, and the conservation of other amenities as justification for growth constraints. If these trends continue, legislative and executive agencies will increasingly shape land use decisions.

Minorities: "Snob Zoning" and "Exclusionary" Laws

Minority groups, particularly civil rights organizations, view community growth constraints with utmost suspicion because these policies can become, deliberately or unwittingly, instruments of social discrimination. Citizens promoting growth controls in the name of "ecology," "preserving open space," or "keeping a decent neighborhood," may be using social welfare as a camouflage for social prejudice.

The typical community now developing growth restraints is fairly homogeneous and socially distinctive; predominately white, affluent, suburban, and small or moderate in size. It often seems to the disadvantaged that these are embattled middle-class enclaves determined to preserve their social identity. One result is the unusual alliance between homebuilders and other development interests working with minority groups to challenge the constitutionality of growth restraint measures. Since the courts have demonstrated a readiness to strike down quickly such proposals if they appear to be "exclusionary"— that is, to discriminate against the disadvantaged—almost all current challenges to community development constraints are likely to allege that they will become discriminatory in some manner.

In fact, growth controls can readily become exclusionary, however unintentionally this may occur. Planned growth, or growth caps, will often drive up the cost of available undeveloped land and existing residential housing in a community when it becomes apparent that new housing in the community will be scarce. In the two years after Boca Raton, Florida, announced its intention to cap its residential development after 40,000 units, the price of vacant land within the city boundaries rose 25 per cent and existing homes increased 15 per cent in value.[21] Such price escalation can soon place even modest housing beyond the reach of moderate- or low-income groups. Large-lot zoning—"snob zoning" to its critics—has a similar effect. Communities committed to "phased growth"—in which extension of community services to new areas is planned years in advance and limited to those areas for which community services are already available—often do not provide for low-cost housing or moderately priced apartment complexes likely to appeal to the less affluent.

Beyond the effect on property values, spokesmen for minorities usually assert that any constriction of a society's economic growth will immediately and severely penalize the disadvantaged through its impact upon governmental budgets. Explains Bayard Rustin, director of the Urban League:

> A healthy rate of economic expansion is a precondition for the success of manpower and service programs that are directed to the special needs of the poor. Without substantial growth, we simply will not have enough jobs for those individuals who have undertaken training programs as a means of overcoming the effects of poor educational opportunity. Nor will government have the resources to build the housing, supply the medical services, and upgrade the schools in the inner cities.[22]

In light of the great discriminatory potential to be found in any proposal to limit community growth, it is understandable that the courts have very carefully scrutinized almost all such plans brought to the bench and have usually placed upon the authors a responsibility to demonstrate that such plans will not unfairly discriminate against the disadvantaged. Those growth management plans the courts have found acceptable, such as ones adopted in Ramapo, New York, and Petaluma, California, have carefully included provisions for housing and other services benefiting the less affluent. At the same time, newer proposals for growth control can be expected, almost routinely, to mobilize opposition from blacks and other minorities until the proponents can demonstrate (if they can) that their plans are not social discrimination dignified as social planning.

Government against Government

In a recent speech appealing for comprehensive federal land use planning, Senator Henry Jackson (D.-Washington) decried "the near-anarchy of present land-use decision-making policy."[23] Many experts have condemned the fragmentation of land use authority among many thousand local governments, the fifty states, and Washington. Such segmented decision-making, they assert, thwarts comprehensive planning and rational evaluation of land use. As communities begin to initiate growth control measures, conflict between governmental units has intensified and the need for comprehensive approaches seems increasingly urgent. Presently, local communities find themselves in constant conflict with one another and with the states in their attempts to make land use decisions.

Local governments are legally creatures of the states. Communities derive their authority, including the police powers and other authority utilized for land use control, from state governments. But for more than a century, the states have delegated great discretion to communities for land regulation so that local agencies have come to regard local control of land use as their prerogative and the essence of "democracy." Most local governments, resenting any state policy that seems to diminish local control of land use, vigorously resist attempts to bring local land planning within the ambit of higher planning authorities. Local governments commonly condemn, with equal vehemence, neighboring governmental policies that appear to encroach upon their own freedom of action in land use. Such mutual jealousy sets the stage for inevitable discord when one agency's land use decisions affect another's territory—an unavoidable situation, quite often, because the effects of land use decisions radiate far beyond the jurisdiction of a single local government. In particular, local governments committed to growth constraints often provoke opposition from adjacent communities because of the alleged "spillovers." County and city governments bordering on the St. Petersburg urban area, for example, attacked that city's proposed growth cap because, they alleged, it amounted to dumping unwanted population upon other communities and intensifying demands for costly services. Often, cities or counties committed to discouraging heavy industry find themselves condemned by their neighbors for pushing pollution problems upon other governments.

Growing discord between communities over land management has led many states to initiate comprehensive land use programs aimed at preventing incompatible or undesirable land use programs between local governments. In Table 7 can be found a recent inventory of these state land use laws. The table indicates how many states have provided "enabling legislation" for local governments to plan land use and what types of "functional programs" exist for land management at the state level. State efforts to regulate land use, or to place local land use decisions under some more comprehensive authority, usually provoke strong opposition from city, and sometimes county, governments. When California and Delaware enacted comprehensive regulations for coastal land development, a multitude of seaboard communities joined land developers and industry in combating the measures through state legislatures and the courts. Using authority conferred by Florida's new Land and Water Management Act (1972), the state cabinet in 1975 declared the ecologically endangered Florida Keys an area of "critical state concern" in an effort to prevent Monroe County and the Key communities from further damaging the islands by careless development. This, asserted the Monroe County Chamber of Commerce, was equivalent to Hitler's marching into Poland. Local governments declared political war upon the "invasion."[24]

Growing conflict between governmental units over land use reflects the deep contradiction between the historical direction of governmental land use policy, which favored its fragmentation and concentration at the local level, and the growing need for comprehensive, centralized controls over land planning. This is evident not only in the urban areas but also along the nation's coastal lands. Coastal zone

TABLE 7. Status of Land Use Legislation, April, 1975

State	Enabling legislation					Functional programs							State land use program[2]
	Munici-palities	Counties	Regional agency advisory only	Regional agency review authority	Procedures for coordination of functional programs	Land use-value tax assessment law	Surface mining	Flood plain regulations	Power-plant siting	Wet-lands manage-ment	Critical areas	Coastal zone[1] management program participa-tion	
Alabama	Yes	Yes	Yes	No	No	No	Yes	No	Yes	No	No	Yes	1
Alaska	Yes	Yes	N/A	N/A	Yes	Yes	Yes	No	Yes	No	No	Yes	2
Arizona	Yes	Yes	Yes	No	Yes	No	No	Yes	Yes	No	No	N/A	2
Arkansas	Yes	Yes	Yes	Yes	No	Yes	Yes	Yes	Yes	No	No	N/A	2
California	Yes	Yes	Yes	Yes	Yes	Yes	Yes	Yes	Yes	No	No	Yes	2
Colorado	Yes	Yes	No	Yes	No	Yes	Yes	Yes	Yes	No	Yes	N/A	3a-c
Connecticut	Yes	N/A	Yes	No	Yes	Yes	No	Yes	Yes	Yes	No	Yes	2
Delaware	Yes	No	Yes	No	Yes	Yes	No	No	No	Yes	No	Yes	2
Florida	Yes	Yes	No	Yes	Yes	Yes	No	No	Yes	No	Yes	Yes	3a-e
Georgia	Yes	Yes	Yes	No	Yes	No	Yes	No	No	Yes	No	Yes	2
Hawaii	No	Yes	N/A	N/A	Yes	Yes	No	Yes	No	No	No	Yes	3a-e
Idaho	Yes	Yes	Yes	No	No	No	Yes	No	No	No	No	N/A	2
Illinois	Yes	Yes	Yes	No	No	Yes	Yes	No	No	No	No	Yes	2
Indiana	Yes	Yes	Yes	No	Yes	Yes	Yes	Yes	No	No	No	N/A	2
Iowa	Yes	Yes	Yes	No	No	Yes	No	Yes	No	No	No	N/A	2
Kansas	Yes	Yes	Yes	No	No	No	Yes	No	No	No	No	N/A	2
Kentucky	Yes	Yes	Yes	No	No	Yes	Yes	No	Yes	Yes	No	N/A	2
Louisiana	Yes	Yes	Yes	No	No	Yes	No	No	No	Yes	No	Yes	2
Maine	Yes	Yes	Yes	No	Yes	Yes	Yes	Yes	Yes	Yes	Yes	Yes	2

Maryland	Yes	Yes	Yes	No	Yes	Yes	Yes	Yes	Yes	Yes	3a–c
Massachusetts	Yes	Yes	Yes[3]	No	No	Yes	No	Yes	No	Yes	2
Michigan	Yes	Yes	Yes	No	No	Yes	Yes	No	No	Yes	2
Minnesota	Yes	Yes	Yes[4]	No	No	Yes	No	No	Yes	Yes	2
Mississippi	Yes	Yes	Yes	No	No	No	No	Yes	No	Yes	2
Missouri	Yes	Yes	Yes	No	No	No	No	Yes	No	N/A	2
Montana	Yes	Yes	Yes	No	No	Yes	Yes	Yes	Yes	N/A	2
Nebraska	Yes	Yes	Yes	No	No	Yes[5]	No	Yes	No	N/A	2
Nevada	Yes	Yes	Yes	No	Yes	Yes	No	Yes	No	N/A	3a–c
New Hampshire	Yes	Yes	Yes	No	No	Yes	No	Yes	No	Yes	2
New Jersey	Yes	No	Yes	No	No	Yes	Yes	No	No	Yes	2
New Mexico	Yes	Yes	Yes	No	Yes	Yes	No	Yes	No	N/A	2
New York	Yes	Yes	Yes	Yes	Yes	Yes	No	Yes	No	Yes	3a–c
North Carolina	Yes	Yes	Yes	No	No	No	Yes	No	Yes	Yes	2
North Dakota	Yes	Yes	Yes	No	No	Yes	No	No	No	N/A	2
Ohio	Yes	Yes	Yes	No	No	No	No	Yes	No	Yes	2
Oklahoma	Yes	No	Yes	No	No	Yes	Yes	No	No	N/A	3a–c
Oregon	Yes	Yes	Yes	No	No	No	No	Yes	No	Yes	2
Pennsylvania	Yes	Yes	Yes	No	No	Yes	No	No	Yes	Yes	2
Rhode Island	Yes	N/A	No	No	Yes	No	No	Yes[6]	No	Yes	2
South Carolina	Yes	Yes	Yes	No	No	No	No	No	No	Yes	2
South Dakota	Yes	Yes	Yes	No	No	Yes	Yes	No	No	N/A	2
Tennessee	Yes	Yes	Yes	No	Yes	No	No	Yes[7]	Yes	N/A	2
Texas	Yes	No	Yes	No	Yes	Yes	No	No	No	Yes	2
Utah	Yes	Yes	Yes	No	Yes	Yes	No	No	Yes	N/A	3a–e
Vermont	Yes	N/A	Yes	No	Yes	Yes	Yes	Yes	No	N/A	2
Virginia	Yes	Yes	Yes	No	No	Yes	No	No	Yes	Yes	2

TABLE 7. Status of Land Use Legislation, April, 1975 (cont.)

| | Enabling legislation | | | | | | Functional programs | | | | | | |
State	Munici-palities	Counties	Regional agency advisory only	Regional agency review authority	Procedures for coordination of functional programs	Land use-value tax assessment law	Surface mining	Flood plain regulations	Power plant siting	Wet-lands management	Critical areas	Coastal zone[1] management program participation	State land use program[2]
Washington	Yes	Yes	Yes	No	No	Yes	Yes	Yes	Yes	Yes	No	Yes	2
West Virginia	Yes	No	Yes	No	Yes	No	Yes	Yes	No	No	Yes	N/A	2
Wisconsin	Yes	No	Yes	No	Yes	Yes	Yes	Yes	Yes	No	No	Yes	2
Wyoming	Yes	Yes	No	Yes	Yes	Yes	Yes	No	Yes	No	No	N/A	3a–d

[1]No state has an approved coastal zone management program at present.

[2]State land use program code

1. No activity at state level
2. Study (executive or legislative) or state legislative consideration in progress
3. State land use program legislation enacted

Authorization for:

(a) inventorying existing land resources, data and information collection
(b) policy study or promulgation by agency or commission
(c) identification of land areas or uses of more than local concern
(d) regulation or management of land areas and uses identified
(e) direct state implementation or state review of local government implementation.

[3]Areawide Council for Martha's Vineyard has authority to administer controls.

[4]Twin Cities Metropolitan Council has regulatory authority.

[5]Must be ratified in a referendum to take effect.

[6]In the coastal zone a development permit from the Coastal Council is required.

[7]Powerplant siting is conducted by TVA only.

SOURCE: Council on Environmental Quality, *Environment Quality: Sixth Annual Report* (Washington, D.C., 1975), pp. 185–86.

management takes on a special environmental significance because coastal lands are among the nation's most precious ecological resources and the most highly stressed by developmental pressures.

THE COASTAL ZONE

The nation's coastal lands are profusely productive. "Salt marshes in temperate zones and mangrove swamps in the sub-tropics are among the most productive environments in earth," notes the Council on Environmental Quality. "Their output of plant material equals that of tropical rainforests; they are twice as productive as ordinary farmlands."[25] A serious deterioration of sheltered estuaries could easily become an economic, as well as ecological, disaster; two-thirds of the commercially valuable fisheries on the U.S. Atlantic Coast and the Gulf of Mexico are in such estuaries. More than half the American population also lives in coastal counties bordering the Great Lakes, the Gulf of Mexico, and the oceans. Unrelenting pressure to develop the coastal wetlands, continuing unabated for more than a century, has seriously reduced the ecological vitality and availability of coastal land. In the thirty-two years between 1922 and 1954, for example, experts have estimated that the nation's productive coastal wetlands and marshes were reduced by 25 per cent; in this century, a half million acres of wetlands have been lost to ecological productivity along the Atlantic Coast alone.[26] The increasing shrinkage of coastal land more than diminishes the nation's ecological resources; it constricts the land available for public recreational use and often scars the coastline with ugly, ill-planned construction. In spite of frequent warnings by environmentalists and others that the coastlands are too ecologically brittle to sustain constant development, it has been difficult to restrain development until recently because coastal areas appealed to many diverse interests.

The Irresistible Wetlands

It is the misfortune of the coastal zone to offer irresistible attractions for man's business or pleasure. Industry often covets coastal sites; manufacturers like the accessibility to the oceans for waste disposal. Petroleum refiners prefer coastal lands amenable to conversion to accommodate tankers or to receive pumped petroleum from offshore sources. Power generating plants seek coastal locations where water is plentiful for generator cooling. With spreading affluence, millions of Americans look to the coastland for recreation; the most significant new source of pressure for coastal zone development comes from the recreation industry and others who cater to this rapidly expanding consumer market.

Coastal recreational development is now a big business. More than 300 companies, many part of large conglomerates, gross in excess of $3 billion yearly in this enterprise. The new consumer market stimulates ambitious plans and big projects. Seeking to capitalize on the consumer's taste for the tropics, C. Brewer and Co. has planned to develop five separate vacation centers on Hawaii's "Big Island," altogether embracing 7,500 acres of largely coastal land. The projected attractions were to include a $10.7 million Polynesian-style hotel and shopping center, 2,000 condominia, 3,600 vacation homesites, two golf courses, and extensive sports facilities. Although the state of Hawaii eventually reduced the scope of this project through land use regulations, big land developments are increasingly common in that state and others, like Florida, with attractive temperate climates.

Coastal migration involves more than wealthy Americans with visions of condominia in their heads. Developers are catering to an expanding market for modest "second homes," though they be only trailers. Between 5 and 7 million Americans, most with incomes below $15,000 yearly, own second homes or land in a prime recreational area, often in wetlands.[27] These second homes are frequently constructed in fragile areas, like ocean fronts, marshes, or coastal foothills unsuited to intensive development. In an effort to expand subdivision lots, builders have frequently dredged and filled estuaries, marshes, and tidal basins without regard to ecological consequences. This relentless dredging and filling, in particular, prompted the state of Florida to impose developmental constraints on the Florida Keys before their unique coral reefs were irretrievably lost; most of this filled land accommodated trailers.

As open coastal land simultaneously decreases in area and increases in value, its owners—like the owners of farmland on the city's periphery—are strongly tempted to sell their property. The owner of Kiawah Island, one of the largest among the lovely islands of the South Carolina outer banks, purchased his property for $125,000 in 1952 and sold it to developers for $17 million in 1973; it is not uncommon for vacant coastal land to appreciate several hundredfold in value over a ten-year period.[28] So long as thousands of individual property owners, businesses, land buyers, and development companies determined the pattern of coastal development through their own economic behavior—restrained, if at all, by the often feeble regulation of local governments—the continual disappearance of open wetlands was inevitable. Within the last decade, federal and state authorities have, for the first time, intervened to regulate coastal zone use; local governments, traditionally indulgent of land development, have lately demonstrated an awakened concern for their coastal jurisdictions. In reversing the historic trend of coastal land use, these governments have collaborated in the nation's first concerted governmental effort at land use planning.

The Awakened States

Recognizing the rapidly growing peril to their coastal wetlands, eighteen of the nation's twenty-one states bordering on the oceans and the Great Lakes now have legislation intended to regulate further coastland development or to control "critical areas" of which coastlands are among the most important. This assertion of inherent state authority over land use, though sometimes welcomed, has more often precipitated political conflict between state and local governments and between state authorities and development interests over coastal land use.

Two states, California and Delaware, have demonstrated special determination to control rigorously further coastal development and have become examples of strong regulatory programs. California has become, as in many matters of ecological policy, the leader. The California Coastal Zone Management Plan, passed through an initiative measure in 1972, created a twelve-member citizen panel, the California Coastal Zone Conservation Commission, with an interim three-year authority to restrict or otherwise regulate all development along the state's Pacific coast. This authority, exercised through the issuance of building permits by six regional subcommissions, covers an area from mean high tide to 1,000 yards inland. During this initial three-year period, the commission is also responsible for writing, for consideration by the state legislature, a long-range development plan, covering the entire coast from 3 miles at sea to 5 miles inland. The commission's operation has been predictably controversial. Developers assailed the plan as a "no-growth" policy. Coastal communities, facing the prospect of a permanent preemption of their land use authority by state and regional agencies, customarily condemned the measure. During the first three years of its implementation, however, there was little evidence that the plan had inhibited coastal development or had deflated property values, although several large developments with potentially serious aesthetic and ecological damage were prevented or seriously modified in order to receive the required permits. Hostile interests were, however, successful in preventing the passage of a comprehensive coastal zone management program in the 1976 California legislature. Although the state's coastal zone management commissions continue to exercise temporary regulation of coastal development, the struggle for a comprehensive plan continues in Sacramento.

Somewhat less complex than California's approach, the Delaware Coastal Zone Act categorically prohibits any industrial development along a 2-mile-wide coastal margin and also bars any offshore bulk transfer facilities for crude oil. Despite an effort to repeal the measure in 1974, the Delaware plan remains operative over the strong objections of industry, most coastal communities, and other developmental interests.

Unlike California and Delaware, many states with coastal zone management plans on the books have become embroiled in conflicts with powerful alliances of local government sufficiently strong to frustrate effective state regulation of local land use policy. Maine's local governments, predominantly small but fiercely independent, have been especially recalcitrant to yield any significant planning authority to state agencies even though state officials, mindful of local sentiments, have sought to dampen opposition by emphasizing the "essentially local" character of coastal planning under the state's new Shoreland Zoning Law. A number of other states, like North Carolina and Oregon, have temporarily avoided a confrontation with local authorities by confining state coastal plans to land use inventories, proposals for future development, advisory opinions, and state assistance to local planning entities. Caution, in this case, may buy little but time. As competition and conflict over land use intensify, clashes between state and local agencies over ultimate management authority for the coastal zone will be inevitable in all coastal states.

An Ambivalent Uncle Sam

The coastal zone presents two different, and somewhat inconsistent, images to Washington. It is an endangered, critically valuable ecological resource. It is also the repository of potentially vast petroleum reserves to slake the nation's enormous energy appetite. Caught in the cross pressure of ecological concern and energy needs, Washington has attempted simultaneously to encourage coastal land preservation and to stimulate offshore petroleum exploration. To the coastal states, many coastal communities, and numerous ecologists, Washington cannot long continue this dual commitment without having to decide whether energy or ecology will have the priority. States and local communities along the coastlands are now engaged in intense efforts to preserve a voice in how the issue will be resolved.

In an effort to promote wise coastal land use, Washington has, for the first time, directly attempted to shape the course of state land management. In 1972, Congress passed the Coastal Zone Management Act, a modest incentive to the states to assert their inherent authority over coastal areas.[29] The act, creating a federal planning grant program, offers the carrot of federal funds as an inducement to state participation. Essentially, coastal states wishing to qualify for grants are required to identify the boundaries of their coastal zones for planning purposes, to identify and rank coastal land and water uses according to desirability (beneficial, benign, tolerable, or adverse), to locate "critical areas," and to indicate how the states propose to implement land controls. However, the act does not require state participation and carefully avoids dictating how the states should define their coastal areas—in effect, it is a gentle nudge toward coastal planning. Although all the coastal states have indicated a desire to participate in the program, none has yet produced a plan conforming to the act's strictures. Thus, the impact of the act remains uncertain.

While Washington promotes coastal land planning, it is also resolutely spurring the development of oil and gas production along the nation's Outer Continental Shelf (OCS). Gas and oil have been pumped for decades from wells in the Gulf of Mexico and along the Pacific Coast. Federal authorities are now briskly selling exploration rights to many hundred thousand acres of OCS in such virgin areas as the Atlantic Coast and the Gulf of Alaska. Estimates suggest that between 20 and 200 billion barrels of recoverable oil may lie in these untapped reserves—by the most optimistic estimates, as much new oil as the nation has produced to date.[30] Behind this new exploration boom lies the nation's growing energy problems. Alarmed when the Arab states' oil embargo of 1973 demonstrated the nation's increasing dependence upon imported oil and its vulnerability to foreign energy blockade, President Nixon in his 1974 Energy Message committed the federal government to achieving "energy self-sufficiency" by 1980—a program called Project Independence. To accomplish this, the President pledged his administration to leasing 10 million acres of OCS for exploration beginning in 1975. Subsequently, President Ford reaffirmed this pledge. Although it proved impossible to sell exploration rights at the rate anticipated by Nixon, the Ford administration began in 1976 to implement the exploration program as completely as possible. By 1980, perhaps three-fourths of the original acreage scheduled for leasing may be actively explored.

The prospect of an unprecedented exploration boom along the OCS from Maine to Florida and beside Alaska's ecologically brittle coast alarms many conservationists. Summoning the specter of the huge 1969 Santa Barbara oil spill, they assert that new spills would be inevitable from 50,000 or more new wells, particularly because violent weather and earthquakes are common in the unexplored regions. Coastal states and communities regard the prospective OCS development with ambivalence. State and local agencies, apprehensive about potential environmental disasters, want federal assurances that rigorous environmental standards will govern any federal leasing and production permits; they want guarantees, moreover, that exploration will not proceed where ecological risks are severe. Local communities likely to bear the economic impact of sudden offshore exploration and production want influence, and sometimes a veto, over the siting of production facilities. These communities are particularly concerned lest they be exposed to a boom-and-bust cycle: Towns may first be inundated by new residents and new construction as exploration begins, but later their population may diminish when exploration ends or refining facilities, requiring a small work force, are all that remain. Many communities, jealous for their existing character, find the prospect of a sudden growth and the passing of their life style abhorrent. Then, too, there are the unavoidable dangers of oil spills. At the same time, both state and local officials recognize the economic benefits to be realized from OCS exploration; many states and communities would welcome the revenues directly and indirectly generated provided they could be sure they will not pay a steep ecological cost for them.

Since new exploration of the OCS seems inevitable, the political conflict will turn upon how authority over exploration permits and the siting of production facilities will be apportioned between Washington, the coastal states, and local communities. Washington has assured concerned state and local officials that their legitimate interests will not be submerged in a rising tide of offshore petroleum. But the implementation of this commitment—that is, the creation of institutional and political structures for controlling exploration—have yet to emerge. At the moment, no one can predict confidently whose interests will dominate the new oil boom.

NEEDED: FEDERAL LAND USE PLANNING

As the nation attempts to plan its future land use and, in so doing, to strike the difficult balance between developmental and ecological values, it has become obvious that Washington must participate directly and continually in the task. Almost all planning experts now recognize that land use planning can no longer proceed, as it has done historically, under the fragmented control and often parochial viewpoints of fifty states and more than 80,000 local governmental units. The need to reconcile competing and conflicting land uses, to balance economic, environmental, and developmental interests, and to anticipate thoughtfully the future direction of land use in order to shape it —all these require comprehensive planning viewpoints and wide-ranging public authority that transcend the limited jurisdictions of most state and local public agencies. In short, the need for a national framework within which state and local land use decisions are to be made seems imperative.

There can be little doubt that some form of comprehensive federal land use legislation will emerge within the next few years. We have seen that urban growth management and coastal zone planning both lead naturally toward more comprehensive planning concepts, and these, in turn, encourage the gravitation of authority toward Washington where such comprehensive power can be exercised. Indeed, attempts have already been made to bring Washington into the business of national land use planning. In a sense, the federal government has always exercised influence over national land use—albeit almost always on the side of development. Federal tax policy, for instance, encourages home building and buying because it permits an income tax deduction for mortgage payments. Depreciation provisions in existing tax laws encourage rapid property turnover and discourage the renovation of existing older property. In the early 1970's, Congress twice attempted unsuccessfully to formulate a comprehensive federal land use law to bring federal influence to bear on the side of land conservation, modest growth controls, and greater attention to aesthetic considerations in city planning. A comprehensive federal land law, first proposed in President Nixon's 1971 Environmental Message, has been subsequently suggested in every annual administration legislative program.

The details of any federal land law will be intensely controversial; a vast range of options have been considered. However, the proposals generally contain some common elements. These can be considered the essential ingredients in a federal land use program:

1. Requirements that the states inventory their existing land uses, identify critical land areas, project future land use, and establish priorities for land development which attempt to protect ecological and aesthetic values as well as economic interests.

2. A comprehensive land use plan for that one-third of the nation's area controlled by federal agencies—the 450 million acres of "public domain." This plan should include provisions for the preservation and enhancement of environmental values. It should also identify ways in

which Washington can encourage wise private land use through administration of the public lands.

3. Requirements for ecological controls on surface and underground mining. With the growing pressure for massive strip mining west of the Mississippi, such a national regulatory program is imperative to protect western lands from ecological devastation.

4. The discouragement of settlement or industrial development in the coastal zones and on flood plains. Presently these are among the most desired developmental sites in the nation.

5. A requirement that states regulate the siting of power plants, or other production facilities, in a manner consistent with their comprehensive land use plans and with respect to the danger to any "critical areas" identified in these comprehensive plans.

These, in the view of environmentalists, are little more than the bare bones of a satisfactory national land use plan. Significantly, they do not directly discourage rapid economic expansion, nor do they force the state to intervene in local land use planning, although both procedures would be listed high on the priorities of ecologists. These proposals do accept the reality of continued economic growth and the need to balance environmental goals against others with equal importance to millions of Americans. Regardless of the substance of any future national land use policy, it seems evident that the country has passed into a new era when, for the first time, growth and expansion no longer have a sovereign claim on the conscience of public officials.

CONCLUSION

As the nation enters its third century, it appears that land is no longer considered as largely a private good, a commodity to be owned and distributed according to the economic advantage or private whim of its owner. Slowly, the nation and its public officials are coming to regard land as a public resource and to see its use in terms of public impacts and long-range repercussions. This is leading, slowly and unevenly, toward a transfer of control over land use from private to public agencies. It is evident today in the first appearance of public constraints on land development—constraints imposed by public agencies acting under community authority. As the nation continues to reflect upon the values traditionally, and uncritically, accepted in the term "growth," an opportunity is provided for ecologists to influence public opinion in the direction of greater land conservation and more restraints upon unplanned economic expansion. The frontier has finally disappeared, it seems, in the public imagination as it long ago disappeared in fact.

NOTES

1. Fletcher Knebel, "The Greening of Fletcher Knebel," *New York Times Magazine,* September 17, 1974, p. 37.
2. These early comments cited in David M. Potter, *People of Plenty* (Chicago: University of Chicago Press, 1954), p. 78.
3. Figures on land use cited in Council on Environmental Quality, *Environmental Quality: Sixth Annual Report* (Washington, D.C., 1975), chapter 2.
4. *Ibid.* Other figures cited may be found in Council on Environmental Quality, *Environmental Quality: Fifth Annual Report* (Washington, D.C., 1974), chapter 1.
5. California and Florida statistics taken from *New York Times,* Sept. 3, 1973; Houston's growth is examined in *New York Times,* December 4, 1975.
6. U.S. Environmental Protection Agency, Office of Research and Development, *Environmental Management and Local Government* (Washington, D.C., 1974), pp. 23–30.
7. *New York Times,* May 7, 1973.
8. The Rockefeller Brothers Fund, Task Force on the Use of Land, *The Use of Land: A Citizen's Policy Guide to Urban Growth* (New York: Thomas Y. Crowell, 1973), p. 17.
9. *Ibid.,* p. 14.
10. *New York Times,* May 25, 1975.
11. Council on Environmental Quality, *Fifth Annual Report,* p. 61.
12. A useful summary of the indictment against rapid suburbanization and its attendant ills may be found in Edmund K. Faltermayer, *Redoing America* (New York: Harper and Row, 1968), chapters 6 and 7.
13. These environmental costs are suggested in Council on Environmental Quality, *The Costs of Sprawl: Detailed Cost Analysis* (Washington, D.C., 1974), pp. 69–74.

14. The impact of growth in Florida's water supply is extensively explored in Luther J. Carter, *The Florida Experience: Land and Water Policy in a Growth State* (Baltimore: The Johns Hopkins University Press, 1974), especially chapters 5–8.

15. Cited in Council on Environmental Quality, *The Costs of Sprawl,* chapter 5.

16. *New York Times,* September 28, 1974.

17. A useful summary of current local land use constraints may be found in U.S. Environmental Protection Agency, Office of Research and Development, *Promoting Environmental Quality through Urban Planning and Controls* (Washington, D.C., 1974). See also Council on Environmental Quality, *Sixth Annual Report,* pp. 138–88.

18. Fred Bosselman, David Callies, and John Banta, *The Taking Issue* (Washington, D.C.: Government Printing Office, 1973), p. 17. Unless otherwise noted, the discussion of the taking issue draws from this source.

19. *New York Times,* September 4, 1974.

20. Cases cited here are, in order: *Construction Industry Association of Sonoma County* v. *City of Petaluma,* 7 ERC 1001; *Salamar Builders Corp.* v. *Tuttle,* 325 N.Y.S. 2d at 936; *Steel Hill Development, Inc.* v. *Town of Sanbornton,* 496 F. 2d at 961.

21. *New York Times,* February 9, 1973.

22. Bayard Rustin, "No Growth Means Less is Less," *New York Times Magazine,* May 2, 1972, p. 13.

23. *New York Times,* June 11, 1972.

24. *New York Times,* April 22, 1975.

25. Council on Environmental Quality, *Sixth Annual Report,* p. 141.

26. *Ibid.*

27. Council on Environmental Quality, *Fifth Annual Report,* p. 21.

28. *New York Times, August 7, 1974.*

29. The act is summarized in Garrett Power, "The Federal Role in Coastal Development," in Erica L. Dolgin and Thomas G. P. Guilbert, eds., *Federal Environmental Law* (St. Paul, Minn.: West Publishing Co., 1974), pp. 831–36.

30. Figures cited in Congressional Quarterly Service, *Continuing Energy Crisis* (Washington, D.C.: Congressional Quarterly Service, 1975), pp. 43–48.

8. Black Gold and Green Wastes : Energy, Ecology, and Surface Mining

. . . the United States must embark upon a major effort to achieve self-sufficiency in energy, an effort I have called Project Independence.

Richard M. Nixon, Message to Congress, January 23, 1974

Strip mining means just what it says. It strips the people of everything they have.

Joe Begley, Letcher County, Kentucky

In late 1973, King Faisal cut the American jugular and it bled oil. Brief but total, the Arab embargo on American oil inspired by the Saudis depleted U.S. imports by 2 million barrels daily. The public and its officials were shocked into recognizing the widening gap between domestic energy consumption and available resources. The economy was threatened. But Washington was particularly chilled by the revelation of national vulnerability to external energy blockades. Federal officials announced an "energy crisis" and preached energy conservation, but it was new energy development they most wanted. Thus was born Project Independence, which, President Nixon promised, could bring the nation by 1980 to the place where it was "no longer dependent to any significant extent upon potentially insecure foreign energy supplies."[1]

No policy declaration in the 1970's stirred more widespread misgivings among environmentalists than the White House commitment to energy "self-sufficiency." The project, to be sure, is still mostly rhetoric. Even zealous energy developers disagree about the feasibility of U.S. energy self-sufficiency. The Ford administration, heir to President Nixon's energy commitment, could not fashion an energy program even approximately conforming to the Nixon proposals. But Project Independence has become the catalyst for the formation of a powerful energy coalition embracing the major electric utilities, the economy's fossil fuel sector, diplomatic and military strategists, the White House, and numerous legislators—all with visions of soaring new national energy production. Taking advantage of a prevalent public mood that new energy development is imperative, the project has become a rallying point for a politically potent alliance of interests prepared to initiate a broad new onslaught upon national resources in the name of energy security.

Ecologists fear that Project Independence, in some permutation, will unleash a pervasive assault on the environment. They warn that the chimera of energy self-sufficiency, together with the powerful appeal to national security and economic development, will become an ominous justification for the energy sector to emasculate environmentally protective legislation and to override ecological safeguards in the quest for new energy sources. At the core of this apprehension lies coal. More than any other resource, coal is the fuel that feeds the conflict between environmentalist and energy developer. Coal, the nation's most plentiful energy reserve, is an "energy pariah" whose mining technology is the most ecologically virulent of all energy sources. The White House is heavily committed to ambitious new coal production; so prominent is coal that all White House energy programs assume its plentiful availability. Early in 1974, the Federal Energy Administration announced that "all the current scenarios for dealing with the nation's long-range energy needs include coal as one essential element." Early in 1975, the President's Energy Message placed "heaviest new emphasis" on coal development; in late 1975, the President elevated coal to "*primary* reliance" in future energy plans.[2]

New coal production today will require surface mining on an unprecedented scale. No issue stirs greater passion among environmentalists than surface mining, possibly because surface-mined land is so often utterly devastated when the miners abandon it. To understand the fury of the ecologists' indictment and the political complexity of new coal mining proposals, it is essential to examine the technological and environmental impact of surface mining and to appreciate its national pervasiveness in any new coal boom.

THE DIRTIEST DECLARATION OF INDEPENDENCE

Coal is cheap, coal is abundant. With half the globe's coal reserves, the United States possesses recoverable deposits equal to four times the energy potential of all Arabian oil fields; estimates suggest these deposits might fuel American technology for 300 to 800 years. Coal is cheaper to burn than oil or natural gas, and huge low-sulfur reserves of the western states could be consumed with greatly reduced risk of violating the new federal air emission standards. Current coal production supplies less than a fifth of the nation's energy needs, but more than half the country's electric power is generated by coal, and industrial demand, particularly for metallurgical coal, is rising.[3] Coal is the one energy reserve immune to foreign blockade and the most likely to supplement or supplant diminishing supplies of other fuels; in fact, the United States currently exports 10 per cent of its yearly production. Nuclear power, once the "energy of the future," will be no significant energy source in this century because the nuclear power industry is beset with technical and economic problems adding strong disincentives to rapid expansion. Supplies of domestic natural gas, already partially rationed, are not likely to increase appreciably in the future.[4]

Were it not for surface mining, coal would soon replace oil as the nation's "black gold." But a coal boom today would become a surface mining boom. The new technology would spread across the nation in epidemic proportions; Project Independence would signal a potentially vast devastation of land and water, leaving most of the nation's mined land a sterile waste.

What Surface Mining Means

Several methods of mineral extraction are known collectively as surface mining.[5] Open pits, varying from a few hundred feet to more than a mile in depth and diameter, recover minerals from earth through a series of descending terraces. Minerals are often claimed in and near water bodies by dredging moist bottomlands; huge hoses are sometimes used to wash soil from hills and mountains, which is then sifted for minerals. The most important forms of surface mining economically and environmentally, however, are strip mining and the closely related "auger mining." On largely level ground, stripping is done by making a rectangular "box cut" that exposes mineral seams below the surface; minerals are then extracted from the exposed seams along the walls and the "spoil" (discarded earth) is thrown into the open cut as mining proceeds through the seams. In this manner, mining may proceed for a mile, leaving in the wake a deep, wide trough filled with a series of spoil deposits resembling, from the air, "the ridges of a giant washboard." On hills and mountains, "contour stripping" is used. A bench is blasted into the hillside after all topsoil and vegetation are scraped clear by bulldozers. This bench creates a "highwall," exposing mineral seams to extracting equipment, which removes the ore and commonly piles the spoil below the cut on the hillside. A bench may extend along a mountain's contour for many miles, others may be cut above and below, and mining continues until all extractable coal has been captured. Augering, the common companion to stripping, is "a method of producing coal by boring horizontally into a seam, much like a carpenter bores a hole in wood." Augers may be 7 feet in diameter and drill holes 200 feet deep and, in all cases, produce coal that is collected like shavings from a carpenter's bit.

Stripping was a negligible industry until the early 1950's because most of the nation's coal—the principal mineral recovered by stripping—was taken from deep mines. Then seams that could be mined profitably from deep shafts began to diminish at the same time the coal demand rose, sending mine operators in search of new recovery techniques that eventually led to the stripping boom. One incentive to stripping's growth was the appearance of new machines that greatly increased productivity and lowered costs. Bulldozers, leaders, scrapers, graders, and trucks of up to 100-ton capacity became available for strip mining, together with shovels of gargantuan proportions. Shovels capable of lifting 115 cubic yards of earth in one "bite" are not rare; at least one 185-cubic-yard bucket exists and a 200-yard bucket is on the drawing boards. This technology reaches its zenith in a mechanical behemoth, the Central Ohio Coal Company's "Big Muskie," operating near Cumberland, Ohio. Thirty-two stories tall, its base larger than a football field, its bucket lifting 325 tons of soil in one bite, it weighs 27 million pounds; placed in the middle of Ohio State's 81,000-seat football stadium, it would rise above the topmost seats and stretch beyond the bowl's edge.[6] With increased coal demand and this new technology, coal stripping produced far greater ore recovery than underground mining and was safer and generally cheaper on a per unit basis. The rising stripped coal output was further elevated in the late 1960's by the growing demand for electric power, the prospect of a process called "gassification" that converts coal to natural gas, and demands for low sulfur fuels to reduce air contamination.

The nation is becoming progressively more dependent upon stripping for coal and other minerals; more than 80 per cent of all ores and solid fuels used by American industry are currently produced by stripping, which also accounts for more than half the nation's coal supply. Stripped coal output has increased in great surges; between 1969 and 1970, the national output increased by almost 25 per cent, most of this originating in Appalachia, where stripped coal volume doubled between 1970 and 1971 in eastern Kentucky. By 1970, almost 6,000 square miles of American earth were affected by surface mining, almost all this land the property of mining companies. Several states now depend heavily on strip mining, particularly the economically depressed states of West Virginia and Kentucky, where mining is practically the only important industry. Estimates suggest that the loss of strip mining to West Virginia would cost the state as much as $200 million yearly and idle 8,000 workers. Even now no state is unaffected by surface mining in some form. At least ten states have more than 100,000 acres disturbed by surface mining; since the last careful estimate of surface-mined land is now over a decade old, newer studies will surely reveal startling increases in the extent of surface mining nationally.

This vast, growing industry is dominated by a handful of large mining companies, most of which are subsidiaries of petroleum industries or parts of vast corporate conglomerates. The corporate interlock between strip mining and the nation's great industrial enterprises is further extended by frequent "mine-mouth" arrangements whereby large electric utilities generate much of their power directly from the coal-mining sites and by long-term leases upon unstripped coal reserves owned by major utilities throughout the nation.

"An Imminent and Inordinate Peril"

Surface mining produces an immediate, violent, pervasive metamorphosis in the land it affects. Critics predict that stripping will yield a malevolent harvest of devastated land on an unprecedented scale if a new coal boom starts in the United States. "Surface mining frequently shocks the sensibilities," declares the Department of the Interior. "Some of the surface evacuations are so vast as to resemble craters of the moon. . . . Square miles of land may be turned over to a depth of 100 feet or more and valleys rimmed by mile after mile of contour benches."[7] It is a minor irony of environmentalism that the Kentucky legislature, so often the indulgent and protective guardian of mining, should have written one of the most brutally accurate, concise descriptions of stripping's impact in the preamble to a bill requiring the "restoration" of stripped land:

> The General Assembly finds that the unregulated strip mining of coal causes soil erosion, stream pollution, the accumulation of stagnant water and the seepage of contaminated water, increases the likelihood of floods, destroys the value of land for agricultural purposes, counteracts efforts for conservation of soil, water and other natural resources, destroys or impairs the property rights of citizens, creates fire hazards dangerous to life and property, so as to constitute an imminent and inordinate peril to the welfare of the Commonwealth.[8]

Stripping makes coal unique among the nation's major fuel sources because its extractive costs, in environmental terms, are extremely high and inflicted directly upon the producing jurisdictions. Appalachia was first to pay the price for unregulated stripping. As strippers cut their way through Kentucky, West Virginia, and Tennessee behind their gargantuan shovels, the verdant, rolling landscape was transformed into thousands of acres of sterile wastes. When stripping became Appalachia's major industry, state governments fully embraced its economic benefits and looked the other way when the environmental toll rose. This proved to be a perilous indifference.

Appalachia today is a national showcase for strip mining's environmental impact, particularly in West Virginia and Kentucky, where stripping is most intensive. Across the Appalachian region spread 18,000 miles of spoil, 20,000 miles of highwalls that isolate mountaintops from their lower levels, and 4,000 miles of streams polluted by mine drainage. Throughout the area are more than 20,000 surface acres of impoundments and reservoirs affected by mine drainage and siltation. Impoundments laid across the region's numerous hollows to control spoil erosion and mine drainage are a menacing presence to people in the valleys. Impoundments sometimes collapse, breached by heavy rains or the pressure of accumulated wastes, sending a cascade of destruction through the hollows. Such a catastrophe occurred on February 26, 1972, when a waste impoundment broke at Buffalo Creek, West Virginia, unleashing 5 million cubic feet of water that killed 117 persons and erased several small hamlets in its path. Only a third of this surface-mined land has been "reclaimed" in any manner; the greater portion, a ravaged waste, would now reach across the United States in a swath more than a mile wide extending from New York well beyond San Francisco.

The Vulnerable West

The American land now surrendered to surface mining will pale to insignificance beside the projected future toll. If Project Independence becomes a reality, the United States is expected to witness an explosive new growth of surface mining—stripping especially—west of the Mississippi River. According to a government geologist, "We are on the brink of, not years, but generations of strip mining for coal that will make the evacuation of the Panama Canal look like a furrow in my backyard vegetable garden."[9] Seventy per cent of the nation's strippable coal reserves—the target of Project Independence—lies to the west. The Fort Union Coal Formation straddling the Powder River alone contains about 40 per cent of these reserves; in Wyoming, estimates suggest that mining the state's portion of the Formation would profoundly disturb 756,000 acres of farm and grazing land.[10] The Sierra Club predicts that western stripping could constitute "the most massive industrial development of a rural area within a short period of time that has ever occurred in this country."[11] Compounding the ravages of stripping would be the secondary environmental effects from "mine-mouth" generating facilities and industrial plants likely to locate near abundant coal supplies.[12]

The Four Corners Project, located where the borders of Utah, Arizona, New Mexico, and Colorado meet, indicates the size to which these mine-mouth projects can grow and graphically illustrates their environmental impact. Begun by a consortium of twenty-three power companies, the present two generating facilities are expected to grow to six large plants and several smaller ones generating 40,000 megawatts of power. Today, the smoke emissions from the existing facilities have been seen as far as 215 miles west in Bryce Canyon and 150 miles south in Albuquerque. If all six large plants were operating at full capacity, their estimated daily emissions of fly ash, sulfur dioxide, and nitrogen oxides would exceed the load of these pollutants found daily in New York and Los Angeles air combined.[13] The largest plant, yet to be constructed, will cool its generators yearly with enough water to supply San Francisco's annual requirements. Together, the six plants will consume 2,000 railroad cars of stripped coal daily.

Nearly all the 193,345 square miles of western coal deposits are federally owned. Under the Homestead Act, this control embraces the minerals under the land already sold to farmers and ranchers and includes Indian lands. Washington has already sold, or is considering the sale of, 500 leases covering about 760,000 acres upon which mineral exploration and mining might rapidly evolve. Washington has repeatedly assured the affected states that it would not permit expansive new mining on federal lands without consultation with state authorities. However, Washington's clear jurisdictional authority over this coal and its commitment to new domestic energy development cause continuing concern, as we shall observe, among state officials who fear that their lands will be sacrificed to stripping in the name of the greater national good.

Western coal, Appalachian devastation, energy hunger, ecologists, strip miners, public officials—from these ingredients has been fashioned the current struggle to secure an effective national regulatory policy for surface mining. It confronts policy-makers at both state and federal levels with perhaps the most difficult of all environmental "trade-offs": ecological preservation against energy needs. It has drawn powerful political and economic interests into the fray; it pits states against one other and, quite often, states against the federal government. The urgency of finding a satisfactory solution is underscored by the fact that the nation now has no national surface-mine regulatory policy.

THE STRUGGLE FOR REGULATION

Surface mining commanded little serious governmental concern until recently. It was tolerated in Appalachia. Washington seemed largely indifferent to its environmental consequences. Virtually no research was conducted into techniques for reclaiming the land destroyed by stripping—if, indeed, it could be reclaimed. Only since the late 1960's has the environmental toll of stripping become an issue on the national political agenda. The actors in the current struggle include the mining companies, often working in alliance with corporate energy consumers, the state governments, Washington, and environmental interests.

The Mining Industry

The surface-mine industry, especially strip mining, is dominated by a handful of corporations. Most strip mines are controlled by eleven companies. In order of their coal production, these are Peabody Coal (subsidiary of Kennecott Copper), Consolidation Coal (subsidiary of Continental Oil and known in the trade as Consol), Island Creek Coal (part of Occidental Petroleum), Pittston, U.S. Steel, Amax Coal (part of American Metals Climax), Bethlehem Mines (a facet of Bethlehem Steel), Eastern Associated Coal, General Dynamics, and Old Ben Coal (part of the Standard Oil complex).[14] In their confrontation with ecologists, these companies commonly speak through representatives of their trade associations, particularly through the National Coal Association—which led the public debate over recent federal regulatory proposals—the National Association of Coal Lessors, and the American Metals Congress. Even this list of politically powerful groups fails to portray fully the industry's political strength. The industry commonly enlists the economic and political support of the parent corporations and many other major industries that depend on coal and other surface-mined minerals as a primary fuel. In short, ecologists face the mining companies, as well as the political power of the whole "fuel complex," when they enter the political arena against the surface miners.

Until very recently, the strip miners and their allies fought savagely and effectively against governmental regulation. In Appalachia, the story of stripping's progress across the Cumberlands was a bleak chronicle of the land's dismemberment almost unrelieved by any government restraint or corporate environmental responsibility. In their eagerness to strip the hills, the mining industry often appeared so callous that they finally provoked a movement in West Virginia and Kentucky to require some "restoration" of the wrecked sites. The mining companies' arguments against stringent regulation in Appalachia were similar to those put forth when the matter was raised elsewhere. The industry's principal assertions were that restrictions on surface mines would impose an "undue burden on the industry," would force operators out of business and thus create an economic depression in the region, and would drive industry from the state or earn the state an anti-business reputation.

Since strip mining flourished in Appalachia, the mining companies' warning of the economic damage from stringent regulation struck a responsive cord among many Appalachian businessmen, public officials, and citizens. Without mining, most of Appalachia's already depressed areas would be further impoverished for many years: Many impartial, competent studies indicate that sharp cutbacks in stripping would indeed be serious. But without tough environmental controls, the land might be ruined. It is this cruel dilemma—or at least a belief in it—that the region's public officials often cite in explaining their reluctance to force stringent cutbacks in strip coal production. Appalachia and its leaders are confronted with perhaps the starkest conflict between environmental protection and economic costs of any region in the United States and, consequently, are less indifferent to the industry's mood than state officials elsewhere.

Given its great economic importance throughout the Cumberlands, the industry might have weathered the assault of environmentalists and deflated the national campaign for its regulation if it had shown more restraint. However, mining companies provoked a growing outrage among numerous residents of Appalachia—many of whom fully realize the industry's economic importance—by their characteristic insistence upon access to coal at any cost. More than anything else, the miners' use of "broadform deeds" and other legal devices has brought a citizen uprising against the industry. Kentucky has seen this tactic used most conspicuously. Between 1880 and 1900, mining-company lawyers ranged the hills, purchasing mineral rights to thousands of acres of land through broadform deeds running to many pages of fine print. These deeds customarily declared that the mineral rights so obtained could be assigned to new owners forever, that the companies and their successors could do "any and all things necessary, or by him deemed necessary or convenient in mining and removing the coal," and that the new owner was immune from lawsuits for damage arising out of the extractive process. These documents were often signed by illiterates; their "X" on the deed brought many as little as 50 cents for each acre they surrendered. Neither they nor the coal companies could have foreseen the impending coal boom or the physical damage that might follow; stripping was wholly unanticipated.

Citing the broadform deeds, the mining companies now insist on their right to extract coal, even when the total destruction of the land follows—this despite their legal claim to only the minerals. Kentucky's high court proved a sympathetic ally. It has consistently upheld the legality of the broadform deeds to the extent that the mining companies have been permitted to ruin almost any land upon which they hold the mineral rights.[15] The court has interpreted the deeds to mean that a coal company engaged in deep-shaft mining on land where it owned only mineral rights could nonetheless cut as many trees as was necessary for underground props. In another ruling, the court declared the right of a mining company to "divert or pollute" all water "in or near" the land on which it was operating. When stripping began, the high court held that all environmental damage was a permissible result conveyed by the broadform deeds, even though lawyers for the landowners argued that the deeds were written when stripping could not have been imagined and other state courts recognized no right to coal at the cost of the property owner's land. In many western states, as in Appalachia, stripping has often resulted in the total destruction of land upon which only mineral rights were sold; while state courts have sometimes insisted on compensation to the landowners (as sometimes occurred in Appalachia), they have done little to restrain the destruction of the land itself.

In addition, the miners commonly failed to restore the lands they had mined, even when they were publicly pledged to restoration or forced by law to make the effort. Through such indifference, the mining companies alienated much of the Appalachian public that had been its political ally; a new climate of opinion materialized, and protest movements gathered momentum. The companies had also forced growing national attention upon themselves and had fashioned an image that often seemed an amalgam of avarice, ruthlessness, and environmental recklessness. Their spokesmen seldom seemed concerned. As late as 1969, a vice-president of giant Consolidation Coal felt it appropriate when addressing the American Minerals Congress to call those demanding a restoration of mined lands "stupid idiots, socialists and Commies who don't know what they're talking about. . . . I think it is our bounden duty to knock them down and subject them to the ridicule they deserve."[16]

By the early 1970's, however, the industry could ill afford its image. As the miles of highwalls and spoil banks mounted together with the environmental damage in Appalachia and elsewhere, the need for environmental regulation seemed ever more obvious to many observers. The environmental movement had gathered force. The companies' past behavior was an easy target of criticism to which public officials, increasingly interested in a positive environmental image, were more receptive. Beginning in 1972, therefore, spokesmen for the National Coal Association and other mine groups dropped the harsh, unyielding attitude toward regulation and, instead, appeared more enlightened by admitting that "reasonable regulation" might be needed. While they have continued to decry the "national hysteria" over surface mining, leaders of the mining industry have expressed general agreement that reasonable regulations might include a uniform federal strip-mine law to prevent fifty different state laws, a requirement that stripped lands be "restored," and that the mining companies be subject to performance bonds and, perhaps, to cease-and-desist orders for noncompliance. But the industry has fought tenaciously against the prohibition of strip mining on steep slopes, arguing that this would virtually wipe out strip mines in Appalachia and severely curtail stripping elsewhere. Moreover, it has contended that the "restoration" standards that environmentalists hope to impose upon the industry are unduly harsh and economically dangerous to many companies.

The mining industry continues to assist other members of the "energy lobby" in their campaign to begin widespread coal exploration and production in the West. Coal producers and consumers, almost without exception, repeat as litany the American Electric Power Company's widely advertised admonition to Americans: "We have more coal than the Arabs have oil, so let's dig it." The mining industry, in common with its allies in the energy coalition, also supports amendments to the Clean Air Act to relax emission standards for sulfur oxides and to ease pollution control requirements on "new sources" of air pollution—electric generating plants, for example—so that energy consumers could more readily utilize coal as a primary fuel. Thus, while strip mining interests may now accept the legitimacy of some regulation, they clearly oppose any controls that, in their view, would seriously diminish their opportunities to extract western coal.

The States

To speak of the states' role in surface-mine regulation is mostly to confront a vast silence. Every state is disturbed by surface mining; only a few have regulations dealing with its environmental impact, and these confine themselves largely to requirements, or exhortations, that the surface miners "restore" their damaged land. Until 1970, only three states permitted or ordered their officials to require restoration as a condition of mining on public lands; nine states did attempt to regulate stripping and other surface mines on private property by ordering, or encouraging, "restoration."[17]

In the 1970's, the states began to awaken, slowly and unevenly, to the environmental menace inherent in strip mining. The political opposition to surface mining had begun first in Appalachia, where stripping's profound ecological damage was most fully revealed. It has started shortly after stripping began its expansion in the mid-1950's. In the beginning there were only isolated, futile protests, such as those of widow Ollie Combs, a stoic little woman who, by lying down in front of bulldozers about to strip her land in 1954, caused practically the first stir of national attention to stripping. Isolated opposition throughout Kentucky and West Virginia coalesced to form "Save Our Kentucky" in the early 1960's, the first alliance of citizens, conservationists, and public officials dedicated to controlling strip mines. As stripping's ruin marched across the Appalachian hills, the protest was swelled by the Sierra Club, Wilderness Society, Audubon Society, Izaak Walton League, and other groups with a national constituency. In the late 1960's, the legal talents of the Environmental Defense Fund and the Natural Resources Defense Council were added to this alliance in an effort to sharpen the legal attack upon surface mines. As environmentalists publicized their indictments, an effort was made to create a national environmental coalition capable of pushing regulatory legislation through Congress. This resulted in the Coalition Against Strip Mining, formed in 1971 with Washington headquarters, which drew together a multitude of regional and national conservation groups in the legislative struggle. At the same time, the number of national organizations and meetings to protest unregulated surface mining is growing. In 1972, for instance, the National Conference on Strip Mining—held, appropriately, in Kentucky—brought together citizens, public officials, and scientists to study and publicize the ecological consequences of surface mines.

The growing revelation of surface mining's environmental impact together with the rise of the environmental movement appeared to reinvigorate some state interest in regulation and to persuade other states to initiate regulation in the early 1970's. The Kentucky legislature toughened its lackadaisical restoration law. West Virginia, which wrote the nation's earliest restoration act but produced largely a vague, unenforced memorial to good intentions, suddenly renewed its attack. In 1971, the state legislature created a tough new law banning stripping in twenty-two counties for several years and permitting it in productive coal seams only after performance bonds and restoration plans were produced by the mining companies under careful state supervision. One immediate result was a rise in state prosecution of mining companies for environmental damage and a sizable drop in coal production and new mining starts, partly traceable to the economic pinch some operators were experiencing from restoration costs. Many companies tolerated the law (if only because it quieted the clamor to ban stripping entirely), but the industry's sudden, if modest, economic retreat sent ripples of unease through many sectors of the state. Between 1970 and 1974, six new states enacted laws requiring strippers to restore mined lands on public property, private land, or both. This modest increase in state concern over stripping was significant, but only one state west of the Mississippi, where stripping is expected to boom, had enacted comprehensive strip-mine controls by 1974.

Only since the announcement of Project Independence have public officials in the West reacted vigorously to the impending stripping of their land. Leaders in midwestern and western states facing the strip mine now frequently assert that Project Independence will leave them little more than a choice between status as an "energy exporter" (if coal mining alone were permitted) or an "energy province" (if mine-mouth electric generating plants proliferate, as the utilities would prefer). The alarm was sounded at the Western Governors' Conference in late 1975 when New Mexico's Governor Jerry Apodaca indicted the White House for its lack of "energy conservation." "We do not want to become an energy colony for the rest of the nation," he complained. In Montana, where half the nation's unmined sub-bituminous coal resides, the administration has repeatedly warned Washington that "it will not see itself ripped-off, its land unreclaimed, its life-style disrupted" by stripping.[18] The vigor of this dissent arises from the broad alliance between environmentalists and a coalition of farmers, animal grazers, and foresters; the anticipated land disturbance and water contamination from stripping are projected to leave many hundred thousand acres of western farm and grazing lands, as well as subsurface and surface waters, sterile and unreclaimable.

As the West confronts the implications of stripping, a broad national coalition of eastern and western states now seeks both state and federal constraints on strip mining. Agitation for comprehensive regulation of stripping has forced attention upon the appropriate kinds of regulation. This, in turn, has raised a vexing, and ominous, new issue: Is it possible to "restore" or "reclaim" stripped land? In the view of some experts, stripping may be a distinctively malevolent form of resource recovery because virtually no technology capable of restoring the ravaged land to ecological vitality within acceptable time limits may exist. Other experts assert that restoration is possible but at a staggering cost. Still others suggest that stripping, when confined to appropriate terrain, can be rendered ecologically safe and restoration made economically possible.

The Substance of Regulation

Many environmentalists, distrusting state regulatory programs and weary of governmental compromise with the mining industry, want the federal government to ban stripping immediately and totally. One of these is West Virginia's Congressman Kenneth Hechler, who has repeatedly introduced federal legislation to eliminate strip mines. No national political figure is identified more closely with the battle against stripping than is Hechler, whose rage against the mine operators reflects the feelings of many citizens throughout Appalachia. He told his Congressional colleagues during a fiery floor speech:

> I have seen what havoc and obliteration is left in the wake of strip mining. It has ripped the guts out of our mountains, polluted our streams with acid and silt, uprooted our trees and forests, devastated the land, seriously disturbed or destroyed wildlife habitat, left miles of ugly highwalls, ruined the water supply in many areas and left a trail of utter despair for many honest and hard working people.[19]

Behind this indictment lies the frustration of many who have witnessed the frequent impotence of state regulation over stripping in the face of the economic and political power of the coal corporations. In the past, states that made an effort to require land reclamation were usually waging a paper war. This restoration was seldom more than a gesture, rarely returning the land to a condition remotely resembling the original. Harry M. Caudill, who etches a haunting portrait of Appalachia's social and physical disintegration, describes in his sad chronicle what "restoration" often meant in Kentucky.

> Under the law strippers are required to replant their wrecked and ravaged acres. The State Department of Conservation recommends short leaf or loblolly pines for spoil banks. Conservationists insist that a full year must pass before the young trees are planted. This delay permits the freshly piled soil to settle enough so the trees can take root. The seedlings are approximately five inches long when planted, supposedly at intervals of six feet. Some ten years must elapse before trees

growing in such impoverished earth will reach the height of a man's head. In the meantime, the rains have clawed the earth about their roots into deep gullies and there is little left for their foliage to protect. Few operators seriously attempt to comply with the reclamation regulations; most are permitted virtually to ignore them.[20]

Reclamation was sometimes attempted elsewhere by treating the spoil with nothing more than huge hoses spraying water mixed with the plant nutrients, grass and tree seeds; even when careful restoration was attempted, hard rains and acid soil conspired to kill much of the new trees and grass, often sparing only a few scrubs and patches of vegetation to eke out a precarious existence. There were, to be sure, more successful efforts by private companies, which testified to the impressive capacity of the miners and their technicians sometimes to salvage the land when money and will were present. Nonetheless, restoration had been largely a fiction or a failure; two of every three acres touched by stripping remained almost totally abandoned.

Unlike Kentucky, some states did include strong restoration provisions in their statutes but failed to provide vigorous budgetary and political support for their enforcement. Administered by agencies that lacked legislative help and adequate personnel, these laws were rarely effective. "Public confidence in State regulation of surface coal mining has frequently been misplaced," noted a Congressional investigating committee. Citing "political influence" and "the continued rapid expansion of the industry relative to the States' capability of managing such mines" as reasons for this failure, the report concluded pointedly: "Subtle or otherwise, political influence is often used to moderate enforcement of state laws. In States where the coal industry dominates the economy as a major source of jobs and taxes, powerful leverage is available."[21]

In light of the states' experience with strip-mine regulation, many public officials and environmentalists have argued that only a strong federal program, with uniform regulatory standards for the nation, is likely to control stripping satisfactorily. Others have asserted that the states should initiate their own programs without awaiting federal action—as, in fact, some states have done. Regardless of which governmental agencies assume the responsibility for enforcing it, most environmentalists assert that a sound regulatory program must include the following provisions:

1. *Spoil banks, and perhaps all strip mining, should be forbidden on slopes too steep and vulnerable to water erosion to be adequately restored.* Many ecologists wish all stripping banned on slopes with gradients of more than 14 degrees; others would settle for a 20-degree limit. In either case, the effect would be to eliminate strip mines throughout large portions of Appalachia and the mountainous West. If stripping is not wholly prevented on steep slopes, environmentalists assert that the spoil banks, at least, must be removed to prevent dangerous erosion, landslides, and visual ugliness.

2. *Restoration should be "concurrent," not "standard."* With concurrent restoration, land removed from coal seams must be replaced as the mining occurs; the "standard" method (so called because it has been customary in state laws) would permit replacement at a much later period and thus would allow open seams to remain exposed to the elements and to bleed their acids onto the soil for many months.

3. *Significant contour restoration should be achieved.* Many experts assert that the ecological viability of any reclaimed land depends, in good measure, upon restoring most of the original land contours. At a minimum, ecologists argue that land on slopes should be terraced and water-gathering depressions eliminated during restoration. Without significant contour restoration, the original topography of the land is so radically altered by filling that surface water, underground water, soil stability, and soil nutrients may be permanently impaired.

4. *Land revegetation must be demonstrated.* This, the most rigorous standard, would require that land removed from mining "cuts" be restored with the topsoil in its original place and with vegetation capable of surviving for a stated period. In effect, this would require miners to demonstrate convincingly that they *can* revegetate the land before they begin mining; otherwise, stripping would be prohibited.

5. *Mining companies must post performance bonds in advance of operations to ensure they restore the disturbed land.* This requirement would make mining companies forfeit their bonds (which should be sizable) when they fail to restore land to required conditions and would enable governmental agencies to issue cease-and-desist orders

when companies do forfeit the bond so that further mining is prevented.

6. *Public notice and public hearings must occur before any mining permits are issued by federal or state agencies.* One objective of this provision would be to assure that administrators charged with responsibility for mine supervision do not deliberately or inadvertently permit stripping where environmental restoration is difficult. Another purpose is to put administrators under pressure to consider environmental interests before granting permits. Not least important, public notice and hearing give environmental groups a chance to mobilize and educate public opinion on their behalf in permit controversies.

At the moment, few states have the majority of these provisions in their mining regulations. As Table 8 indicates, sixteen states concurrently have regulated programs for strip mines; most of them include only one or two of the more demanding restoration requirements. Significantly, some of the least rigorous programs are in the West, where strip mining will become a major environmental problem.

Strip mining companies have professed a willingness to accept "reasonable" regulation but assert that regulatory programs akin to those commonly suggested by ecologists will be prohibitively expensive to the companies and the nation. Generally, the companies argue that programs favored by environmentalists will be so costly that company profits will fall dramatically, that many mines will be closed because of restoration costs, that coal production will be drastically curtailed when mines are shut on steep slopes, and that the nation's energy supplies will, as a result, be constricted. Effective land restoration, when possible, is often a costly business indeed. In Britain, where restoration is uniformly required, as it is in most other nations, the cost often runs to $1.25 a ton for extracted coal—a ratio that might well consume the profit margins of many stripping operations and materially reduce the profitability of others. In Japan, the cost of restoration and the environmental damage of stripping has led to the virtual abolition of strip mines; the Japanese purchase stripped coal from the United States instead. Truly effective restoration in the United States has generally been costly. The Pacific Gas and Electric

TABLE 8. State Surface Mining Reclamation Requirements

State	Timing		Future Land Use	Grading/Backfilling			Revegetation		
	Concurrent	Standard		Approximate Original Contour	Terracing	Rolling Topography	Topsoil Saved	Planting Required	Survival Standards
Alabama		X				X		X	X[1]
Colorado		X	X			X		X	
Illinois		X	X			X[2]	X	X	X
Indiana	X		X			X		X	
Kentucky	X			X[3]	X[4]			X	
Maryland	X		X	X[3]	X[4]		X	X	X
Montana		X	X			X		X	
North Dakota		X	X			X	X	X	
Ohio	X		X	X	X[5]		X	X	
Oklahoma	X		X			X		X	
Pennsylvania	X		X	X	X[5]		X	X	
Tennessee	X		X	X[3]	X[6]		X[3]	X	X
Virginia	X		X		X[7]			X	
Washington		X	X			X		X	
West Virginia	X		X	X[3]	X[8]		X[9]	X	X
Wyoming	X					X		X	

[1] Where soil conditions do not inhibit growth.
[2] Grade to 30 per cent on all outslopes over 40 vertical feet.
[3] Area mining only.
[4] Maximum slope angle limited to 45 degrees.
[5] If approved by administration agency in conjunction with approved land use, slope angle limited to 35 degrees.
[6] Slope angle of highwall and outslope limited to 35 degrees.
[7] Reduce highwall to maximum extent possible, no slope angle limitations.
[8] Slope angle limited to 32 degrees for highwall and outslope.
[9] In acid-producing areas only.

SOURCE: U.S. Department of the Interior, Study of Strip and Surface Mining in Appalachia: An Interim Report to the Appalachian Regional Commission (Washington, D.C., 1966).

Company's extensive reclamation program for its Wyoming mines, generally considered by environmentalists a model corporate endeavor, has cost more than $700 an acre. Any limitation upon the gradients where stripping can be practiced would undoubtedly reduce available coal reserves; how much reduction would result depends upon where the gradient limit is drawn. Using as a guideline a recent Congressional proposal that stripping be prohibited where the land cannot be restored to its original use, or to a higher one, the EPA estimated that this might reduce U.S. coal production by approximately 90 million tons a year, or by 14 per cent of current production.[22] Critics of surface mining commonly have little patience with the industry's warning about reduced profits; they assert that the companies exaggerate the prospective losses, that most can absorb the losses without ill effect, and that reduced profits, in any case, are a small price for avoiding environmental devastation. If energy production is curtailed by regulation, conclude ecologists, it will not seriously impair the economy; moreover, it will force Americans finally to begin curbing their energy appetite.

Beyond arguments over the details of restoration lies a more profound environmental issue. Many experts suggest that it may be difficult, or impossible, to restore western stripped lands to ecological vitality within acceptable time periods. "The potential for rehabilitation of any surface mined land," noted a 1973 study by the National Academy of Sciences, "is critically site specific."[23] Western coal acres receive three to four times less rainfall than eastern mined lands— usually less than 16 inches a year—so that eastern reclamation techniques are seldom applicable to the West. Further, very little experimentation has been conducted in reclamation beyond the Mississippi. The combination of low rainfall and/or high evaporation rates poses "a difficult problem" in the West, according to the National Academy of Sciences:

> Revegetation of these areas can probably be accomplished only with major, sustained inputs of water, fertilizer, and management. Range seeding experiments have had only limited success. . . . Rehabilitation of the drier sites may occur naturally on a time scale that is unacceptable to society, because it may take decades, or even centuries, for natural succession to reach stable conditions.[24]

The House Committee on Interior and Insular Affairs, after reviewing the Academy study and other materials on revegetation of stripped western land, concluded that "the possibility for permanently despoiling thousands of acres of productive agricultural lands is very real indeed."[25] Thus, the West may face the prospect of massive strip mining for which no environmentally acceptable safeguards exist.

Generally weak state regulatory programs and the need for rigorous restoration standards have persuaded most experts that a comprehensive federal program for strip-mine regulation is essential. In this, most coal companies agree; they prefer a uniform set of national standards to a variety of inconsistent state ones. Since 1972, a broad coalition of environmentalists, state interests, and federal legislators has worked diligently, but so far unsuccessfully, to create such a national program.

Awakening on the Potomac

Twice since 1972, Congress has overwhelmingly passed a strip-mine regulatory bill; twice it has been vetoed in the White House. These two bills contained several common provisions: (1) a set of uniform minimum standards for restoration of strip-mined land, (2) a requirement that states adopt the minimal standards or yield regulatory control to Washington, (3) a requirement that all mined land be reclaimed, and (4) a tax on coal production to pay for reclaiming 2 million acres of "orphan banks" abandoned by strip miners in the past. Since the minimum federal standards embraced many elements widely desired by environmentalists, most conservation groups were enthusiastic proponents of the two measures. The first measure was vetoed by President Ford in December, 1974, and the second in April, 1975; both times, Congress failed by a very slim margin to override the veto.

White House objections to the strip-mine measures were that the bills would cause a drastic curtailment in coal production (perhaps as much as 162 million tons a year, or a fourth of current coal production), that more than 36,000 jobs would be lost, and that electric power costs for consumers would be raised. Proponents of the legislation have disputed all these arguments, citing other estimates to suggest that unemployment, production losses, and consumer power costs would all be substantially less than the White House claims. Nonetheless, Congress has yet to pass a comprehensive regulatory program.

The absence of a federal regulatory bill does not leave the federal government without effective means to reduce, or otherwise control, the effects of strip mining across the nation. Washington is in a position to strongly affect the course of strip mining through its control of the public domain, a mineral-rich expanse equal to more than a third of the nation's land on which most coal reserves now reside, through its administration of the Tennessee Valley Authority (TVA), and through preparation of impact statements on all coal exploration leases on federal domain.

For more than a half century, federal officials have possessed a potentially strong weapon to control strip mining on the public domain in the Mineral Leasing Act of 1920. This act confers upon the Secretary of the Interior the authority to grant prospecting and mining permits for minerals on public land, gives him the right to deny permits if mining "would impair other important land uses," and allows him to impose standards for land restoration following mining. The wording of this authority is sufficiently broad to enable the Secretary or his subordinates to promulgate strict restoration standards for stripping on the federal domain or to forbid it whenever satisfactory restoration is deemed impossible; with the current growth of stripping and its westward expansion, this authority assumes great importance, for most of the public domain lies in the West, where extensive mineral deposits constitute an important foundation for the industry.

Until 1969, well after stripping was familiar on federal land, virtually no environmental restraint on surface mining or restoration of stripped land was evident on the public domain; as far as stripping was concerned, the 1920 law had been largely an arrangement for mining's growth but not its control. In early 1969, the Department of the Interior at last seemed willing to draw upon the dormant power of the 1920 legislation to regulate stripping on public lands. Specifically, the department promulgated new regulations that, among other provisions, required (1) that the Bureau of Land Management and the Bureau of Indian Affairs conduct a "technical examination" to determine the environmental impact of a mining operation before issuing a permit, (2) that these agencies establish requirements for reclaiming the mined land in advance of mining, (3) that a performance bond equal to the cost of land reclamation be posted by mining companies, and (4) that periodic reports on environmental damage and reclamation be submitted to the agencies by companies subject to the regulations.[26] Environmentalists were cautiously optimistic about this, encouraged by the intent yet apprehensive lest such "restoration" measures suffer the same haphazard enforcement found in similar state measures.

In late 1972, a careful review of the administration of these regulations, prepared for Congress by the Comptroller General, seemed to confirm these misgivings; enforcement was indifferent, sometimes negligent, prompting some critics to charge that the Department of the Interior was incapable of regulating its own clients. Based on a sampling of leases and permits issued by the department since 1969, the study revealed that in almost half the cases, no technical examination of environmental impact had been conducted prior to issuing mining permits, that the required performance bonds were often unposted, and that periodic reports on mining activity required of the companies were sometimes unprepared.[27] The controversy was further stirred by western conservationists, joined by the governor of Montana, protesting pervasive environmental damage on public lands near Yellowstone National Park caused by mining exploration and operations. Environmental spokesmen, joined by some influential Congressional leaders, argued that control of stripping on public land would have to be removed from the Department of the Interior and vested in the Environmental Protection Agency or a new superagency responsible for all resource matters.

This controversy boiled up simultaneously with growing concern over the environmental damage caused by the giant TVA complex. Built in the early days of Franklin Roosevelt's New Deal, the Tennessee Valley Authority was once primarily a hydroelectric facility symbolizing for millions of Americans the finest achievement of governmental conservation, a monument to wise environmental use bringing economic and physical regeneration to the whole Tennessee River Valley. In the decades since its beginning, however, the TVA gradually shifted to generating 80 per cent of its electric power from coal and, in the process, became the largest single consumer of coal for electric power in the nation, today burning more than 5 per cent of the nation's yearly coal output in huge drafts of 1,600 carloads daily. The focus of the environmental controversy is the TVA's massive demand for strip-mined coal. The facility yearly negotiates thirty to forty strip-mine contracts from which it obtains more than 16 million tons of coal, thus becoming a major stimulant to the growth of surface mining throughout Appalachia. Already the nation's largest producer of electric power, TVA intends to double its output by 1985. This new expansion will thrust TVA's supply lines into the heart of the midwestern coal reserves and thereby encourage expansive new stripping there. Conservationists argue that TVA has been negligent in seeking alternative fuel supplies and in encouraging production methods that do not wreak such environmental damage. They assert that the TVA could, at the very least, use its enormous purchasing power as leverage to force strip miners to practice environmental restoration on mined lands if they want government contracts. Further, many conservationists charge that the TVA has become so consumed with obtaining cheap coal that it drives down the market price, thus denying many coal companies the extra income that might be allocated to environmental restoration. If Washington wants to diminish the environmental degradation of strip mining, say many conservationists, the TVA is a logical place to begin.

In response to this criticism, the TVA's directors announced a new coal-purchase policy in 1972, which, they asserted, would greatly encourage environmental protection from strip mining and diminish their own contribution to environmental negligence. In the future, the TVA would purchase no coal from strippers operating on slopes so steep that the spoil would constitute an environmental hazard, nor would coal be bought from companies operating in scenic and wilderness areas; mines creating water pollution or endangering streams or public water supplies would be similarly excluded from future contracts. Additionally, a portion of the coal supplier's payment would be withheld until he had satisfactorily reclaimed the land disturbed by stripping; failure to meet new restoration standards established by the TVA would result in the loss of a portion of the supplier's usual bonus. These regulations are too newly minted to have proved themselves yet, but conservationists suspect that the results will be no less dismal than those commonly witnessed in other state and federal restoration laws.

Finally, ecologists believe that the Department of the Interior could significantly diminish the environmental ravage of stripping through the careful preparation and consideration of impact statements in connection with the issuance of mining permits on public lands. In recent years, environmental groups have urged that the department draft impact statements not only for each permit but also for groups of permits covering large expanses of adjacent land. When permits are simultaneously granted for large tracts of adjacent land, assert ecologists, the effect is a "regional impact" that should be considered separately from the more limited impact of a single mining operation. Moreover, the argument continues, these impact statements would provide state authorities—already apprehensive, as we have seen, about the consequences of new stripping—with a realistic appraisal of what to expect from new mining operations. Since most environmentalists believe any sound impact assessment would readily reveal the ecological damage of many strip mines, they would then have a potentially persuasive document to use in opposing new mining leases. For all these reasons, the National Resources Defense Council, the Environmental Defense Fund, and the Sierra Club have been especially aggressive in taking the Interior Department to court when it appears that it has produced unsatisfactory impact statements—a common event, according to many ecologists.

Despite the many measures Washington might take to control stripping even in the absence of a national regulatory law, most observers believe that the most satisfactory restraint on stripping must remain a national regulatory program. In its absence, all other measures appear to many environmentalists as weak and ultimately inadequate.

SUMMARY: THE EDGE OF THE ABYSS

Today the nation faces the advent of an unprecedented strip-mine boom, spreading across the midwestern plains to the western deserts, with few effective environmental constraints. Strip mining, possibly the most ecologically pernicious of all technologies endangering the environment, has become the most immediate environmental crisis generated by the nation's growing energy hunger and the first fruit of Project Independence. The states, faced with powerful corporate structures interlocked into an energy coalition, have largely been unable to impose meaningful ecological controls upon stripping. If the massive, and possibly irreversible, ecological devastation following uncontrolled stripping is to be prevented, it appears that Washington must act, soon and incisively, to restrain it. To control stripping is to choose between energy needs and environmental preservation, between conflicting interpretations of the nation's best interests, between powerful and antagonistic political alliances on different sides of the mining controversy. Until recently, government officials went to war against stripping armed largely with pens and brave intentions. Unless vigorous new restraints upon stripping are imposed immediately, the nation may pay for its negligence with many thousand acres of wholly devastated, unrecoverable wastes.

NOTES

1. Project Independence was officially declared by President Nixon in a November 7, 1973, address to the nation. The President's commitment to "energy self-sufficiency" was mentioned in his Energy Message to Congress on January 23, 1974. The detailed program known as Project Independence was created by a federal task force and announced by Federal Energy Administrator John C. Sawhill on November 12, 1974. The report did not urge increased coal production but explored its possibilities; it did assert the potential for doubling U.S. coal production in a decade. However, the Ford administration has generally assumed that production, as explored in the Project, was desirable and possible. Thus, President Ford embraced part of this program on October 8, 1974, when he declared a national goal of eliminating all oil-fired power production by 1980—a step that would dramatically increase coal use.
2. The FEA statement appeared in *New York Times,* January 14, 1974; the President's statements appeared in *New York Times,* October 21, 1974, and March 24, 1975.
3. Figures cited are drawn from Congressional Quarterly Service, *Continuing Energy Crisis in America* (Washington, D.C.: Congressional Quarterly Service, 1975), pp. 2–12, 75–82; Dennis W. Ducsik, ed., *Power, Pollution and Public Policy* (Cambridge, Mass.: MIT Press, 1971); *New*

York Times, February 18, 1974; June 16, 1974; and October 21, 1974; and Federal Energy Administration, *Project Independence: Final Task Force Report* (Washington, D.C., 1974), text and appendix.

4. The demise of nuclear energy as an imminent substitute for coal, oil, and natural gas is discussed in *New York Times,* November 11, 1975. It is also explored in a number of recent Congressional documents including U.S. Congress, House Committee on Banking and Currency, *Oil Imports and Energy Security: An Analysis of the Current Situation and Future Prospects* (September, 1974); and U.S. Congress, Joint Economic Committee, *A Reappraisal of U.S. Energy Policy* (March 8, 1974).

5. This description is adapted from U.S. Department of the Interior, *Surface Mining and Our Environment* (Washington, D.C., 1967), pp. 33 ff. Quotes, unless otherwise noted, are from this source.

6. Described in Harry M. Caudill, *My Land Is Dying* (New York: E. P. Dutton and Co., 1971), p. 23.

7. U.S. Department of the Interior, *op. cit.,* p. 51.

8. Cited in Harry M. Caudill, *op. cit.,* p. 85. Quoted from the dissenting opinion in *Martin* v. *Kentucky Oak Mining Co.,* 429 S.W. 2d (Ky.) 395.

9. *New York Times,* August 22, 1971.

10. *New York Times,* April 11, 1974.

11. *New York Times,* March 24, 1975.

12. The development of "mine-mouth" generating plants has been seriously considered, and indirectly promoted, by the Ford administration. FEA administrator Frank G. Zarb, for example, has advocated concentrating energy facilities at a few regional centers with abundant coal supplies (*New York Times,* December 25, 1975). The North Central Power Study, produced by thirty-five power companies and the U.S. Department of the Interior, suggested forty-two mine-mouth power plants along the Fort Union Formation, which would, when completed, generate 50,000 megawatts of power, consume 210 million tons of coal yearly, and attract perhaps a half million people to the affected areas of Wyoming, Montana, and North Dakota.

13. Congressional Quarterly Service, *Energy Crisis in America* (Washington, D.C.: Congressional Quarterly Service, 1973), p. 30. See also John Holdren and Philip Herrera, *Energy: A Crisis in Power* (San Francisco: Sierra Club, 1971), pp. 160–68.

14. According to National Coal Association figures published in *New York Times,* October 15, 1972.

15. These deeds and court opinions are extensively discussed in Harry M. Caudill, *Night Comes to the Cumberlands* (Boston: Little, Brown and Co., 1963), chapter 19.

16. Quoted in Harry M. Caudill, "Are Capitalism and the Conservation of a Decent Environment Compatible?," in Harold W. Helfrich, Jr., ed., *Agenda for Survival* (New Haven, Conn.: Yale University Press, 1971), p. 177.

17. State performance prior to 1970 is summarized in U.S. Department of the Interior, *op. cit.,* pp. 98–99. Information on state laws since 1970 is taken from Council on Environmental Quality, *Environmental Quality: First Annual Report* (Washington, D.C., 1972), pp. 188–89.

18. The Western Governors' Conference is cited in *New York Times,* September 24, 1975; the Montana quote is from *New York Times,* August 14, 1974.

19. *New York Times,* October 15, 1972.

20. Harry M. Caudill, *Night Comes to the Cumberlands,* p. 316.

21. U.S. Congress, House Committee on Interior and Insular Affairs, *Surface Mining Control and Reclamation Act of 1974* (House Report No. 93–1072), May 30, 1974, p. 61.

22. *New York Times,* June 8, 1975.

23. House Committee on Interior and Insular Affairs, *op. cit.,* p. 57.

24. *Ibid.*

25. *Ibid.*

26. Summarized in U.S. General Accounting Office, *Administration of Regulations for Surface Exploration, Mining and Reclamation of Public and Indian Coal Lands* (Washington, D.C., August, 1972), ch. 1.

27. *Ibid.*

9. The Future as Junk: Solid Waste Management

Standing in splendid isolation atop Mt. Rainier, a companion to wind and perpetual snow more than 14,000 feet above sea level, may soon appear the nation's highest privy. Officials of the National Park Service have been forced to ponder such a possibility because the volume of waste left by climbers on the popular peak has become an acute problem. Such a grotesque monument to human carelessness would be one sign of the rising volume of wastes on the nation's mountains; it would, in turn, testify to the fact that some portion of the continent undefiled by solid waste no longer exists. Trash dumps have been found at the 17,200-foot level on Mt. McKinley; recently, conservationists removed more than 400 pounds of junk from its upper slope alone. In one national park, the debris found at high altitudes included cans, bottles, paper, tools, aluminum chairs, tents, medicine, food waste, and a pornographic library. In the White Mountains National Forest, campers are discouraged from pitching tents above the timberline, for campsite litter and other human damage have seriously impaired the fragile plant and animal life at high altitudes. "People will drop almost anything if they figure they don't have to carry it out," concluded one Park Service official in explaining the mountain litter.[1] As more than 250,000 Americans yearly climb the nation's major mountains, the last barrier to human litter has been conquered; solid waste marches upward.

Below the mountaintops, solid waste has been skyrocketing into a national problem. The garbage dump has become prosperity's boneyard. Fed by affluence, solid waste is accumulating at a rate that many public officials predict will create a disposal crisis within a decade. Public expenditures for solid waste collection and disposal, almost all financed by the average taxpayer, are likely to triple by the century's end.[2] Solid waste is synonymous with visual ugliness, health problems, impaired property value, and extravagant resource and energy consumption. Yet the technology of solid waste collection has been almost static for fifty years; disposal methods are only slightly better and still largely experimental. Only in this decade have public and private agencies begun to explore seriously the promising potential for environmental conservation in the recycling of solid wastes. Indeed, so recently has concern arisen that basic data about solid waste production before 1965 are almost unavailable. The reasons for this tardy attention are complex, related to consumer behavior, the economic structure of waste-producing industries, disposal technology, and the balance of political strength among those interests involved in solid waste control. The nature of the problem and the broad design for its solution nonetheless are quite clear.

THE MAKING AND UNMAKING OF SOLID WASTE

Most Americans associate solid waste with the contents of the garbage dump: glass, plastic and metal containers, food remnants, paper products, toothpaste tubes, perhaps the rusting hulks of mattresses, cars, and metal appliances. This refuse, despite public attention, is only a small portion of all solid waste produced annually in the United States. More than half the nation's solid waste is produced by agriculture, mostly from animals (farm animals alone produce ten times the metabolic waste of the whole U.S. population); an additional quarter of the nation's solid waste comes from mining, principally fossil fuel extraction. Compared to this massive load, the solid materials produced by residential, commercial, and institutional sources— about 250 million tons annually—might seem trivial; this debris, which we shall call "consumer waste," is nonetheless troublesome, expensive, and dangerous. It is often the most difficult to destroy satisfactorily; it commonly accumulates near communities, where it may pose grave health hazards; it almost always insults sight and smell. And this waste, feeding upon our affluence, continues to multiply.

The dimensions of the solid waste problem are writ large in a few statistics. In 1920, the average American threw away 2.75 pounds of garbage daily; in 1970, the figure had jumped to 5 pounds daily. Consumer garbage is expected to mount steadily through the turn of the century. Table 9 presents a conservative estimate for this consumer generation of garbage through the year 1990. In national terms, the nation's urban communities now daily dispose of more than 800 million pounds of solid waste and can expect this mountain of junk to grow in volume threefold by 1980. Many of the collection and disposal problems can be understood by examining briefly the contents of this consumer waste.

Consumer Waste

Consumer waste is extremely troublesome because of its many elements as well as its growing volume.[3] One large component is *packaging material,* which accounts for more than half of all consumer garbage. The most familiar of these packaging materials is the disposable container, primarily metal, glass, and plastic; we now use and discard more than 30 billion glass and plastic bottles and 60 billion cans annually. Another 30 million tons of paper products, much of it wrapping material, ends on the trash heap. To this massive debris is added uncounted tons of foil trays, flashlight batteries, cosmetic sprays, film cartridges, pesticides, and aerosol containers of every sort. This packaging has grown in volume phenomenally over a very short time, increasing at a rate far faster than the gross national product—from 400 pounds per person in 1958, to 578 pounds in 1970, to a predicted 661 pounds by 1976 with no terminal point anticipated. Americans spend more than 3 per cent of the gross national product in producing these materials. This packaging caters to the consumer's affluence and demand for convenience, especially in the food industry, where, for instance, packaging single units or a small volume of items previously sold in bulk has significantly increased the demand for wrapping material.

Another large portion of consumer waste is *organic products* of all kinds, mostly food garbage. Food wastes are biodegradable, creating

TABLE 9.   Projections of Postconsumer Solid Waste Generation
1971–90

	Estimated		Projected		
	1971	1973	1980	1985	1990
Total gross discards					
Millions of tons per year	133	144	175	201	225
Pounds per person per day	3.52	3.75	4.28	4.67	5.00
Less resource recovery					
Millions of tons per year	8	9	19	35	58
Pounds per person per day	0.21	0.23	0.46	0.81	1.29
Equals net waste disposal					
Millions of tons per year	125	135	156	166	167
Pounds per person per day	3.31	3.52	3.81	3.86	3.71

SOURCE: U.S. Environmental Protection Agency, Office of Solid Waste Management Programs, Resource Recovery Division, *Third Report to Congress: Resource Recovery and Waste Reduction* (Washington, D.C., 1975), p. 10. Projections for 1980 to 1990 are based in part on contract work by Midwest Research Institute.

a less difficult disposal problem than other consumer wastes; however, organic wastes usually attract scavengers and vermin, breed many pathogenic organisms, and rapidly become a menace to public health if they accumulate in large volume and are left to stand for long periods.

Having conquered the road, the American automobile is rapidly claiming the land; *abandoned and junked auto bodies* today constitute a growing solid waste problem. No one knows exactly how many junked or abandoned autos exist in the United States. Estimates of abandoned auto bodies along the highways reach as high as 20 million. In Philadelphia, 21,700 cars were deserted in 1971; in New York, 82,000. Altogether, perhaps 7 million autos are abandoned every year. All estimates indicate that abandoned and junked autos will increase for decades, adding millions of metal corpses to the automobile litter already decorating the highways and roadsides. Part of the explanation for mounting auto bodies is the decreasing life of cars, which averaged more than fourteen years between purchase and disposal prior to 1950 but now averages about eight years. Then, too, with growing affluence, the average American buys a car more often; even the relatively poor have little trouble finding the credit to purchase a car of some type. Population expansion alone would greatly increase the demand for new cars and, ultimately, the proliferation of junked ones.

Beyond the consumer waste that can be readily identified are tons of miscellany, still more of our culture's discard pile. During one recent year, Americans tossed away more than 7 million television sets, presumably because they no longer worked. Other appliances— toasters, washers, refrigerators, small motors of all kinds, and ovens —are common fare on any city dump. Grass cuttings, wood shavings, leaves, even animal bodies are also collected and must somehow be destroyed.

The Ecological Cost

The nation's traditional indifference to wise solid waste management has imposed a triple ecological cost upon society. First, unrestrained resource use and discarding of solid wastes deplete the nation's resources by diminishing its supplies of virgin materials. Moreover, solid waste constitutes an environmental hazard whose control costs society billions of dollars. Finally, the nation irretrievably loses the resource potential in recycled wastes so long as it permits them to rot across the countryside.

The environmental toll in past solid waste management policy can be appreciated if one considers the potential recovery value of such waste. According to one recent estimate, the refuse thrown away by Americans during a typical year contains the following recoverable resources:[4]

11.3 million tons of iron and steel
860,000 tons of aluminum
430,000 tons of other metals (mostly copper)
13 million tons of glass
Burnable organic materials equal to 150 million barrels of crude oil or
70 per cent of the annual yield of the Alaskan North Slope reserves

Although all the potential resources in solid waste are never recovered, most can be usefully recycled. This has been done throughout Europe and Asia for decades. The energy potential in solid waste alone should make its recycling attractive. A ton of standard consumer refuse, for instance, has the equivalent heat value of 1.5 barrels of fuel oil; it produces no polluting sulfur oxides and, at current value, could be purchased and burned more cheaply than oil. Smelting a pound of aluminum ore from bauxite requires about twenty times the energy cost of recovering a pound of aluminum from common solid waste; if the aluminum, copper, and ferrous metals now lost through ordinary disposal of solid materials were fully recycled, it would save the energy equivalent of the gas used by all vehicles in the United States for ten days.[5]

Even if the recoverable resources from solid waste were to fall below these estimates—and most experts assert that high recovery estimates are reasonable—the nation would still turn growing attention to its long-neglected solid waste management problems. With recognition of the nation's depleted mineral and energy resources, any promising new sources of energy and resources are bound to generate interest. Moreover, federal air and water pollution laws are gradually eliminating past waste disposal practices; open dumps and incineration, the most common procedures for waste disposal, must meet increasingly rigorous, and costly, environmental standards to avoid polluting air and water. Once cheap and easy, these older methods no longer appeal so readily to public and private agencies as cost and inconvenience rise. Thus, the nation for the first time has begun to ponder a more ecologically and economically profitable method of waste disposal and reuse.

What Needs to Be Done

Among those who have studied consumer waste, there is surprisingly little disagreement about the remedies or the urgency of taking action. Environmentalists might debate the proper order in which these policies should be initiated, but they have generally discovered that the principal problem is to convince public officials that solid waste is now a grave ecological ill that requires the creation of politically difficult but environmentally imperative remedies.

Speaking in the early 1970's, EPA's first administrator, William
Ruckelshaus, summarized the nation's waste management problems
briefly: "The principal obstacles to resource recovery," he declared,
"are economic and institutional, not technological."[6] Unlike many
ecological problems, the technology for effective management is available and proven; it has existed, in fact, for almost a decade. The key
to managing consumer waste lies in three policies: source reduction,
recycling, and sanitary waste disposal. From an environmental perspective, the first two of these are the more desirable because they
intend to conserve scarce or irreplaceable resources. Source reduction
aims at deflating the volume of consumer wastes generated in the
nation by discouraging the production and consumption of materials
commonly ending in the garbage dump or salvage yard: disposable
containers, packaging materials, and large metal items (including auto
bodies) are among the most important. Any proposal for source reduction encounters formidable opposition because it requires government to intervene in the economic marketplace and to obstruct the
smooth flow of disposable goods that American industry produces in
such extravagant amounts. Yet environmentalists maintain that both
American industry and the consumer share a responsibility for generating consumer waste, and both must somehow be discouraged from
this enterprise if the nation's waste problems are to be solved. Industry
too often creates planned obsolescence and caters too diligently to the
consumer's convenience—both producing unnecessary waste.
"Planned obsolescence . . . is a way of life," remarks one solid waste
expert. "The consumer is urged to buy the new and trade in or throw
away the old. The rise of the nonreturnable container despite the fact
that it costs the user more is another example of the close relationship
between market strategy and the generation of solid waste."[7] Essentially, both producers and purchasers of disposable products must be
discouraged from their accustomed behavior if source reduction is
ever to work.

Even a generous reduction in the volume of materials would still
leave an enormous load of consumer waste as a continuing responsibility for government. Today, government seldom does more than
carelessly bury this debris on a constantly shrinking volume of available land—an unimaginative, environmentally damaging practice
that fails to exploit the constructive possibilities for waste use. "The

ideal of solid waste management," declares one ecologist, "would be the disposal of wastes by reuse or recycling, and the disposition of the irreducible residue without insult and perhaps even with enhancement to the environment."[8] No tenet in the environmental movement has been more widely advertised than recycling, currently a glamour concept among ecologists. While there are many economic, technological, and political problems in recycling, which we shall soon examine, there are also many persuasive arguments in favor of recycling refuse as a means of reducing solid waste. Organic materials can be converted into compost and used for fertilizer and soil enrichment, a common European practice. Most of the metal in automobile frames, appliances, and disposable containers can be collected, sorted, melted, and reabsorbed into a great variety of industrial processes. Paper refuse can be sorted, shredded, and treated to make new paper products; each ton of recycled paper can be a substitute for seventeen trees otherwise cut. It is evident from Table 10 that the nation has hardly begun a serious campaign of resource recycling. According to the table, except for paper, virtually no other solid waste material has been significantly recycled, and less than 7 per cent of postconsumer waste has been used again as a "secondary material."

The energy crisis may have persuaded public and private agencies that energy recycling, long technically possible, is now imperative. There are, in fact, at least five ways in which energy can be recovered from wastes. Such waste can be (1) incinerated to generate steam, (2) shredded into light and heavy components that are then used for fuels, (3) pulped and then dried for incineration, (4) chemically treated at high temperature in a low-oxygen atmosphere to produce oil and gas —a process called "pyrolysis," or (5) incinerated with other fuels to generate electricity. Pilot programs in energy generation have been promising. For example, the Coors Brewing Company, near Golden, Colorado, has installed a pilot garbage gassification plant to convert Denver's garbage into fuel for the distillery. If successful, the plant will eventually expand until almost all the city's garbage will be converted to natural gas for energy.

Under the most favorable conditions, however, recycling would still leave a very large amount of waste to be eliminated. There are few ways in which this residual waste can be treated: It can be dumped in landfills, hauled out to sea and then dumped, or incinerated. In the

TABLE 10. Postconsumer Residential and Commercial Solid Waste Generation and Resource Recovery, by Type of Material, 1973 (in millions of tons, wet weight)

Material categories	Gross discards	Material recycled [1]		Net waste disposal	
		Quantity	Percent	Quantity	Percent
Paper	53.0	8.7	16.5	44.2	32.8
Glass	13.5	0.3	2.1	13.2	9.9
Metals	12.7	0.2	1.6	12.5	9.3
Ferrous	11.2	0.2	1.4	11.0	8.2
Aluminum	1.0	0.04	4.0	1.0	0.7
Other nonferrous metals	0.4	0.0	0.0	0.4	0.3
Plastics	5.0	0.0	0.0	5.0	3.7
Rubber	2.8	0.2	7.1	2.6	1.9
Leather	1.0	0.0	0.0	1.0	0.7
Textiles	1.9	0.0	0.0	1.9	1.4
Wood	4.9	0.0	0.0	4.9	3.6
Total nonfood products	94.8	9.4	9.9	85.4	63.4
Food waste	22.4	0.0	0.0	22.4	16.6
Yard waste	25.0	0.0	0.0	25.0	18.5
Miscellaneous inorganic waste	1.9	0.0	0.0	1.9	1.4
Total waste	144.0	9.4	6.5	134.8	100.0

[1] Resource recovery in 1973 included only material recycling.
SOURCE: U.S. Environmental Protection Agency, Office of Solid Waste Management Programs, Resource Recovery Division, *Third Report to Congress: Resource Recovery and Waste Reduction* (Washington, D.C., 1975), p. 10.

past, a number of seaboard communities, including New York and Boston, did haul part of their sewage out to sea and sink it, creating ocean contamination of such magnitude that the federal government prohibited the practice. Today, most communities simply purchase landfills and use them until overflowing; seldom, however, do these

dumps meet the standards of a "sanitary landfill" that environmentalists regard as an essential ingredient in any sound waste-disposal
program. A sanitary landfill, according to the American Society of
Civil Engineers, is one in which refuse is confined to the smallest
practical area, is reduced to the smallest practical volume, and then
is covered with a layer of earth at the conclusion of each day's operation or more frequently if necessary; it is also an expensive, labor-
demanding form of disposal. Because sanitary landfills are costly,
most communities only use open dumps. Seldom carefully managed,
they are commonly rat-infested areas of visual and ecological devastation stretching over many square miles, much of the debris burning
or smoking from deliberate and spontaneous combustion. Although
large incinerators can be a very efficient, environmentally safe method
of waste disposal when properly constructed and supervised, very few
communities have such facilities; instead, the ubiquitous open landfill
prevails. In short, environmentalists have considerable justification
for asserting that the government has yet to invest time or interest in
truly sanitary, efficient waste-disposal methods.

Any survey of existing waste-treatment technology reveals, as we
have seen, an enormous gap between the creative possibilities for solid
waste disposal and existing practices. The reason, in William Ruckelshaus's terms, are "institutional and economic." More precisely, powerful, well-entrenched interests sometimes tenaciously defend the
status quo against a technological revolution in waste disposal; sometimes it is not political opposition but a lack of economic incentives
that discourages more imaginative waste treatment. Sometimes it is
public officials, loath to sacrifice the security of existing policies for
the imponderables of new programs, who prefer to wait until the
nation's wastes reach a critical level before acting. The complexity of
these social forces can be appreciated by examining, in turn, a major
issue in source reduction, the current status of recycling policy, and
the state of the art in landfill management.

THE GREAT BEVERAGE BATTLE

America's major battle over source reduction today is fought with
bottles and cans. The struggle to rid the nation of disposable beverage

containers, which symbolize to ecologists the triumph of convenience over conservation, has spread from Washington to all the states. This, the Great Beverage Battle, demonstrates how vast enterprises, potent interests, and difficult policy options may be involved in disposing of something so apparently simple as a pop-top can.

Bottles, Cans, and Brickbats

In America, disposable containers are big business. Half of the metal and glass manufactured in the United States is used for disposable beer and soft-drink containers; sales of the metal alone produce more than $1.8 billion in annual income to the manufacturers. Beverage manufacturers attribute their steadily rising sales largely to the spread of disposable containers. In 1960, Americans consumed about 4 ounces of soft drinks per capita each day; by 1970, this figure has doubled. With the continued availability of throw-away containers, beverage manufacturers confidently predict that the nation will be awash in the consumption of more than 10 ounces of soft drinks per capita each day by 1980.[9]

Critics of these containers have been increasingly militant since the mid-1960's when the glut of throw-away cans and bottles first appeared. They point out that the containers have become an ugly embellishment to the American roadway and an eyesore wherever people travel. Although the containers constitute less than 8 per cent of all solid waste, they represent from 50 to 70 per cent of the nation's roadside debris. Discarded containers are growing much faster in volume than the nation's beverage consumption; while the nation's beverage intake rose 32 per cent between 1959 and 1972, its container discards jumped by 262 per cent.[10] This, assert the critics, forces government—and, ultimately, the taxpayer—to shoulder the cost of controlling the litter; estimates suggest that the aggregate yearly cost to state and local governments may exceed $500 million. More significantly, ecologists point out that disposable containers waste valuable resources, especially because so few are ever recycled. Roughly 2 per cent of all industrial energy is used yearly in producing beverage containers; the reuse of disposable containers would save the energy equivalent of about 92,000 barrels of oil daily.[11] The 2 million tons of steel and 575 tons of aluminum used yearly in metal throw-away containers could be better used, or saved, suggest environmentalists. Since these containers are so costly in fiscal and resource terms, can be so easily controlled at their source, and cater to a national need no more urgent than consumer convenience, many ecologists argue that the throw-away container is a logical target for regulation. "There are few other instances," noted John Sawhill, former administrator of the Federal Energy Administration, "where energy savings could be achieved so easily."

The Beverage Industry

Any campaign to rid the nation of disposable containers arouses the intense opposition of a powerful industrial alliance known collectively as "the beverage industry." It includes steel and aluminum manufacturers, beer and soft-drink purveyors, can and bottle manufacturers, the unions representing the labor force in these industries, and segments of the retail and wholesale trade marketing products in throwaway containers. The unusual alliance of big business and big unions in defense of disposable containers presents ecologists with a particularly formidable political opposition. Most commonly, the industry viewpoint is expounded by the U.S. Brewers' Association and the National Soft Drink Association; labor is represented by the United Steelworkers of America and Glass Bottle Blowers' Association.

Spokesmen for the beverage industry assert that any significant reduction in the sale of disposable containers could have serious, and perhaps catastrophic, consequences for the industry. They note that the industry's economic structure is dictated in good measure by the logistics of disposable containers. Companies have been able to operate with a few large plants at great distances from their outlets because they did not have to collect and transport returned bottles to the factories. Among other things, this enabled the large national manufacturers to compete with, and often to eliminate, local beverage manufacturers. With returnable containers, the spokesmen note, the industry would have to decentralize, would have to absorb the cost of collecting and transporting returned bottles, and would have to make other technical adjustments costing more than $5 billion. Moreover, the argument continues, the manufacture of metal beverage containers would virtually cease because there is no way yet known to make a metal can returnable and reusable without total (and expen-

sive) recycling. Both union and industry spokesmen emphasize the
loss of jobs inherent in any major reduction of disposable containers.
I. W. Abel, president of the United Steel Workers of America, has
argued that a total prohibition on disposables would eliminate 60,000
union jobs.[12] In the end, suggest spokesmen, the consumer will pay
a cost quite disproportionate to the benefits of a ban. Disposable
containers, they observe, constitute only a small part of the nation's
solid waste problem; for the elimination of this marginal waste the
consumer will have to pay higher costs for returnable containers.
Moreover, many industry representatives assert that regulation will
thwart the nation's traditional deference to the consumer. "The bone
of contention," notes an official of Pepsico, "is really the free enterprise system—shouldn't the consumer be allowed to choose what he
wants?"[13]

The beverage industry maintains that the solution to managing
disposable containers lies in recycling—a policy that would seemingly
retain the throw-away container and still produce significant resource
conservation. Beverage and container interests currently support the
National Center for Resource Recovery in Washington, D.C., where
research and information on recycling are intensively developed, and
several other pilot projects across the country intended to demonstrate the attractions of recycling. Industry spokesmen emphasize,
however, that the center and its related operations are intended to
stimulate state and local governments to assume the responsibility for
container recycling; eventually, the industry expects to phase out the
center when local governments take the major role in recycling. Critics argue that the industry's reluctance to make a large, continuing
commitment to recycling and the uncertain future of recycling among
state and local governments mean, in effect, that the industry will not
seriously undertake the arduous task of creating a major recycling
system for disposable containers in the future.

Governmental Action

Proposals to ban disposable beverage containers have been introduced in Congress, in every state legislature, and in several hundred
county and city legislative bodies. To date, only two states and a few
local governments have enacted these so-called "bottle laws." The
most widely observed law, passed by Oregon in 1972, bans all pop-top

cans and requires a deposit on all glass beverage containers; it encourages the reuse and recycling of containers. The bill mandates a five-cent deposit on all bottles "distinctive to one brand" and a two-cent deposit on standard beer bottles; the lower deposit on standard bottles encourages use of common containers that can be returned anywhere in the state. According to a legislative study conducted a year after the bill's enactment, beverage-related litter declined by 66 per cent across the state; so, too, did profits to beer and soft-drink industries —although not greatly.[14] A South Dakota law, taking effect in late 1976, calls for the complete withdrawal from the market of all nonreturnable and nonbiodegradable cans and bottles.

These states are exceptions to the general failure of bottle laws across the country. All seven state and local referenda on bottle laws conducted since 1970 have been won by the beverage interests. Legislative proposals almost uniformly fail; the opposition is frequently tough and grimly determined. Thus, when a bottle law was proposed in Erie County, Pennsylvania, the Teamsters' Union joined the opposition and intimidated many of its early proponents into abandoning their positions. Local breweries withdrew their advertising from a television station that had editorially endorsed the plan. A local legislator was warned by a large soft-drink manufacturer for whom he worked as a legal counsel that "repercussions" would arise if he supported the bill.[15] To many opponents of bottle laws, far more than ecology and resource conservation is involved; jobs and income are at stake.

At the moment, the nation continues purchasing an ever-growing volume of disposable cans and bottles and throwing away the consequences. There seems little likelihood that Washington, or most state and local governments, will follow Oregon and South Dakota in taking meaningful steps to constrain this massive industrial tribute to the consumer's convenience.

RECYCLING

If the recycling of used materials is to reduce the nation's solid waste significantly, a major alteration in the economics of use must occur in the United States. This alteration would require important changes in the way industry uses and prices raw materials, in the present government regulations concerning transportation rates of raw and used materials, and in the pricing of consumer goods. These are by no means the only economic transformations required to make significant recycling a reality, but they are sufficient to suggest how complex and controversial such a policy is likely to be. Ecologists have, unfortunately, often advertised recycling as a panacea to solid waste problems without enough regard for the harsh economic, technical, and political problems that stubbornly stand between the idea of recycling and its realization. To appreciate the formidable task facing federal policy-makers in creating a recycling policy, let us examine briefly some of the major aspects of a recycling system.

Economic Discrimination

Massive recycling is practical today only when recycled materials can be profitably used; today the government and the economy both discriminate against recycled materials. Federal tax and transportation policies, in particular, create strong disincentives for industry to substitute recycled (or "secondary") materials for virgin resources. Virgin materials, including timber, coal, and iron ore, are treated under federal tax law as capital assets and taxed as capital gains rather than as ordinary income when they are sold for profit; the effect is to encourage sale of these rather than the substitution of secondary materials more harshly taxed. Then, too, the standard depletion allowance has been granted producers of virgin materials as another incentive for their use. Finally, the Interstate Commerce Commission's national rate structure favors the transportation of virgin over recycled materials. It costs about two and one-half times as much to ship recycled ore as virgin ore; in the end, it costs the user about 6 per cent more to use recycled materials in his products than to use virgin ones. According to the National Association of Secondary Industries, a trade group representing producers of recycled materials, almost two-thirds of the nation's recyclable copper is unused because, among other reasons, it costs at least 50 per cent less to ship virgin copper.[16] Substantially the same transportation discrimination exists among all potential recycled materials.

The price of recycled materials fluctuates, often wildly, to such an extent that producers of recycled materials often find themselves in a boom-and-bust cycle. During the energy crisis of late 1974, for instance, the price of processed garbage rose to such an extent that it was profitable to market recycled wastes as fuel; within a year, however, the price had so plummeted that it was no longer profitable to sell garbage for fuel. During 1973, the city of Hempstead, Long Island, was shredding and selling its old newspaper at a modestly profitable $27 a ton; when the recession of 1974–75 came, the price fell to $2 a ton, and the operation had to be closed. Generally, when demand for any resource is high, recycled materials can be sold profitably; when resource demand drops, often only slightly, recycled materials are the first to be scratched from the nation's industrial shopping list. Not least important, the physical accessibility of virgin materials favors their use over recycled ones. Manufacturers using virgin materials commonly locate near their supply source; recycled materials must be transported over longer distances. Paper mills, for instance, are usually sited close to forests rather than close to urbanized areas where recycled wood materials are most likely to be available.

All these factors suggest that there must be some direct governmental intervention in the resource market to encourage more production and use of recycled materials. At the moment, the nation's governments have barely awakened to this need.

Local Governmental Stirrings

State and local governments, slowly running out of space for landfills and facing a rising volume of waste materials, have now begun to explore, very tentatively, the possibilities of recycling their wastes. Only twenty-three states have initiated comprehensive programs of resource recovery, and only thirty-two communities in these states have actually undertaken waste recovery as a result. The most ambitious state has been Connecticut, which plans to create a $290 million system for converting the household and commercial garbage of all the state's 169 towns and cities into low-sulfur fuel for electric generating plants and into commercially marketable scrap iron, aluminum, and glass. The system, handling more than 10,000 tons of refuse daily when completed, would practically eliminate solid waste disposal as a local problem. At the local level, St. Louis, Missouri, plans to complete by the late 1970's a system, constructed by Union Electric Company, to convert almost all the metropolitan residential and commercial garbage into fuel and secondary metals. Handling 8,000 tons of waste daily, it will be the largest municipal operation of its type in the nation. St. Louis is exceptional; only twenty-six other American cities anticipate large resource recovery programs by 1980.

Inertia in Washingtion

However modest may be the results, the performance of state and local governments in resource recovery is impressive when compared with the federal government's record. Aside from issuing periodic pieties about the need for resource recovery—a genuflection toward resource conservation—Washington has done little to encourage recycling of waste materials. An indication of Washington's present mood may be found in the fate of the Resource Recovery Act (1970), a feeble yet mildly constructive Congressional initiative toward waste management. The act required the White House to investigate processes for waste reduction, to study the recovery of energy and other useful products from solid waste, and to provide state and local governments with assistance in developing waste recovery programs. Within a year after its passage and regularly thereafter, the administrator of the EPA, under White House leadership, was to provide an annual report on progress toward these goals. Only in 1973 did the first report appear—a thin 41-page document that, in the opinion of almost all experts, advanced the nation's waste management program not a bit. Avoiding all controversy, the report concluded that "additional Federal incentives for recycling are not considered desirable at this time." As for the nation's current waste problems, the report proposed "further exploration of the problem."[17]

Why has Washington been so indifferent? Solid waste management cannot easily capture public interest nor advance the fortunes of party or politician; it doesn't have political "sex appeal." Then, too, waste problems do not seem life-threatening as do air and water pollution or other environmental hazards. The White House has also been reluctant, especially during the economic recession of 1974–75, to take any measures that might discourage the nation's industrial recovery. Manipulating the comparative market prices of virgin and secondary materials, it has been argued, might produce unanticipated negative effects on users and producers of virgin materials. No doubt, the political weight of the virgin resource producers has been thrown solidly against a national recycling program. "The lobbying power of the virgin resource industries and their record of success against widespread criticism and the demand for reform suggest that major change, in the near future at least, is unlikely." In short, there does not yet exist the political leverage sufficient to move Washington from its present inertia on recycling.[18]

LAND DISPOSAL

With so little interest in source reduction or waste recycling, the country continues to leave state and local officials to dispose of wastes in the traditional manner. If the nation can be said to have any solid waste policy, it is little more than an assumption that solid waste is still only trash, the disposal of which should be left to local communities. The nation's local governments continue, for the most part, to bury this ever-mounting quantity of debris as if the earth could accommodate our garbage indefinitely.

The nation does not lack a large volume of state and local waste laws. It is evident from Table 11 that a great many states have written legislation dealing with solid waste in their jurisdiction; according to this compilation, thirty-two states have at least some general waste management plans or guidelines, forty-two have some specific solid waste regulations, and twenty-five have gone so far as to require permits before landfills and other dumping can be done by municipalities. Unfortunately, these laws are often vague; they frequently lack detailed, operational provisions and are often erratically enforced, largely because enforcement customarily depends on the uncertain will of local governments. Many states have been reluctant to enact provisions that might be enforceable (note that only half the states even require disposal permits from municipalities). In any case, state regulations generally deal with solid waste collection and disposal but not with the management of solid waste volume. The states have so far made little effort to control the volume of solid wastes entering or leaving their borders, or to encourage a significant recycling of materials. But it is doubtful that the states, acting individually or in concert, can contribute much to managing the nation's growing volume of solid waste, for problems of coordination and political obstacles are formidable impediments to a state-by-state effort at waste management. It may well be that any significant regulation of solid waste production must rest with the federal government, which has the necessary power to regulate interstate commerce.

Such state regulations as do exist are commonly administered at the local level, together with any additional laws that municipalities and counties may enact. Governmental waste management on this basis becomes extremely decentralized and fragmented among thousands of municipalities, counties, and special waste management districts. Local officials, customarily strapped with tight revenue sources, concerned with other high-priority programs, and facing very limited technical resources and labor problems, have rarely been innovators in solid waste management. "Local governments," explains the Council on Environmental Quality, "have only limited funds, and municipal officials are timorous about interfering with refuse collection routines for fear of upsetting labor relations and public relations. . . . Even when the evidence is clear that new methods result in improvements, jealousies and fear of adverse employee relations sometimes prevent implementation.[19] A great many municipal governments have almost abandoned the management of solid wastes entirely, turning the responsibility over to private companies operating by governmental franchises.

The majority of local governments are still managing their own solid wastes in the face of growing problems. Collection is one nettlesome task. Cities spend several billion dollars annually simply to haul the garbage to disposal sites—the average community spends about 6 per cent of its total revenues on this alone. Solid waste collection, moreover, is a very labor-intensive activity, requiring much manpower and capital expenditure for equipment; both are sure to rise with growing labor costs and mounting waste volume. Collection technology is largely undeveloped—the compactor truck is practically the only significant innovation in the last half century. Still, many municipalities could greatly improve the quality of their collec-

TABLE 11. Status of State Solid Waste Regulation

	Solid Waste Laws	Rules and Regulations	Disposal Permit Required	Political Subdivisions Technical Assistance	Financial Assistance
Alabama	X	X			
Alaska					
Arizona	X	X			
Arkansas	X				
California					
Colorado	X	X	X	X	
Connecticut	X	X	X	X	X
Delaware		X	X	X	
District of Columbia		X			
Florida		X			
Georgia		X			
Hawaii	X				
Idaho		X			
Illinois	X	X	X	X	
Indiana	X				
Iowa	X	X	X		
Kansas	X	X	X	X	X
Kentucky	X	X	X	X	
Louisiana		X			
Maine				X	
Maryland	X	X	X	X	X
Massachusetts	X	X	X	X	X
Michigan	X	X	X		
Minnesota	X	X	X	X	
Mississippi		X			
Missouri		X			
Montana	X	X	X	X	
Nebraska					
Nevada	X				
New Hampshire	X	X	X	X	
New Jersey	X	X	X	X	
New Mexico		X	X		
New York	X	X		X	X
North Carolina	X	X			

TABLE 11 (cont.)

North Dakota		X		X	
Ohio	X	X	X		
Oklahoma	X	X			
Oregon	X	X	X	X	
Pennsylvania	X	X	X	X	X
Rhode Island	X	X		X	X
South Carolina		X	X		
South Dakota	X	X		X	
Tennessee	X	X	X		
Texas	X	X	X	X	X
Utah		X		X	
Vermont		X	X	X	X
Virginia		X	X	X	X
Washington	X	X	X	X	X
West Virginia		X		X	
Wisconsin	X	X	X	X	
Wyoming	X			X	
American Samoa					
Guam					
Puerto Rico					
Trust Territory					
Virgin Islands					

SOURCE: U.S. Environmental Protection Agency.

tion by purchasing better equipment, hiring more manpower, and arranging more frequent pickups. All this, of course, would mean a major increase in collection costs to be passed on to consumers. The high cost of collection could be somewhat reduced and better service almost ensured if consumers were willing to take several modest steps to simplify collection tasks. Unfortunately, Americans seldom cooperate in such situations. Few consumers, for example, will voluntarily sort organic and inorganic materials into separate containers, a simple act that could vastly simplify municipal garbage disposal and increase its efficiency; few municipalities have the courage to force such action.

Collection seems a simple matter, nonetheless, compared to disposal problems. The essence of the crisis is that land for dumping is rapidly disappearing. Blessed with a seemingly inexhaustible bounty of cheap land, the United States has traditionally depended on land disposal of solid wastes; we are still largely burying our refuse. About 60 per cent of all this solid waste ends up in the ground, most often in open, unsanitary landfills. Although small or impoverished communities are most likely to purchase cheap land for unsanitary dumps, even large cities are sometimes careless about dump siting. The San Francisco Metropolitan Region annually unloads more than 3 million tons of refuse in seventy-seven sites, more than two-thirds of which are along the shoreline of San Francisco Bay, where dump drainage poses a constant aesthetic and health problem. Many large cities, currently pressing the available dumping sites to the limit, may soon face a land scarcity. Estimates suggest that New York City may exhaust its available dumping space before 1980. Other cities, accustomed to using neighboring counties and municipalities for dumps, are now encountering greater resistance to this refuse exportation. San Francisco, already transporting some of its refuse more than 100 miles for disposal in thinly populated adjacent counties, is finding its neighbors increasingly reluctant to accept additional loads.

Ultimately, the amount of land that large communities can use for landfills is finite. Unless a major technological or economic innovation reduces drastically the volume of solid waste now accumulating in American communities, there will be some future point, perhaps not many years hence, when the land is gone. But short-range planning and limited objectives still dominate municipal planning; because dumping is the cheapest form of disposal for most communities, this economic appeal alone often perpetuates it.

NEEDED: A NATIONAL WASTE POLICY

Bury it and forget it—the traditional American approach to solid waste disposal—cannot continue indefinitely. Air and water pollution laws are gradually forcing state and local governments to abandon the open landfill for more sanitary methods. The need to conserve and recover energy and other resources from waste—no matter how slowly the realization is coming to public officials—will eventually force government to consider seriously a national waste management program. As in other environmental matters, most experts believe that Washington should set the broad policy framework in which state and local governments operate in waste management.

The essence of a national waste program, according to most ecologists, should stress resource reduction and recycling—that is, environmentally constructive approaches—over dump siting and management. The funding of such a program could be shared among governments and private interests. Most ecologists suggest that such a program should include the following elements:

1. *A charge, imposed on manufacturers, for the disposal costs of their products to be reimbursed to the extent the manufacturer uses recycled materials.* This would make recycled materials more appealing to manufacturers and would, perhaps, diminish the demand for products whose disposal is unusually difficult or costly. Such a proposal would drive up the cost of nonreturnable containers made with virgin material and encourage the use of recycled materials for their manufacture.

2. *A prohibition on the manufacture or sale of products whose disposal cannot be accomplished technically in a manner protective of the environment.* This would be aimed primarily at "hazardous substances" such as PCBs or other synthetic chemicals for which an adequate recycling system does not exist and at other materials, including perhaps plastics, whose volume is so great that disposal in large quantity produces significant air and/or water pollution.

3. *A prohibition on the use of nondegradable and nonrecyclable materials.* Many packaging materials, among them cellophane and styrofoam, fall into the category of nondegradable and nonrecyclable materials. Such a measure would probably reduce appreciably the volume of solid waste as well as encourage manufacturers to favor degradable materials, such as paper products, for packaging.

4. *Increased federal research into recycling technology and increased federal assistance to state and local governments for recycling systems.* Following the logic of the federal grants for the construction of waste treatment facilities found in the Federal Water Pollution Control Act Amendments, this would provide an incentive to state

and local governments to begin recycling systems by defraying some of the costs. It is the carrot to accompany the stick of other regulatory laws intended to reduce solid waste.

What is the likelihood that any of these measures will become law in the next few years? Environmentalists usually reply that the chances are almost nonexistent. The most optimistic perspective on the matter is provided by the energy crisis. To the extent that the nation feels the need to find major new energy sources rapidly, solid waste recycling may hold out attractions. Indeed, it has been almost entirely within the context of future energy policy that the White House has given any significant attention to recycling technology. Without the goal of energy needs, the solid waste problem is likely to languish, probably until the nation is literally buried in its own refuse.

NOTES

1. *New York Times,* September 5, 1972.
2. Estimated by John E. Bryson, "Solid Waste and Resource Recovery," in Erica L. Dolgin and Thomas G. P. Guilbert, eds., *Federal Environmental Law* (St. Paul, Minn.: West Publishing Co., 1974). p. 1292.
3. This discussion is largely drawn from William E. Small, *Third Pollution* (New York: Praeger Publishers, 1971).
4. Boyce Rensberger, "Coining Trash: Gold Strike on the Disassembly Line," *New York Times Magazine,* December 7, 1975, p. 31. Figures quoted are extrapolated from EPA estimates.
5. Figures cited by the president of the Combustion Equipment Associates, Inc., and reported in *New York Times,* January 22, 1973.
6. *New York Times,* February 4, 1973.
7. Rolf Eliassen, "Solid Waste Management," in Huey D. Johnson, ed., *No Deposit—No Return* (Reading, Mass.: Addison-Wesley, 1970), p. 57.
8. *Ibid.,* p. 63.
9. Data taken from *New York Times,* April 10, 1973; July 8, 1974.
10. Data on containers may be found in Philip Nobile and John Deedly, eds., *The Complete Ecology Fact Book* (New York: Doubleday Anchor Books, 1972), pp. 364–79.
11. On energy costs of solid waste disposal, see also Council on Environmental Quality, *Environmental Quality: Fifth Annual Report* (Washington, D.C., 1974), pp. 131–39.

12. *Washington Post,* July 1, 1975.
13. *Ibid.*
14. *New York Times,* September 4, 1974.
15. *New York Times,* September 8, 1974.
16. On costs of transportation, see John E. Bryson, *op. cit.,* pp. 1299 ff.
17. *Ibid.*
18. *Ibid.,* p. 1300.
19. Council on Environmental Quality, *Environmental Quality, 1970* (Washington, D.C., 1970), pp. 118–19.

10. The Unplanned Revolution: Ecology as a Subversive Movement

The environmentalist may well be a revolutionist disguised as a reformer. The movement is more than a crusade to change public policy; it is a thrust at the institutional structure underlying public policy. Environmental spokesmen commonly assert that policy change and institutional transformation are inseparable, that durable alterations in the nation's environmental policy are impossible without redesigning governmental structures. "The structures of laws and public institutions have evolved on the basis of assumptions and objectives that . . . cannot be relied upon to cope with the environmental problem in present or future," writes Lynton Caldwell. "Because man has not heretofore recognized a problem in the relationship of society to its total environment, he has not organized his public institutions to deal with it."[1] Measured by the vast social upheavals commonly called "revolutions," what environmentalists seek seems modest. In the context of traditional American political practice, however, it is major transformation.

The political struggle for environmental conservation is particularly arduous because its success will turn, ultimately, on major institutional changes. This provokes between ecologists and their opposition a different order of conflict from that involved in policy change alone. It is characteristic of American politics that governmental structures become citadels of group privilege; organizational arrangements become the base for group influence. Interest groups, acquiring power in Congress, bureaucracy, and the White House, because they have learned to accommodate themselves to existing

structures and then to exploit them, fiercely resist institutional reor-
dering. To lose a policy battle is a setback; to lose one's existing power
base may be a profound defeat. Thus, groups are far less willing to
compromise or bargain over major institutional changes than over the
substance of policies. To the extent that the environmental movement
seeks to redesign institutions, it assures itself a particularly resolute
opposition and a politically costly fight.

The structural changes sought by environmentalists run against the
grain of American political tradition in several respects. The movement seeks to create and maintain effective environmental planning.
It promotes the coalescence of public authority in national and regional agencies administering environmental programs. It seeks to
change the political style of public officials. In these respects, ecologists are "subversives"; often unintentionally and unwittingly, they
are conspiring to create a major transformation in American public
institutions.

THE PLANNING PROBLEM

American public institutions ceaselessly produce plans—thousands
of them yearly. Yet America's governments do not ordinarily plan
well. Throughout most of America's history, this was not a serious
problem because public agencies had few managerial functions; government was limited, most social functions were in the hands of
private institutions, and people preferred this arrangement. Beginning
with the New Deal in the 1930's, governmental agencies have collectively inherited so many social welfare responsibilities that social
planning has become an expected governmental activity. Thus, public
institutions—particularly federal ones—are expected now to do what
historically they were not designed nor expected to do: develop and
implement comprehensive social programs.[2] This is particularly important to environmental management. The environment, as the
Council on Environmental Quality has observed, is a "totality," and
public officials must "perceive the totality of the environment and the
inter-relationships of pollutants in all media."[3] Environmental problems cannot be effectively attacked as isolated phenomena but rather
must be treated holistically; ecological management must be compre-

hensively planned. Such planning requires a number of elements: agencies equipped with adequate authority to create and implement comprehensive environmental measures, adequate coordination and oversight of plan implementation, leadership with the will and capacity to make planning commitments a reality, resources to underwrite planning goals, and, finally, "a sense of purpose and continuity of purpose."[4] It has often seemed that American government is a conspiracy against sound planning structures.

Governmental Fragmentation

Perhaps the single most formidable obstacle to sound environmental planning is America's governmental fragmentation. The dispersion of authority across governmental levels—the federal dimension—and the pluralism of governmental authorities at county and community levels—the local dimension—are continual impediments to a national environmental management plan. This problem is increasingly recognized. The Council on Environmental Quality has consistently identified governmental pluralism as a major structural problem in new ecological programs. A recent survey of city and county governments revealed, characteristically, that "fragmented authority" was considered by a majority to be a major obstacle in better environmental management.[5]

America's governmental pluralism is an environmental problem because this fragmentation works magnificently, as it was intended to do. Governmental pluralism has been a device to magnify the influence of local interests, regional groups, differing communities, and other discrete geographic viewpoints in the national political process; it invests this multiplicity of interests with an institutional base and continuing visibility in national government. Inevitably, it also encourages competition and jealousy between governmental units and, quite often, reduces efforts at governmental collaboration to bickering among governmental entities, each protective of its powers and accountable only to its own constituency. Thus, any comprehensive planning that appears to require the surrender or reduction of some governmental powers by one unit in favor of another is likely to be seen as an erosion of authority and a threat to some public agency and its clientele. We have seen the outbreaks of these institutional conflicts in the administration of the Coastal Zone Management Act, the Clean Air Amendments, and the Federal Water Pollution Control Amendments. States, protective of their own powers, frequently resent "federal interference" in the name of environmental management; the states, in turn, reap a harvest of recrimination from the local governments who fear usurpation of their own powers.

It has been customary for federal officials to soften these conflicts by bargaining with state and local agencies over the details of policy substance and implementation. Each governmental unit is likely to extract some concession as the price for its collaboration in national environmental programs. In effect, national officials often pay a tribute to state and local pluralism by modifying the law to accommodate the viewpoint of local governments; in the process, it becomes difficult to keep policies firmly directed at clear and consistent goals. Indeed, writes Ralph Huitt after long study of the American political process, "What is least feasible is what requires serious, responsible consideration of some unitary conception of national need."[6] In the end, America's governmental pluralism, with its strong separatist tendencies, forces upon the nation's planning process such constraints that all long-range plans become, in fact, tentative and negotiable.

The Embattled Planner

Environmental management requires the professional planner. The planner has traditionally been a stepchild in American governmental circles. Professional planners have been incorporated within governmental administrative structures only within the last several decades; especially at the local level, many community governments still have no professional planning staffs. Moreover, planning agencies are inevitably "staff" entities with little, if any, operational authority over programs. Planning agencies may sometimes influence the deliberations of elective officials and other bureaucrats, but they seldom have the legal or organizational resources to argue their viewpoints forcefully or to compel a measure of deference to their views.

More importantly, the planner and the elective official tend to think quite differently.[7] Elective officials are sensitive to public moods and responsive to shifts in public sentiments; they may talk of programs meant to span years or decades, but their operational planning horizons may span only the time that separates their last election from the next one. Dependent upon public support for office, they cannot afford to stray too far from majority sentiments, nor leap too ambitiously beyond public thinking, nor commit themselves so firmly to programs that they cannot change their mind in the face of new political realities. In contrast, the planner tends to judge his programs by professional and technical standards, to think in terms of generous time frames for program implementation, to be absorbed more in problem solving that in its political logistics, to seek consistency, predictability, and continuity in program design. Unlike elective officials, the planner and his staff seldom have a constituency to mobilize in support of their work; indeed, planners who attempt to fashion a political base are often soon unemployed.

Out of these differing perspectives frequently grows an implicit conflict between planner and elective official. Elective officials want a planning process firmly in their control so that any governmental programs for which they must be accountable meet the test of "political feasibility." Further, plans once accepted must be continually monitored and are always susceptible to modification when political expediency so dictates. This often leads the elective decision-maker to tinker endlessly with programs and to regard all programs as provisional and amendable. Substantially the same viewpoint may be found in the higher echelons of local, state, and national administrative structures. Middle- and upper-level management is usually the "political executive" class. Ostensibly administrators, they usually think like elective officials because their job is usually to preserve and promote the political fortunes of their agency. The political executive, consequently, often imposes the same constraints upon program planning as the elective official to whom, quite often, he is likely to feel especially responsible.[8]

Given the constraints imposed by public officials and his own weak political position, the environmental planner commonly operates under formidable handicaps. He must, insofar as possible, satisfy the technical and professional requisites for his tasks, must meet the broad needs to which his programs are directed, and must still accept the political ground rules that will ultimately govern program implementation. In practical terms, this means that the planner's work is usually subordinated to the politician's viewpoint. This is not necessarily a prescription for failure—planners, after all, can be wrong and politicians right about the substance of programs—but it often leads to bad plans and poor planning. Especially in the case of environmental management, sound programs may require great continuity, dependable implementation, and substantive features without strong public support—indeed, necessary programs may directly contradict majority opinion or move beyond existing public understanding. In short, environmental management may have to proceed by the creation of plans violating customary concepts of "political feasibility." An effective environmental administration apparently will require a vigorous and continual growth in the resources and influence of the planning professionals in the legislative and administrative process.

Professional Experts and Legislative Generalists

Environmental planning increasingly requires legislators and executives not only to declare the objectives and priorities within programs but also to specify how environmental goals will be achieved. This means that legislators, especially, now make technical judgments upon the proper technologies and scientific framework with which to approach environmental issues. Thus, Congress not only has ordained that the nation shall achieve "swimmable and fishable waters" by 1983 and shall control all hazardous air pollutants within the decade, but also has decided that this shall be done by effluent controls on pollution sources and shall involve the application of specific control devices by specified deadlines. This means that legislators, who are essentially scientific amateurs, are now in the business of prescribing scientific solutions to environmental ills; Congress, and many state and local legislative bodies, now mandate both the "what" of policy (that is, goals and priorities) and the "how" (the technical means). Speaking specifically of air and water pollution laws, Kneese and Schultz describe a situation common to most environmental policy: "When the federal government sets about dealing with situations that are inherently complex, and that involve literally millions of interactions among individuals, state and local governments, and business firms, then *how* becomes as critical as *what*. Furthermore, since *how* can greatly influence costs, it becomes intermingled with the question of *what*."[9]

Environmental spokesmen often assert that elective decision-makers, and Congress particularly, must accept the need for greater reliance upon the advice of scientific and economic experts in the design of environmental programs. Kneese and Schultz, for instance, insist that congressmen and their staffs are not presently equipped by training or temperament with the skills to evaluate or to prescribe technologies for pollution abatement; rather, they choose solutions by a logic that unnecessarily drives up treatment costs and frustrates adequate pollution regulation.[10] Essentially, assert Kneese and Schultz, congressmen choose programs according to those provisions that will win majority support in legislative chambers and prove acceptable to influential constituencies. Legislators, in any case, are often uninformed on the technical aspects of the programs. Congressional staffs, moreover, do not compensate for this lack of technical expertise because they are usually selected for their skills in compromise and negotiation. Since bureaucratic experts are often committed to White House programs or defend their own agency interests, they are often not sufficiently nonpartisan to offer a reliable assessment of program alternatives. What seems necessary, claim many environmental experts, is much greater legislative receptivity to the advice of scientific professionals outside government and greater legislative experiments with new approaches to policy implementation lying outside the traditional framework of legislative thinking.

To expand the role of scientific professionals, economists, and other technical experts in legislative planning for environmental programs would, as in the case of the professional planner, reverse the traditional balance of forces in public agencies. It would, conceivably, create a new technocratic bloc within the governmental process and invest it with an uncommon measure of political influence. To many environmental experts, the alternative is to rely upon traditional decision-making procedures now increasingly inappropriate to the requirements of environmental management.

NEW ADMINISTRATIVE STRUCTURES

It has become obvious that effective environmental management requires more than a more coherent planning process; a major alteration in governmental structures is imperative. The nation's public institutions are not, on the whole, well designed to deal with environmental problems, because governmental powers and structures are organized around geographic jurisdictions that seldom coincide with the ecological dimension of a resource problem.[11] The administrative implementation of environmental protection, in particular, appears to require very significant strengthening of national administrative powers and the development of regional administrative units—both of which would grow, in all probability, at the expense of state and local governmental autonomy and authority. This erosion of local powers is already under way, in fact, even as federal officials deny it or, alternately, assert that it is only temporary. This growing intrusion of national and regional entities into state and local jurisdictions, justified on the basis of ecological needs, appears to be one of the unavoidable, yet controversial, results of a national environmental management program.

Regionalism

One remarkable aspect of current environmental analysis is the unanimity among most experts, who otherwise disagree on many matters, that sound public programs for environmental protection require, in most cases, the creation of regional authorities to plan and implement programs. This conclusion arises because major environmental problems develop heedless of existing governmental jurisdictions; they may sprawl geographically over a multitude of cities, counties, or even states. Nonetheless, such problems are often fashioned from a complex set of interdependent factors that must be treated together. Water pollution is often best approached through a comprehensive river basin or watershed management program; air pollution control may require treatment of a whole "airshed" stretching over several states. In these instances, it appears that regional administrative entities, embracing parts of states or interstate jurisdictions, are a logical solution. Regionalism has been suggested by such diverse organizations as the Committee on Economic Development (a business group), the Brookings Institution (a private research corporation), and the President's Council on Environmental Quality.[12]

The growth of regional environmental administration would constitute a major transformation in American administrative structures. Few such regional entities now exist. With the exception of the Tennessee Valley Authority, a federal enterprise, only a handful of regional administrative agencies with ecological responsibilities can be found; these deal almost wholly with river basin management. Perhaps the best known, the Delaware River Basin Commission, has functioned reasonably well so long as it confined itself to those operations acceptable to its governing board representing all the states affected by its work. However, regional authorities in the United States have been historically hobbled because they represent a confederation of state and local governments, each willing to surrender a small portion of authority through a "compact" to the regional entity for a specific purpose (such as river basin development) yet determined to keep the captured authority within narrow limits. Usually, member governments enjoy a veto power over regional projects; as a rule, only modest environmental regulation is tolerated. Generally, these regional agencies exist for purposes so narrowly defined and carefully hedged by veto groups that they cannot be considered as significant environmental regulators. Most state and local governments, in fact, have been too protective of their powers to accept membership in regional compacts. In short, regional environmental administration has been hardly more than an ecologically marginal experiment.

Regional environmental authorities must overcome more than an instinctive state and local aversion to any diminishing of authority. In all probability, regional authorities will have to exercise some meaningful control over land use if they are to be effective; land use powers are perhaps guarded as jealously as any in the possession of state and local officials. Indeed, one suspects, land use controls would be the last authority that local officials would wish to see in the hands of regional entities. Land use control is becoming an essential component of environmental management for several reasons. Non-point water pollution such as agricultural wastes, fertilizers, urban stormwater, and sedimentation—all major water contaminants that must be managed —can perhaps be controlled only through land use; no available technologies to manage such pervasive contaminants originating at such widely dispersed and numerous locations presently exist. In the case of "point" pollution sources such as an industrial outfall or a municipal waste treatment plant, it is often necessary to control their siting by land zoning. Further, the Clean Air Amendments require the EPA (and presumably any administrative agency acting under the EPA's pollution authority) to control the development of shopping centers, stadiums, and parking lots or other facilities that encourage vehicle use, traffic congestion, and the resulting increase of air pollution loads. Any regional agency with such responsibilities would, in effect, have to control zoning or other land use in order to determine where such "complex sources" of air pollution could appear. Indeed, there is a growing volume of evidence to suggest that the control of both air and water pollution from new sources can be best managed through land use constraints with technological procedures, like effluent controls, as a secondary strategy. All of this argues powerfully that land use management would have to become a major tool in the hands of any administrative agency with a significant environmental regulatory program.

In one respect, any discussion about regional authorities is still speculation; the nation has just initiated a comprehensive attack on air and water pollution, has no national land use policy, and has proceeded cautiously with other environmental management policies. Federal officials, hard pressed to implement the mandates in existing environmental laws, have been extremely wary about promoting, or even proposing, regional arrangements sure to arouse animosity among many state and local governments already disgruntled with existing environmental programs. Nonetheless, the argument for regional administration in environmental management has been advanced so often and so persuasively that its advocacy now constitutes a continuing theme in discussion of future environmental policy. Moreover, it may well be that experience with environmental management will convince decision-makers at the national level that satisfactory management is so difficult, if not impossible, without regional arrangements that the case for them will become compelling and their appearance unavoidable.

Growing Federal Authority

If laws told the truth, one would not doubt that the nations state and local governments are still influential architects of the nation's environmental policy politically, legally, and administratively. In writing the host of new environmental laws it has produced since

1970, Congress has been at pains to declare its zealous regard for state and local authority. The Clean Air Amendments announce that "the prevention and control of air pollution at its source is the primary responsibility of states and local government." The Federal Water Pollution Control Amendments echo the theme: "It is the policy of the Congress to recognize, preserve, and protect the primary responsibilities and rights of the States . . . to plan the development of land and water resources."[13] Despite these elaborate protestations, the course of federal environmental programs has been resolutely to absorb, at a differing pace and in different degree according to which laws one examines, traditional state and local discretion over environmental management. Careful studies of both the Clean Air Amendments and the FWPCAA suggest that Washington now exercises considerable control over the interpretation and implementation of air and water pollution control programs at lower levels. Harvey Lieber's conclusion concerning the FWPCAA can stand for the Clean Air Amendments as well—and in spite of Congressional declarations to the contrary: "Perhaps the administration of pollution control has remained local but only in the sense that most of the work is still being done on that level. However, the directions come from Washington. . . ."[14]

The gradual coalescing of environmental regulatory authority in Washington has proceeded much further in air and water pollution control than in other environmental areas, so that large areas of independent state and local authority still exist—as in land use. However, air and water pollution programs suggest the developmental pattern likely to unfold in other environmental areas: from gentle and conservative federal encouragement for state and local regulation to increasingly vigorous federal controls to constrain, or replace, local measures. This growing federal presence in environmental programs constitutes, as many commentators have noted, a quiet but continual restructuring of American federalism through ecological management. Increasingly, it appears, Washington's formal commitments to preserve a vigorous federal scheme for environmental administration —that is, arrangements involving power sharing and generous provisions for independent local initiatives—obscure the reality of a growing national regulatory approach federalized, if at all, only during enforcement.

This continuing nationalization of environmental administration constitutes a historical departure from the nation's past disaggregation of environmental authority and represents a countervailing force to the governmental fragmentation that impedes the environmental planning process. At the same time, it is a real shift in the locus of authority among America's governments and does represent a major structural alteration in national governmental powers. The causes of this change are complex. Partially, it results from the inability, or reluctance, of state and local officials to act incisively to curtail environmental degradation in the face of powerful political opposition; but many states, including New York, California, Texas, and others, have vigorous traditions of effective environmental management. In many cases, the change reflects the limited resources available to state and local governments in the face of pervasive environmental ills requiring comprehensive, massive resources to control. It also indicates, as we have observed, that many environmental problems defy the jurisdictional limits and multiplicity of local governments seeking to deal with them. In any case, it seems more evident with the passage of time that environmental protection is a major incentive, if not a compelling force, in redirecting the distribution of powers across the federal system. For better or worse, Washington has gained and local governments have lost in the new design of environmental authority created by the unfolding environmental movement.

POLITICAL STYLE: ENDING SUBSIDIZED DEGRADATION

American public officials, like politicians everywhere, approach decisions with a "political style"—that is, a set of informal norms, often inarticulate, that determine the manner in which they apply their political values to concrete political situations. Faced with a matter to decide, they apply a set of ground rules that seem to them acceptable and appropriate for translating into practice such abstractions as "democratic," "fair," or "just." American politicians, for instance, are generally "pragmatists" in political style; they "evaluate problems in terms of their individual merits rather than in terms of some preexisting comprehensive view of reality."[15] Few American officials will test any decision according to how well it fits into some philosophic framework such as conservatism, socialism, or something else; "one deals with the issue at hand, perhaps in terms of some guiding principles, but not as an instance of some overall scheme."[16] Political styles become important because they tend to become the routine, the expected approach to policy issues; eventually what decisions are made by governmental institutions may largely reflect the policy style of the decision-makers. In brief, style shapes policy.

The environmental movement seeks not only to recast formal governmental organizations but also to alter the traditional manner in which officials approach decision-making—another type of institution. In an important sense, the two are related; institutions influence the political style of their members and nations often design institutions to suit their political style. The political style of American public officials has long concerned ecologists because many of the premises upon which politicians have traditionally acted have been incompatible with sound environmental management. This, in part, explains the particularly low regard with which "politicians" are held by many environmentalists; they identify the essence of political style with bad environmental management. Although this depreciating view of the political vocation is unfair in many respects, it emphasizes the movement's concern with altering not only formal institutions but the manner in which politicians *think* about environmental issues.

Congress has historically sought to buy its way out of environmental dilemmas by using the federal treasury to prevent, or delay, coming to terms with environmental conservation. Though new ecological sensitivities have apparently developed in Washington, old political styles also stubbornly persist. Even as Congress writes new measures intended to reverse past ecological mistakes, it continues, quite often, to subsidize further environmental degradation.

Congressmen tend to use federal subsidies, grants, public works, and other federal investments in two environmental situations: first, when the private sector creates, or intensifies, environmental problems and some controls must be applied and, second, when it appears that Washington must choose between environmental protection or economic development. These investments are often advertised as a means to "solve" or "ameliorate" the problems thus created—that is, as a step toward an environmentally sound solution. Quite often the procedure only delays the harder, but unavoidable, choices and permits in the meantime further environmental deterioriation. Thus, federal investments often buy only time before the inevitable reckoning when public officials will have to confront the need for better environmental management. For obvious reasons, however, this style appeals strongly to public officials. It seems to give something to everyone. It avoids what politicians dread: having to choose between two powerful interests. It glosses the issue with a veneer of resolution that subdues further agitation for a while.

One can observe this Congressional strategy in a number of recent policies. First, the massive $18 billion construction grant program attached to the Federal Water Pollution Control Act Amendments appears to be a procedure for encouraging state and local compliance with water pollution regulations at the expense of environmentally and economically sounder measures.[17] This huge public works enterprise is widely regarded as the federal sop to mollify state and local governments' resentment of the amendments' regulatory features. Many economists have asserted that the program has been so designed that it will unintentionally result in many large new waste treatment plants where they are not needed, will prevent other, less costly forms of pollution management from being adopted by private industry, and will discourage the industrial development of less environmentally dangerous technologies. Moreover, the critics assert, this $18 billion is only a down payment; many more billions in federal money will be poured into the program when Congress, once having committed itself to underwriting the new facilities, finds it politically difficult to withdraw even though costs will constantly escalate. In spite of these deficiencies—many of which were brought to Congressional attention during hearings on the amendments—it was difficult for Congress to resist the new program. Not only did it undercut opposition to the new water pollution regulations, it also appeared "equitable" by having Washington accept a large share of the cost for pollution controls it was now imposing on state and local governments. And it brought public works—federal pork—to hundreds of local communities.

Floodplain management is another policy domain in which federal subsidies replace environmentally better controls. Operating through the Corps of Engineers, the Bureau of Reclamation, and other water resource agencies, Congress continues to rely upon public works to protect private and public property endangered by flooding rather than to discourage development of floodplains or to promote the resettlement of individuals and institutions situated on floodplains. Confronted by communities or businesses facing serious water damage, Congress commonly authorizes the creation of dams, dikes, stream channelization, or other devices dependent upon public investment. This procedure becomes an implicit encouragement for the development of floodplains, many of which would be environmentally better protected through alternative uses (for example, as recreational areas). Any public officials determined to change this logic must move the weight of almost two centuries of political tradition. Floodplain projects have always been one of the most readily available, and easily justified, means of getting federal money into local constituencies; congressmen will not easily abandon so generous a larder of federal pork upon whose delivery to their constituents their own political fortunes may rest.

Finally, current federal policy concerning the development of the Outer Continental Shelf (OCS) shows signs of developing into another example of federal dollars delaying better environmental policies. As we saw in Chapter 8, federal officials have been strongly disposed to promote extensive, immediate development of offshore oil wells along the Atlantic Coast in hope in tapping what may be huge new oil reserves. This, an aspect of Project Independence, would presumably diminish U.S. dependence on foreign oil and thereby reduce balance-of-payment deficits and increase American military security. We have seen that this policy, with its resulting thousands of new offshore oil wells, petroleum storage facilities, and onshore petroleum processing installations, has created strong misgivings among environmentalists and the communities affected, or likely to be affected, by the OCS activities.

Recently, Congress passed and the President signed the Coastal Energy Impact Bill, which, among other things, "authorizes Federal financial assistance to build roads, schools, hospitals, sewage systems and water purification facilities for communities on the coasts of the oceans and Great Lakes whose populations might expand because of the energy projects."[18] Viewed superficially, this appears a reasonable, even judicious, measure. Not only does it seem to assist local communities in adjusting to the sudden influx of population with the sharp increase in services it will demand from communities affected by OCS activity, but it also contains other provisions that apparently ensure that no local community will be forced to accept an offshore energy development unwillingly. However, there is a less benign aspect. In effect, the bill is also a strong solvent to local opposition to offshore energy development. It erodes local dissent by appearing to lift from communities a major buden imposed by OCS oil drilling; it holds out the promise of federal dollars—perhaps huge subsidies—for local development if OCS activity is permitted. And it discourages alternative approaches to energy development which would emphasize energy conservation—controlling demand rather than increasing energy supply—and environmental conservation by keeping OCS drilling on a limited scale. Few communities, when given a choice between generous federal subsidies and refusing them in favor of some alleged long-range environmental good, will find the decision easy. Especially if local officials believe they can have environmental safety and federal subsidies, too (the current Washington argument), there may seem no reason to refuse federal assistance. Nonetheless, it can also be argued that this new federal grant program, however well motivated, is another instance of Washington's buying its way out of a difficult choice between energy development and energy conservation. The threat of offshore oil spills, the depletion of irreplaceable oil reserves, and the continual feeding of the nation's huge energy hunger are all environmentally undesirable results of OCS development. New energy sources and less need to restrain national economic development are the rewards. To many congressmen and the White House, the new bill circumvents the politically difficult choice between such alternatives; apparently, one can have both.

So long as the political style of public officials favors the use of such generous federal funding to avoid difficult but environmentally constructive policies, the nation will be locked into an environmentally pernicious political logic that delays full governmental and public acceptance of the responsibilities inherent in sound environmental management.

AN END OF THE BEGINNING

Measured in historical terms, the environmental movement is still only a historical episode. Despite brave and passionate rhetoric, re-

gardless of the promises and programs grandly proclaimed by politi-
cans, environmentalists and their allies have no assurance that the
movement will not be swallowed up in some imperious new national
issue or emergency demanding attention. Alternately, it may suffer
the slow attrition, the gradual loss of faith and will for the cause, that
often afflicts movements as they mature. Still, one can be sure that the
beginning of the movement is behind; it has appeared, has prospered
in some respects, and may yet prevail.

Two incidents come to mind. A prominent environmentalist, asked
how he could be certain the nation would sustain its new environmental sensibilities, suggested that the country required an environmental
disaster of shocking magnitude every three years. Three years, he
suggested, was the proper interval because it took about that time for
public enthusiasm for a new issue to lapse into boredom and because
it took that long for public officials to lose the sense of urgency about
any newly important matter. A new environmental tragedy, he commented, would convince the public that the issue was still urgent, and
a new attention cycle would begin.

The great Canadian physician Sir William Osler once told a medical school graduating class that 50 per cent of what they had been
taught was probably wrong. Unfortunately, he added, his teachers did
not then know which 50 per cent. Moreover, he continued—and this
was the real point—no one seriously expected doctors to abandon
their vocation because they might be unwittingly ignorant in some
aspects of its practice.

One hopes that it will not require further environmental deterioration, perhaps mounting into a tragedy, to keep public and private
commitments to ecological preservation steadfast. It is in the nature
of most political movements that their drastic predictions and impas-
sioned rhetoric soon seem stale; the worst never seems to happen or
the rhetoric seems only dramatic. No prophecy seems more certain
than this, however. Further environmental neglect is a down payment
on a future disaster. However slowly the intricate pattern of ecological
causality may move toward its end, we can be certain the environmental disasters predicted by responsible ecologists will happen if the
movement's major spokesmen are not taken seriously.

Perhaps, as William Osler suggests, the experts will be wrong in the
details. Perhaps the ecologist will err in his prescriptions for dealing

with particular problems. He may misapprehend the complexities of many issues. If so, time will eventually reveal the truth. But the movement must prevail. We may not again have the opportunity to begin with so many possibilities for environmental protection still open to us. If not to ourselves, we owe it to generations unborn, whose only voice and power are our own, to protect this Spaceship Earth, upon which, so far as we yet know, the only human life in the universe exists.

NOTES

1. Lynton K. Caldwell, "Achieving Environmental Quality: Is Our Present Organization Adequate?" in Leslie L. Roos, Jr., ed., *The Politics of Ecosuicide* (New York: Holt, Rinehart and Winston, 1971), p. 84.
2. This point has been made often and emphatically. See, for example, Donald N. Michael, *The Unprepared Society* (New York: Harper Colophon Books, 1968), and "Governmental Structure for Planning," in H. Wentworth Eldredge, ed., *Taming Megalopolis,* Vol. 2 (Garden City, N.Y.: Doubleday and Co., 1967), pp. 667–724.
3. Council on Environmental Quality, *Environmental Quality: Second Annual Report* (Washington, D.C., 1972), p. 341.
4. William K. Reilly, *The Use of Land* (New York: Thomas Y. Crowell, 1972), p. 211.
5. U.S. Environmental Protection Agency, Office of Research and Development, *Environmental Management and Local Government* (Washington, D.C., 1974), pp. 209–10.
6. Ralph Huitt, "Political Feasibility," in Ira Sharkansky, ed., *Policy Analysis in Political Science* (Chicago: Markham Publishing Co., 1970), p. 410.
7. The conflicts between planners and public officials are explored perceptively in Britton Harris, "Planning Method: The State of the Art," in D. R. Godschalk, ed., *Planning in America* (Washington, D.C.: American Institute of Planners, 1974), pp. 132–49.
8. This argument is explored in Theodore J. Lowi, *The End of Liberalism* (New York: W. W. Norton and Co., 1969), part 2.
9. Allen V. Kneese and Charles L. Schultz, *Pollution, Prices and Public Policy* (Washington, D. C.: The Brookings Institution, 1975), p. 9.
10. *Ibid.,* pp. 114–16.
11. This argument is forcefully made in Lynton K. Caldwell, *Environment* (New York: Doubleday and Co., 1971), part 4.

12. See Kneese and Schultz, *op. cit.;* also Committee for Economic Development, *More Effective Programs for a Cleaner Environment* (New York: Committee for Economic Development, 1974).
13. Clean Air Act Amendments of 1970 (Pub. L. 91–604), Sec. 101; Federal Water Pollution Control Act Amendments of 1972 (Pub. L. 92–500), Sec. 101(b).
14. Harvey Lieber, *Federalism and Clean Waters* (Lexington, Mass.: Lexington Books, 1975), p. 199.
15. Sidney Verba, "Comparative Political Culture," in Lucian W. Pye and Sidney Verba, *Political Culture and Political Development* (Princeton, N.J.: Princeton University Press, 1965), p. 545.
16. *Ibid.*
17. See Kneese and Schultz, *op. cit.*
18. *New York Times,* July 26, 1976.

Selected Readings

Bruce A. Ackerman et al. *The Uncertain Search for Environmental Quality.* New York: Free Press, 1974.

A careful, detailed study of difficulties in enforcing water quality legislation in the Delaware River Basin. A useful examination of the relationship between political and technical aspects of pollution control.

Lynton Keith Caldwell. *Environment.* Garden City, N.Y.: Doubleday, 1971.

A political scientist's examination of the political and administrative problems associated with achieving environmental protection.

Harry M. Caudill. *My Land Is Dying.* New York: Dutton, 1971.

Caudill is a Kentucky lawyer and legislator who writes with passion and precision about strip mining's impact on Appalachia. The pictures accompanying the story say volumes in themselves.

Barry Commoner. *The Closing Circle.* New York: Knopf, 1971.

An internationally known environmentalist's explanation for our growing environmental ills. Written for the laymen, it nonetheless contains a useful scientific introduction to ecological protection.

Matthew A. Crenson. *The Un-politics of Air Pollution.* Baltimore: Johns Hopkins Press, 1971.

One of the few careful studies of how community political structures have affected environmental policy. Suggests how the political system can create, or stifle, environmental issues.

Council on Environmental Quality. *Environmental Quality.* Washington, D.C.: Government Printing Office.

Issued annually, this provides a yearly update on trends in pollution and other environmental matters. Contains a review of the past year's governmental efforts in the environmental field. Packed with useful data.

J. Clarence Davies, III. *The Politics of Pollution.* 2d ed. New York: Pegasus Press, 1975.

The author has a fine sensitivity to the political process inherent in enforcing pollution legislation. A good, thorough introduction to the intricacies of water and air pollution laws.

Erica L. Dolgin and Thomas G. P. Guilbert, eds. *Federal Environmental Law.* St. Paul, Minn.: West, 1974. Published for the Environmental Law Institute.

A comprehensive survey of major federal environmental legislation to 1975. Especially useful in explaining the logic and legislative intent behind the legislation.

Cynthia H. Enloe. *The Politics of Pollution in Comparative Perspective.* New York: McKay, 1975.

Studies the development of environmental policy in the United States, Western Europe, and several Asian and Middle Eastern states. Very informative in accounting for differences in national attitudes toward environmental protection.

Harry Foreman, ed. *Nuclear Power and the Public.* Garden City, N.Y.: Doubleday, 1972.

A collection of informative articles on all aspects of the nuclear power controversy. Somewhat technical but not difficult.

Marshall I. Goldman. *The Spoils of Progress.* Cambridge, Mass.: MIT Press, 1972.

One of the few careful, extended studies of environmental ills in the Soviet Union. Links political structures with environmental problems with particular clarity.

Donald R. Kelley, Kenneth R. Strunkel, and Richard R. Wescott. *The Economic Superpowers and the Environment.* San Francisco: Freeman, 1976.

Compares pollution policy among the major industrialized nations. Points to common technical and political problems as well as national differences.

Allen V. Kneese and Charles L. Schultze. *Pollution, Prices and Public Policy.* Washington, D.C.: The Brookings Institution, 1975.

A critique of our present federal approach to air and water quality management with a proposal for an alternative scheme based upon taxing effluents. Brief, readable, and provocative.

Grant McConnell. *Private Power and American Democracy.* New York: Knopf, 1966.

A sweeping, reasoned explanation of why the United States has permitted private interest groups to penetrate the political process so effectively. Particularly helpful in exploring the impact on resource management.

Donella H. Meadows et al. *The Limits of Growth.* New York: Universe Books, 1972; and H. S. D. Cole et al. *Models of Doom.* New York: Universe Books, 1973.

The first book is the famous Club of Rome study which utilized computer simulation to predict a coming massive, worldwide environmental crisis after the turn of the next century. The second book includes a number of articles critical of the study. Disturbing, but highly provocative reading.

Arthur W. Murphy, ed. *The Nuclear Power Controversy.* Englewood Cliffs, N.J.: Prentice-Hall, 1976. Published for the American Assembly.

The nuclear power controversy without hysterics. A collection of articles on the legal and political problems associated with nuclear power development in the United States.

David M. Potter. *People of Plenty.* Chicago: University of Chicago Press, 1954.

A classic study of the "psychology of abundance" which shapes American character. A seminal study in explaining the American attitude toward resources.

William K. Reilly, ed. *The Use of Land.* New York: Thomas Y. Crowell, 1973. Published for the Rockefeller Brothers Fund, Task Force on Land Use.

One of the first and best studies of the "new mood" in American land use. Explores in depth and breadth the problems and options in dealing with land management during the next several decades.

Charles ReVelle and Penelope ReVelle. *Sourcebook on the Environment.* Boston: Houghton Mifflin, 1974.

A concise summary of the major components of environmental pollution. A layman's scientific guide to environmental problems, with useful illustrations.

Stewart L. Udall. *The Quiet Crisis.* New York: Holt, Rinehart and Winston, 1968.

A readable account of past American environmental policy with attention to how it relates to present environmental ills.

Lettie McSpadden Wenner. *One Environment Under Law.* Pacific Palisades, Calif.: Goodyear, 1976.

A brief but informed and informative study of the options facing policy-makers in controlling air and water pollution. Very good at exploring the economic aspects of pollution control and relating them to political problems.

Index

Walter A. Rosenbaum is Professor of Political Science at the University of Florida in Gainesville. He received his doctorate from Princeton University. Professor Rosenbaum has worked as a policy analyst and consultant to the U.S. Environmental Protection Agency. He has contributed numerous articles on environmental policy and politics to professional journals and is co-author of *Analyzing American Politics* and co-editor of *Political Opinion and Behavior: Essays and Studies.*